KU-713-490

Power and Christian Theology

STEPHEN SYKES

WITHDRAWN FROM THE LIBRARY
UNIVERSITY OF WINCHESTER

continuum
LONDON • NEW YORK

Continuum International Publishing Group
The Tower Building, 11 York Road, London SE1 7NX
80 Maiden Lane, Suite 704, New York NY 10038

www.continuumbooks.com

© Stephen Sykes 2006

All rights reserved. No part of this publication may be reproduced or transmitted in any form or by any means, electronic or mechanical, including photocopying, recording, or any information storage or retrieval system, without prior permission in writing from the publishers.

First published 2006

British Library Cataloguing-in-Publication Data
A catalogue record for this book is available from the British Library.

ISBN: 0–8264–7651–1

Typeset by Kenneth Burnley, Wirral, Cheshire
Printed and bound in Great Britain by MPG Books Ltd,
Bodmin, Cornwall

Contents

Foreword

On the face of it, a faith in which God is worshipped as a 'God of power and might' has every reason to think long and hard about the relationship of power and theology. This is especially the case in a context in which the very idea of power has pejorative connotations. It has to be asked, indeed, whether the Christian Church has any business with power? Or is it the case that 'worldly power' is one thing, and 'spiritual power' quite another? In the West, and especially in Europe, both East and West, one is inevitably conscious of the long association of the Church and the power of the ruler. It includes episodes of such authoritarian misrule and institutional abuse of freedom that Lord Acton's celebrated dictum ('power tends to corrupt and absolute power corrupts absolutely'[1]) scarcely seems adequate. Is it not power itself which is the problem? Some have thought so, and have not hesitated to draw the conclusion that a 'God of power and might' is in urgent need of demythologization.

The invocation of 'spiritual power' provokes further questioning. It has become unmistakably clear that the domestic life of the Church and the existence in it of sacramental or spiritual authority creates the conditions in which abuse can occur. Appalling cases of paedophile activity have been exposed and admitted in the Catholic Church in recent years.[2] But a large penumbra of abusive activities have also been identified in other churches.[3] These facts prompt the searching question, whether it is not the very existence of power which is the problem?

The cumulative impact of the political, social and psychological misuse of power has assisted the radical theological case for the option of 'powerlessness', the renunciation of power and might pioneered by the one nailed for our sakes to the cross. Could it be that Christians are being summoned to have literally nothing to do with 'worldly' power, but instead voluntarily embrace the 'power of weakness'?[4] On the face of it a substantial case could be made for regarding the Emperor Constantine as the fountain-head of a disastrous turning point for the Church, when under his direction it achieved the status of an established religion.[5] A bishop in the Church of England has a special duty to take such a possible conclusion seriously.[6]

At the same time another consideration arises. It would be understandable if a church which was in a strong majority in a country took a robust view of its opportunities for exercising direct forms of power, whereas a church in decline or in a weak position saw the attractions of more subtle modes of influence. A somewhat similar thought has struck a recent political commentator. In his provocative and widely discussed essay, Robert Kagan has argued that European and American perspectives on power, its efficacy, morality and desirability, are sharply diverging. More precisely, the attitude towards power which was once a feature of American politics has now taken up residence in Europe, and vice versa. The reason for this ideological exchange, he holds, is that the actual power equation has shifted:

> When the United States was weak, it practised the strategies of indirection, the strategies of weakness; now that the United States is powerful, it behaves as powerful nations do. When European great powers were strong they believed in strength and martial glory. Now they see the world through the eyes of weaker powers.[7]

As the gap in military technology and competence widens, so Europeans express a correlative commitment to international law and institutions – structures for which 'hard power' matters less than 'soft power'. The European argument is in its own strategic interest. But this internationalism was precisely what Americans wanted in the eighteenth and nineteenth centuries, 'when the brutality of a European system of power politics run by the global giants of France, Britain and Russia left Americans constantly vulnerable to imperial thrashing'.[8] Having earlier invented the 'raisons d'état' of power politics, Europeans have now turned themselves into 'born-again idealists', suspicious and fearful of American world dominance.[9]

There is something intuitively persuasive about the thought that the political disposition of a nation should correspond to its capability. A saying which Kagan quotes runs as follows: 'When you have a hammer, all problems look like nails'; but equally, as he observes, when you don't have a hammer, you don't want anything to look like a nail.[10] It sounds cynical, as though political argument was always the cover for self-interest. But one does not have to be unduly cynical to think that the way one construes and analyses a problem may correlate to some degree to the resources one has for dealing with it. This is particularly likely when one is dealing not with an individual's reasoning and motivation, but what is thought to be a collectively appealing course of action in a democracy. In such a context, what is urged in public argument will have to be widely persuasive. What a nation's capabilities actually are will be widely known through the public media. The analyses and arguments which have an obvious public appeal will be those that society has the best chance of carrying out successfully.

Arguments about power also concern theologians, They do so in at least three ways. The 'power of God' is a traditional phrase both in the Bible and in the worship of the Church, and 'Almighty God' is a traditional mode of address; secondly, the power of the 'power of the Church' in, for example, its influence in society has obviously been a reality, for good reasons or bad; and thirdly, 'power in the Church', the distribution and exercise of power by various members of the Church, whether hierarchical or not, is similarly a fact, even if it is a problematic fact. But is the way in which power is conceptualized in the Church, in some way or all of these ways – which we will be dissecting in this book – subject to the same correlation, that Kagan observes in the case of political power? Is it, for example, the weakening of the Church's influence in Western Europe which has suggested to it that it has no business with that kind of power at all? Are the theological analyses and arguments about power current in the Church, those which Christians have the best (indeed, in the case of a comparatively weak institution, the only) chance of carrying out successfully? And can one trace a similar history of correlation in the case of theology, to that to which Kagan points in the case of politics? Was a strong and influential Church, deeply entwined with the structure of government, inclined to look positively at the phenomenon of power, whereas a weak, marginalized Church has had all manner of anxieties and reservations about the same subject?

Relevant to these questions is the thesis of a second recent book on the subject of political power, Joseph Nye's *Soft Power*, with its alluring subtitle, 'The Means to Success in World Politics'. Nye argues that political power is changing in character in the modern world as a result of the global revolution in information technology. What constitutes a nation's power resources changes over time. It is not that 'hard power', the power to command and coerce backed up by military might, has ceased to matter. But other resources have risen in importance, notably 'getting others to want the outcomes that you want'.[11] Nye envisages a spectrum of power behaviours. On the 'hard' side lie command, coercion and inducement; on the 'soft' side, agenda setting, attraction and co-option. The resources needed for the different behaviours likewise vary. 'Hard' power requires force, sanctions, payment and bribery; 'soft' power relies on institutions, values, culture and policies. In a global information age the 'relative importance of soft power will increase'.[12]

Again there is something intuitively persuasive about the idea that what counts as a power resource should vary over history. The connection between science, inventiveness and military technology has existed (and varied) for centuries. And if indeed 'the pen is mightier than the sword', then the rapid circulation of ideas and images throughout the world is bound to have an effect on people's attitudes and intentions. The intriguing question again arises whether and to what degree theology is influenced by the rise of 'soft' power. The Church is, after all, an institution with values, a culture and policies. It is more used to persuasion than to coercion, though as we shall see, an immensely influential argument in favour of coercion was advanced shortly after that became indirectly available as a resource. Now that 'soft' power is rising in importance, is this the moment at which the Church is in a position to denigrate its past association with 'hard' power – or even to deny it has any business with power at all?

The rootedness of particular arguments in history seems, on the face of it, as intuitively persuasive in the case of theology as in the case of politics. On the other hand, the sceptical possibility that theological ideas are 'nothing but' the elaborate disguise of self-interest provokes alarm and anxiety. Has theology no basis in truth? Are the ideas on this subject to be found in Scripture merely a wax nose to be turned this way and that in the light of prevailing conditions? Are the political, social and psychological understandings of power in any way relevant to the use of the word and concept in theology? Does the history of the way power has been understood in non-theological contexts affect (and change) theological ideas? Or is it, perhaps, possible that the influence flows the other way, from theology into politics, sociology and psychology?

These are among the large questions to be raised in this book. Because they are so large, I have attempted to write as succinctly as possible so that the argument does not sink beneath the details.

After considering to what extent a careful definition of terms can help us (Chapter 1), I attempt (in Chapter 2) a kind of map of the territory occupied by the terminology of power in Christian theology. Then two different tendencies are identified in the way in which power has been handled in theology. The first, which I entitle, 'the affirmation of power', celebrates divine power, and sees no particular difficulty in its human embodiment or instantiation (Chapter 3). On the other hand, there is also at least an ambivalence about, and on occasions a plain antagonism to, what human beings characteristically make of power. I call this 'the rejection of power' (Chapter 4), though what takes place is often its re-evaluation.

These two chapters (3 and 4) suggest that the history of theological attitudes to power is multifaceted, not uniform; and it is this multifaceted tradition which encountered the radical re-evaluation of power in early modern European political thought and the attendant rise of sociology (Chapter 5). The theological centrality of power is explored in Chapter 6, which focuses upon the centrality of the idea of sacrifice in Christian thought. These two chapters (5 and 6) concern the power (or powerlessness) of the Church in public life, and the fundamental idea of the power of God. The third area for the language of power is in relation to the distribution and exercise of power inside the Church (or its desirable absence), and this is treated in the final chapter.

The view which I take of this matter may be described as 'realistic', in that I hold it to be impractical to attempt to dissociate oneself from the existence of powers (in the plural). There is such a thing as the abuse of such powers, but that is not avoided by denying their reality or illegitimacy. The Christian faith sponsors a dramatization of human life which should alert the believer to the seriousness of the struggle against evil powers, a contest which cuts through the middle of a believer's life. The theme of sacrifice emphasizes the costliness of what is involved. At the same time to believe in God's almighty power is to be rescued from despair or fatalism, and makes the victory of resurrection available, even within apparent or public impotence.

This realism embraces the likelihood, even necessity, of exercising power within the Church. A white, male, Anglican bishop can only admit to such an opinion together with a severe health warning. But I have come to the view that the health of the Church is more threatened by the disguise of power than by its open acknowledgement. It seems simply foolish and delusional to deny that the life of the Church includes what is ordinarily called politics. The abuse of power is better avoided by those who are completely aware of the temptations and have taken realistic steps to arm themselves against them. Far from it being the case that with Constantine in the fourth century the Church first encountered these problems, it is clear that even in the letters of the New Testament the possibility of the misuse of power is adumbrated; and from the fifth century onwards the Church has possessed a dossier of extraordinary insights into the self-deceptions into which Church leaders (and others) tumble on acceding to office. A revisit to this text occupies much of Chapter 7.

1

Power: An Essay in Definition

It may seem dull to begin a book by discussing the definition of terms, but in the case of 'power' it is unavoidable. It is unavoidable because in one of the main areas with which we shall be concerned, namely power in societies, the literature is vast and the complexities formidable. Despite this fact, the purpose of this chapter is to ask the reader's permission to use 'power' in the way it is used in ordinary speech, that is, with a certain imprecision.

We use the word 'power' in a great variety of ways. It can designate both a person and a thing, a power like a state, or even like an angel or deity. It can be a quality or property, such as an ability to do something or a faculty of body or mind. 'Power' can belong to inanimate things as well as to persons or groups. It can be used to signify the possession of control or command over others, and in this sense be synonymous with 'dominion', 'rule', 'government', 'domination', 'influence', 'control' and 'authority'. Quite commonly it has a negative ring about it, for reasons which will emerge in Chapter 3. When we say of people that they are 'power-conscious', or still worse 'power-hungry', we intend no compliment. Playing personal 'power games', in international relations, 'power-politics', both have strongly negative connotations – except for those who have more or less consciously opted for the more or less unconstrained pursuit of personal or national self-interest. There are occasions when we use 'power' synonymously with 'domination', 'force' or even 'violence'.[1]

But the breadth of ordinary use is not confined to the negative end of the spectrum. We can tell this because of the way we employ 'powerless' to mean that the subject, a person or collectivity, has no way of exerting any influence upon a situation; this may describe a state of affairs, but not (we often imply) a desirable one. It is paradoxical to deplore 'powerlessness' but to speak negatively about 'power'. 'Influence', of course, is one of the broadest terms we have and it includes completely benign capacities, which 'power' can share. To say that something is within a person's power to carry out is a neutral statement. These neutral usages can be qualified in a positive way. There is nothing paradoxical in speaking, appreciatively, for example, of a person's intellectual power, or powers of concentration.

The very breadth of the word 'power' makes it handy in rhetorical contexts. 'Experience shows that when you give people power they generally take it', I read recently in a newspaper report of a speech to the Church of England's General Synod. The speaker, no stranger to power himself, intended to hint at the probable abuse of power; and he could do so without being so negatively specific, or without troubling to consider whether there might not also be a benign use of power, merely by allowing the darker connotations of 'power' to colour his sentence. On this phenomenon Raymond Aron has appropriately written:

> The words 'power' and '*Macht*', in English and German, '*pouvoir*' and '*puissance*' in French, continue to be surrounded by a kind of sacred halo or, it may be preferable to say, imbued with mysterious overtones that have something terrifying about them.[2]

But what are we to say of well-established phrases like ' the power of God', 'power from on high' (Luke 24:49) or even 'the powers that be' (Rom. 13:11)? This last was a brilliant invention of William Tyndale in his translation of the New Testament (1524 onwards; revised 1534), and was perpetuated in the King James (Authorized) Version of 1611.[3] It has lodged itself in ordinary English usage to designate governmental authority or powerful people in a slightly ironic manner. But all of these phrases are, in their original contexts, positive. Of course in speaking of God or the gospel they extend the usage of the word 'power' beyond that of social relations. But that is true of 'power' in any case. 'Power' is a term used in science, mathematics and engineering, both technically and non-technically, completely without negative connotations. We have no reason to create an artificial precision about how the word is going to be employed, if that precision makes doubtful the use of the word in many contexts of everyday speech.

At this point we can pause to consider some etymological information. The English 'power' is derived from the French '*pouvoir*'. As we have already seen it is mainly used in theology as the English translation for two Greek words, *exousia* and *dynamis*, both of which are variously translated in the standard Latin version of the Bible, the Vulgate (for the most part carried out by Jerome of Bethlehem, c.342–420) by *potestas* or *virtus*. There is perhaps a slight difference of emphasis in Greek between *exousia* and *dynamis*, in that the former is sometimes the potential energy, so to speak, which may manifest itself in the latter, in works of power.[4] But the words are also used synonymously, and the Vulgate translates them both as either *virtus* or *potestas* indiscriminately. 'The powers that be', for example, are in Greek *exousiai* and in Latin *potestates*. When Jesus is said, unlike the scribes, to teach with *exousia*, again the Vulgate uses *potestas* (Mark 1:22).

This last passage is of particular interest because the English translations have varied. The context is Jesus' visit to Capernaum where he entered the synagogue and taught. A modern translation reads: 'They were astounded at his teaching, for he taught them as one having authority, and not as the scribes' (Mark 1:22, NRSV). 'Authority' was the term also preferred by the seventeenth-century Authorized (King James) Version, and it strikes modern ears as appropriate. But Tyndale in fact had employed the word 'power': 'And they marvelled at his learning. For he taught them as one that had power with him, and not as the scribes.'[5]

In a certain way Tyndale's rendering may be said to be justified, in that no sharp difference between authoritative teaching and acts of power existed in the minds of Jesus' hearers. When Jesus immediately follows his public teaching by healing a person with an unclean spirit, the people respond: 'What is this? A new teaching – with authority (*exousia*)! He commands even the unclean spirits and they obey him (Mark 1:27, NRSV).' Again Tyndale translates *exousia* as 'power'. Oddly, in a parallel passage in the Gospel of Luke, the Authorized Version adopted Tyndale's 'power' for the Greek *exousia* ('and they were astonished at his doctrine for his word was with power', Luke 4:32).

Imprecision about how this group of words is to be used has, therefore, a long history in theology. It would be convenient were we able rigorously to differentiate between 'power' and 'authority', perhaps particularly if we could load the former with all the unacceptable negative connotations like a scapegoat, and push it unceremoniously into the wilderness. But the feeling that there is, or should be, a difference between the two terms persists; and it is undoubtedly the case that because 'authority' is the benigner word there is a tendency to want to use it in association with religion. Moreover this feeling corresponds to a distinction of usage between *auctoritas* and *potestas* in Roman civil law. *Auctoritas* meant a variously based capacity to influence. A consul had *auctoritas* after his nomination, but *potestas*, the right to issue legally enforceable injunctions, only after he took up office. The Senate, which only delivered itself of weighty advice, had *auctoritas* not *potestas*. In the Roman Empire, the Emperor brought together in his own person both *potestas* and *auctoritas*. The reality of the latter enabled him to intervene in matters over which strictly speaking he had no jurisdiction.[6]

Auctoritas was also a word widely used outside government. Parents had *auctoritas* over their children; it was also attributed to the old and wise. The gods and priests are said to have *auctoritas*, and in that sense their relationship with ordinary mortals is less one of command than of advice, admonition and warning. We have, nonetheless, to face the fact that in the Latin Bible *auctoritas* is never ascribed to God, but *potestas* and *virtus* (strength). We shall see that although it looks as though a late-fifth-century papal author is going to distinguish the *auctoritas* of the Pope and clergy from the *potestas* of the Emperor, he fails to be consistent, and speaks of both Pope and Emperor as *potestates*.[7] And throughout the medieval period literally dozens of treatises were written dealing with the relationship between royal and papal or spiritual power (*de potestate regia et papali*).[8] However the respective spheres of government were to be separated or ranked, they were discussed with the use of the same Latin term, a convention consistent with the Scriptures on which the arguments were mostly based.

In beginning to discuss the relationship between 'power' and 'authority' we are already impinging on territory long occupied by modern sociology, which is chiefly responsible for the massive effort given to precise and distinct definitions. For Hobbes, indeed, the foundation of all true ratiocination is the 'settled significance' of words, and the whole possibility of a rational political science depends upon the sovereign's enforceable definition of terms. Of course we would not deny that where words shift disconcertingly in meaning there is a real need for authors to make clear how they are employing the terms in question, and then to be consistent in all subsequent usage. But the problem in the case of power is not merely that in ordinary usage it is imprecise; it is also that there is no general agreement about how it should be defined with precision.

We may begin with Hobbes' own definition: 'The POWER of a Man, (to take it Universally) is his present means, to obtain some future apparent Good. And is either *Originall*, or *Instrumentall*.'[9] Because power gives rise to competition and conflict between people pursuing incompatible apparent goods, there has to be a sovereign power to whom people voluntarily submit for the sake of limiting the damage they can do to each other. Though Bertrand Russell, like Hobbes, thinks that the chief desires of human beings are for power and glory, and also holds that power is 'the fundamental concept in social science',[10] his definition is more inclusive than Hobbes': 'Power may be defined as the production of intended effects.'[11] The work in question, *Power: A New Social Analysis*, was written in 1938 with the explicit purpose of articulating a basis for the taming of power in the face of both Nazism and Communism. It ignored most of the new literature in social science, which had already made considerable efforts to attain a higher degree of precision.

Notable among these was the formidable scholarly achievement of Max Weber (1864–1920). This was, of course, in German and the terms discussed, namely *Macht* and *Herrschaft*, have their own distinctive background in German culture. In an essay dealing with the distribution of power (*Macht*) within the political community, Weber writes as follows:

> The term *power* will be used to refer to every possibility within a social relationship of imposing one's own will, even against opposition, without regard to the basis for this possibility.[12]

Although this is the most commonly used definition of power, it has been subjected to hefty criticisms. One important strand of these responses asks why power should necessarily be thought of as involving deliberate decision making. The 'present means' of a person (Hobbes), 'intended effects' (Russell), 'realizing their own will' (Weber), all focus upon individual human agency. But should we not also take into account the power of institutions to prevent or manipulate conflict in their own interests? Are there not serious but latent power-conflicts which never reach the level of decision making, precisely because they are implicit and suppressed?

Another criticism of Weber's definition focuses specifically on the issue of conflict. The definition appears to involve the overwhelming of opposition, as if the very concept of power implied the kind of brute force we associate with Nietzsche: 'the strongest are able to make their values count by crushing others'. The irrationality of this assumption was pointed out by the American sociologist Talcott Parsons (1902–1979), who was among those primarily instrumental in introducing Weber to an American audience. His complex definition of power, which retains the possibility, but not necessity, of conflict, illustrates with some clarity how easily definitions by social theorists become the means for advancing their favoured theories:

> Power then is generalized capacity to secure the performance of binding obligations by units in a system of collective organization when the obligations are legitimized with reference to their bearing on collective goals and where in case of recalcitrance there is a presumption of enforcement by negative situational sanctions – whatever the actual agency of that enforcement.[13]

The distinctive elements in this typically convoluted sentence are the references to 'a system of collective organization' and 'collective goals'. Power, Parsons held, was like money in an economy, circulating within a relational context under certain rules and conventions, and enabling the entire economy to achieve things. Conflicts occur, of course; but the point of money (and power) is not perceived by focusing on conflicts, but on the collective goals of the society.

Needless to say this definition too has raised a host of objections, many of which concern its inbuilt tendency to defend, even to disguise, the interests of the main power-holders in a collectivity to minimize or mitigate conflict. As we shall see in Chapter 5, a history of modern sociology can be written on the basis of a distinction between two accounts of power. One of these, by attending principally to actual or potential conflicts, emphasizes that some people have relatively more power, while others have relatively less; the other stresses, by contrast, the benign or communal functions of power.[14] Once it is realized how this disagreement is constructed, the question obviously arises whether some way exists of combining the two traditions in a single theory which relates structure and human agency to each other. But would there emerge, in that case, a non-controversial or neutral definition of power? It is hardly foreseeable. Again, despite objections, it would seem that there is more than a little to be said for the view that all definitions are related to theory, explicitly so in the case of those, such as Weber or Parsons, with a theory to advance; implicitly in the cases of their knowing or unknowing disciples.

Steven Lukes, who has done more than any other contemporary scholar to make the arguments about power accessible, is one of those who holds that 'power' is 'an essentially contested concept'.[15] By this he does not mean to wash his hands of all definitions out of sheer weariness. He intends to draw on a rather precise and significant argument developed by a philosopher of history, W. B. Gallie, in his book, *Philosophy and the Historical Understanding*. The essentially contested concept is, typically, a term which occurs again and again in the history of the discussion of a subject, and yet about which there is chronic disagreement. The meaning of the term is embedded within these disagreements. As a result an historical understanding of how the term has been employed is a prerequisite for clarifying it philosophically.[16] As examples of essentially contested concepts Gallie instances the concepts of 'science', 'fine arts', 'religion', 'justice' and 'democracy'. To them, on exactly the same kind of evidence, in another place I have added 'Christianity'.[17] About all these, as about the concept of 'power', there has always been, and there ought always to be, sharp disagreement. Their essential contestability proves the need for philosophy of a vitally combative kind.

Lukes believes that instead of asking for a precise definition of power, we can focus instead on the question. 'What interests us when we are interested in power?' He believes we can get an adequate start on the subject by accepting what he calls a 'very thin suggestion: that to have power is to be able to make a difference in the world'.[18] Living with this kind of initial imprecision does not excuse one from careful subsequent analysis and rational argument. And it helps one keep an open mind to the variety of manifestations of power, familiar and unfamiliar, which the history of its discussion brings to one's attention. Of course it may be properly asked whether any of the major concepts of social theory are uncontested.[19] But the answer to that question, which seems to be that the very notion of a value-neutral science of society is mythological, supports rather than undermines Gallie's main point. This is, that the student of such a concept must recognize from the start the variety of evaluations which have informed the very way we argue about it.

The viewpoint of this book is that the conceptual imprecision which is already obvious in the formative documents of the New Testament is not an unnatural state of affairs to be briskly remedied by a definition.[20] Indeed we shall argue that the Christian tradition itself sponsors diverging views of power, not wholly dissimilar from the conflictual and the collective types identified by Lukes. Only a 'thin suggestion' will launch us without undue presuppositions onto our subject-matter, which has to be treated, as Gallie insists, in part from an historical point of view. A 'thick' definition, by contrast, would be necessarily lodged in one part of that history, rather as a 'thick' understanding of justice would have to be built up on the basis of particular circumstances within a given society. The relationship of 'thick' and 'thin', however, is not that 'thick' definitions are elaborated instances of 'thin', universal principles.[21] The case is the other way round. One needs to be open to particular ways in which power has been understood in specific contexts in order to appreciate what is involved.[22] One need not, indeed one should not, start from an attempt at over-precise definition.

But that is obviously not all one can say by way of introducing the concept of power. The term is plainly one of a group of words, including violence, force, domination, manipulation, influence, authority, persuasion, and others which the English language has at its disposal for speaking of how agencies, both personal and collective, make a difference in the world. A favourite way of organizing the terms is to locate power on a spectrum between, on the one hand, force, and on the other, authority – (1) in the figure.[23] Another is to use power as a general term, embracing four sub-types, namely, force, manipulation, persuasion and authority (2).[24] A variant on this makes influence the over-arching general term, and power and unintended influence its two main sub-types (3).

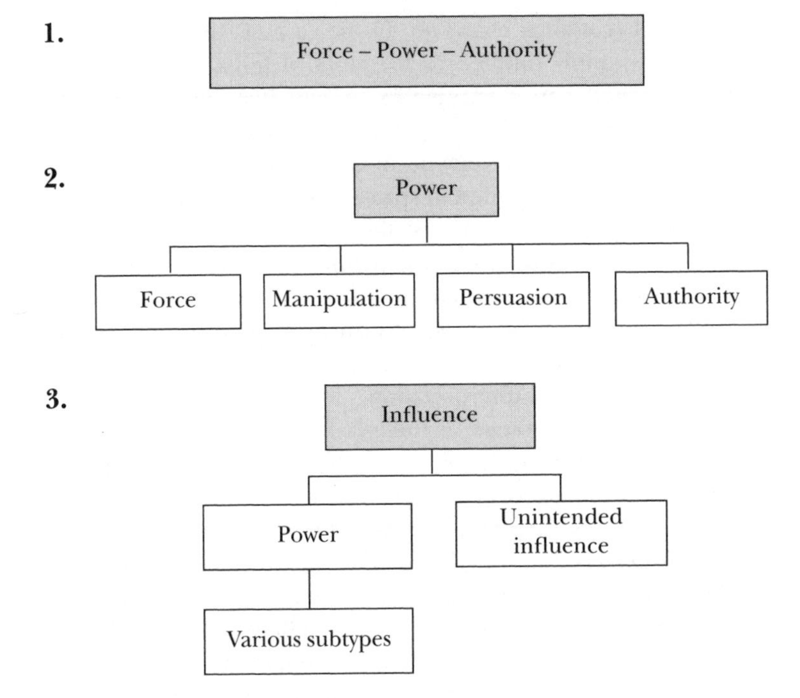

One of the points of contention in such schemes is precisely how authority is to be related to power. Another is whether power necessarily implies the capacity to invoke sanctions of whatever kind in order to exact compliance, and if so how it differs, if at all, from domination. These are questions not lightly satisfied by schematic definition. It is enough that we become alert to the fact that the use of the word 'power' relates in a variety of ways to the use of other words with similar, more or less benign connotations. This too reinforces the argument for accepting imprecision as inherent in the word.

Finally, a theologian has a specific reason for taking 'power' as an essentially contested concept, which is closely connected to the reasons for arguing that 'Christianity' is another example of the same class. Gallie attempts to show the difference between pointless wrangles about terms and proper arguments about essentially contested concepts. He does this by laying down a series of conditions which the latter must fulfil. The first two of these conditions are that the concept should be appraisive in signifying or accrediting some valued achievement, and that that achievement should be of an internally complex character. In the case of 'Christianity' that condition is amply fulfilled by the story of Jesus. In the case of 'power' a theologian is entitled to ask whether the creation and redemption of the world may not be considered that valued and internally complex achievement. In Chapters 5 and 6 of this book we shall see what is entailed in speaking of the power of God. No one, for example, who uses the book of Psalms as texts for the praise of God can fail to be aware of the themes of creation, deliverance and final judgement as instances of God's power, and the consequential relativity of the power of princes. Indeed so fulsome are the praises of God they give rise to suspicion, which is an inevitable consideration in their interpretation.[25]

It would seem, of course, as though that, by insisting on including 'the power of God' within the field of study, a theologian is provoking the parting of the ways between those who see the point, and those who see no point, in speaking of God. But although the argument here is that it makes a difference to take the power of God into account, it does not necessarily follow that the difference can only be seen as the difference between believing or not believing in God. It may present itself, for example, as the difference between different kinds of ethical commitments. In that case the decision to include speech about the power of God will not mean that non-theists have the perfect excuse to abandon the book forthwith. The point is rather, that it will have been made clear that an ethical point of view informs this study of power (and in Chapter 7 I will make an attempt to illustrate the consequences of that viewpoint for the life of a Church). But that should not in itself be a surprise or provoke an ending to the discussion. All the evidence suggests that there is, in each case, a connection between the way in which power is analysed and the political and ethical commitments of the student. My hope would be that non-theists would suspend their disbelief until it becomes clear whether or not the resources of the Christian tradition contribute significantly to the understanding of this complex matter.

That tradition is unequivocal on one vital point, that is, that there exists a plurality of 'powers'. Whatever is said about God's final judgement and the 'putting of all things in subjection under his feet', it is nonetheless the case that here and now human beings live within a network of powers, some of which are malign and exert immense leverage upon them. The power of God is not the fiat of sheer omnipotence. We are caught, so the Christian account insists, in a web of conflicting and contradictory influences. This is a picture which shares a close affinity with a post-modern critique of the myth of sovereignty, but which does not accept the abandonment of the quest for value and truth within the historic process, both personal and communal. Along with the imprecision of the term 'power' in ordinary speech, I am claiming it to be an advantage of the Christian tradition that it recognizes powers of various kinds from which the authors of books on the subject can claim no Olympian detachment. We are in the thickets and we have no compass. Even so, and starting from where we are, map making may not be impossible.

2

Power and Christian Theology: A Map

I

On the basis of our 'thin' suggestion that power always involves the ability to make a difference in the world, it is evident that we have a substantial subject on our hands. Common sense suggests that there are three rather different fields in which power is bound to be discussed in Christian theology. First and foremost is the unblushing ascription of power to God; 'for thine is the kingdom, the power and the glory' is the text of one version of the Lord's Prayer (Matt. 6:13).[1] In the Revelation to John a chorus of angels, living creatures and elders sing, 'Worthy is the Lamb that was slain to receive power, and riches, and wisdom, and strength, and honour, and glory, and blessing' (Rev. 5:12, KJV). In the creeds in Greek and Latin God is entitled, 'God the Father Almighty'.[2]

Then, secondly, there is the obvious involvement of the Church in power. You cannot read or see the historical plays of Shakespeare without noticing that the medieval bishops have their fingers firmly in the political pie with varying degrees of effectiveness. Indeed since the days of the first Roman Emperor to proclaim himself a Christian some 1,600 years ago there has been an intense discussion of the proper relations of Church and the 'powers that be'.

Common sense also tells us that in the third place, there is a distribution and exercise of power, indeed struggles for power, inside the Church. It may be that this ought not to be the case; more doubtfully, it may even be possible for the Church to live wholly uncontaminated by power. But at the very least there is something here to discuss, because we can still recognize what looks remarkably like the frankly admitted dispute among Jesus' closest disciples 'as to which one of them was to be regarded as the greatest' (Luke 22:24). On its own account the Church is certainly not just another organization. But it can scarcely be denied that it has internal problems with the distribution and exercise of power at least analogous to those of other organizations. And it does not seem to cope with these better by denying that they exist, or refusing to see where they come from.

So far common sense. Beyond it one needs only a slight acquaintance with the English text of the Old and New Testaments to come across some important and initially puzzling phrases using the term 'power' or a cognate word. Jesus himself is termed 'a prophet mighty in deed and word' (Luke 24:19). He is born of the Virgin Mary whom 'the power of the Most High' overshadowed (Luke 1:35). He is filled with 'the power of the Spirit' (Luke 4:14). 'With authority and power' he casts out evil spirits (Luke 4:36). On performing a miracle he notices that 'power' has gone out of him (Luke 8:46).

Then again there are demonic powers ranged against Jesus and his kingdom; a whole series of passages in the New Testament letters speak obscurely of 'principalities and powers' who are to be finally overthrown and set under the dominion of Christ (Eph. 1:20–23; 1 Peter 3:22). In this connection it is intelligible why Paul would speak of the gospel as 'the power of God for salvation to everyone who has faith' (Rom. 1:16); or the author or Ephesians vividly depict the Christian life as a struggle against 'the cosmic powers of this present darkness, against the spiritual forces of evil in the heavenly places' (Eph. 6:12).

These are, of course, uses of the word 'power' or a cognate word in English translation. Modern Biblical scholarship has studied the terminology with minute care and rightly points out the contextual and other differences of use.[3] But it is still relevant to observe that for centuries the biblical text was quarried for significance without benefit of such semantic precision. In our way of seeing things there would be no reason to assume that all these uses of a single word must be instances of a single unified thought or concept, to be explained by a single definition.[4] But the biblical text has not always been treated in so differentiated a manner. Part of our problem will be the exposition of a tradition which not merely used the Bible as a single-authored book, but also one where single sentences in one part were thought to be illuminated by single sentences in another.

It would be insulting and inaccurate to suggest that ancient scholars were unaware that there are plenty of nouns in human language which have a wide range of meanings, and whose precise signification can only be determined by the context in which they are used. But in truth the first instinct of our biblical scholars is to distinguish where the ancients harmonized. At the same time our task is not merely to observe that there is no necessity for 'God of power and might' to carry the same sense of 'power' as 'the cosmic powers of this present darkness' or 'to all who received him . . . he gave power to become the children of God' (John 1:12). It is also to understand the way a tradition of understanding was shaped by those who looked for consistency in all the references of the sacred text.

Uncovering both that variety and the way Christian theology attempted to shape the topic is one of the reasons for the title of this book, *Power and Christian Theology*. It is not presumed that the subject-matter can be unified under the banner of 'a theology of power' – a heroic attempt indeed.[5] As we have already admitted, of course, the power, almightiness or omnipotence (the words carry different connotations) of God is an entirely proper 'theological' subject, in the literal sense. There are formidable, philosophical questions to discuss under this heading, relating to evil, providence and human freedom.[6] But though proposed resolutions to these difficult matters bear upon the way in which the Church is involved in questions of power, they by no means determine the discussion. It is relevant, as we shall shortly see, that the power of God has, in Christian theology, to be related to the humility and crucifixion of Christ; but the inescapable pressures and demands of human life exert their own leverage upon the life of the Christian Church. It is this mutual, two-way influence which makes this topic so complex and fascinating.

Bearing in mind the negative or 'realistic' connotations of the word 'power', which we shall have reason to explore further in Chapter 3, there is something challenging about associating it with the supposedly soft idealism of 'theology'. My first appointment as a young clergyman was to the office of Fellow and Dean of a Cambridge College. My predecessor in that office had been the College's disciplinary officer, as well as the priest responsible for the worship in College Chapel. He had been a naval chaplain during the war, and was perfectly used to the misbehaviour of young males;

only meanness of spirit shocked him. But there were those in the College who held it inappropriate for a priest to be a disciplinarian, and at my appointment the offices were separated. As a parent, the cogency of the reasoning eluded and still eludes me, however relieved I was at the time not to assume the office's heavy responsibilities.

A moment's thought reveals that any dualism of areas of 'hard' and 'soft' thought and activity has very serious consequences for both sides. The 'real' world of 'power politics' will come to be thought of as exempt from ordinary moral judgement or constraints. The 'ideal' world, on the other hand, will tend to be seen as only applicable at particularly favourable moments. Under pressure the mask will slip, and 'realism' will prevail.

The challenge to this common way of thinking, for which indeed modern Christian theology is itself partly responsible, has to consist in two procedures. First, earlier traditions of Christian thinking about power need to be excavated. Part of the task will be carried out in the present chapter, where a systematic attempt will be made to expound in a map the implications of the dramatic framework which the biblical documents provide for the living of human life. As we have already seen, there are a lot of uninhibited references to power in the New Testament. The typology which I propose to offer is, of course, modern; but it has the possible advantage of helping to explain two somewhat diverging traditions in pre-Machiavellian Christian theology.

Then we shall need to see with some clarity how it was that Christian theology gradually ceased to be an effective contributor to the public discussion of power, under pressure from the new standards of 'realistic' or 'scientific' discourse on the subject. Here I shall try to offer a rather new narrative of that history, whose intention is to liberate theology for a reappraisal of the subtlety of the biblical accounts of the matter. Of course I do not want to claim too much too facilely. For all its contradictory diversity the modern sociological analysis of power extends and deepens all pre-Enlightenment Christian theological treatments of the subject. But that same diversity makes it possible for a theologian to offer, as a contribution to public discourse, an account of power which is both recognizable as Christian, and at least plausibly 'realistic'.

II

That, at least, is the goal of this book. But as the first subject for reflection I propose to consider the extent of Christian responsibility for an exercise of power in its most unacceptable guise, namely, in and after the Nazi *Machtergreiffung*. On the face of it, how could a Christian be anything other than appalled and repelled, both by the attendant circumstances and by the sheer contradiction between Christ's innocent suffering on the cross and the masterful opportunism of an incipient dictator? But all is not what it seems. The narrative of the crucifixion is, of course, bound to be central to a Christian's understanding of power. To put it mildly, there are conceptual difficulties to tackle if one is to say that the only-begotten Son of Almighty God was crucified, died and was buried. Paul does not exaggerate when he says that 'Christ crucified' is 'a stumbling block to Jews and foolishness to Greeks' (1 Cor. 1:18–23); but he then adds, with some emphasis, that to those who understand the matter aright Christ is both the power and the wisdom of God.

How can the crucifixion be spoken of as the power of God? There is evidence within the narratives themselves that considerable thought had been given to this paradox. The Gospels underline the irony of the reversal of the power claim by highlighting Pilate's interrogation of Jesus over the title, 'King of the Jews', properly bestowed upon Herod the Great (Mark 15:26; Matt. 27:37; Luke 23:38). The inscription 'King of the Jews' was fixed to Jesus' cross in mockery (John 19:19). In the Gospel of John the chief priests are said to have protested that they had no king but Caesar (John 19:15). The same gospel has a story of an exchange between Pilate and Jesus on the subject of power in its grossest form. Pilate asks Jesus if he does not realize that he has the power to crucify him. Jesus replies: 'You would have no power over me unless it had been given you from above' (John 19:11). Pilate subsequently refuses to alter the inscription on the cross to, 'This man said, I am King of the Jews' (John 19:21).

The same narratives, indeed, even go out of their way to emphasize the power of God. Not merely is God said to be the source of the power which Pilate wields; Jesus is also presented as having, so to speak, resources in reserve – 12 legions of angels (Matt. 26:53). Furthermore an eschatological reversal is envisaged; those who now exercise their limited mundane powers will in due time 'see the Son of Man seated at the right hand of Power [here a significant periphrasis for "God"] and coming with the clouds of heaven' (Mark 14:62). According to John's still more explicit account, Jesus says to Pilate: 'My kingdom is not from this world. If my kingdom were from this world my followers would be fighting to keep me from being handed over to the Jews' (John 18:36). Violence, then, does not have the last word. That belongs to the final judgement and the establishment of God's kingdom; and the evidence for the reality of both is the resurrection and the sending of God's Spirit, 'power from on high' (Luke 24:49; Acts 1:8).

It is obvious from what we have briefly noted about the narratives of the crucifixion that they are not innocent of reflection upon the power of God. Nonetheless on the face of it we are at the opposite pole from any violent *Machtergreiffung* but for two potentialities in the stories. In the first place the very lack of ultimacy accorded to the powers of 'this world' implies both a distinction between this and another world, and with it the possibility of passive resignation in the face of injustice and oppression. Martin Luther had explicitly taught a doctrine of two kingdoms (*Zweireichenlehre*), which we shall have cause to consider in Chapter 4. It seems that he should not be blamed for the misunderstanding which was prevalent among many concerned German protestants that the *Machtergreiffung* was merely another episode in a this-worldly history of governmental wrong-doing, which Christians were called on to endure. We shall see that there is a long pre-history to the debate about rebellion against unjust government and the nature of the states' powers of coercion.

There is a second problem. In his compelling study of Hitler, *Hitler: The Fuhrer and the People*, Joseph Peter Stern pointed out the formidable attractions of what he called 'the sacrifice syndrome', 'the death wish at the heart of the will to power', to which Hitler's speeches and the autobiographical writings of individual members of the Nazi Party bear testimony.[7] The rhetoric of sacrifice is powerful for people brought up as orthodox Catholics or Protestants. It is part of their belief system that the death of Christ is the true sacrifice atoning for human sin; and they are taught to offer themselves as a sacrifice. Moreover centuries of association have sanctified the giving of one's life in defence of kith and kin as a way of following Christ's example. The verse, 'Greater love hath no man than this that a man lay down his life for his friends' (John 15:13) is invariably quoted in support, though death in military service could scarcely have been further from its original meaning. When Hitler began to call on Germans to make sacrifices for the good of the nation as a whole, first economic sacrifices, then sacrifices of ordinary civic rights, he was tapping a rich vein of associations. Whatever judgement is made upon the dispositions and actions of the leaders of the churches in Nazi Germany, it is undeniable that Hitler's self-presentation in the language and rituals of a Christian religious messianism had much to do with the recognition he elicited among ordinary churchgoers. Such is the sensitivity of the post-war German theologian to this history that orthodox treatment of the death of Christ as sacrifice for sin has become a difficulty – for Protestants with their greater theological freedom of interpretation, virtually an impossibility.

The 'sacrifice syndrome' is by no means a problem restricted to Germans. The shedding of blood and 'sacrificial' death is written indelibly into the history of Irish nationalism.[8] Indeed the early Church taught on the basis of the example of Stephen that to die a martyr's death was to be baptised in Christ's own blood, and to be guaranteed immediate entry into Christ's kingdom.[9] The identification of a national cause with Christ's own cause has, in Christian history, frequently proved irresistible. The evidence in twentieth-century British history, especially during the First World War, is all too plain.[10]

Feminists also identify sacrifice as a negatively powerful concept for women. Particular biographical studies, and ordinary female introspection, identify women as particularly susceptible to the idea that they ought to 'sacrifice' themselves, their own careers, interests, sense of worth, and even their own bodies to God, or the Church, or their husbands and offspring. In doing so, of course, it is said or implied that, in a uniquely female way, they are imitating or participating in the self-abnegation and sufferings of Christ. It raises suspicion, to say the least, that for centuries these teachings have been heard largely from men, though they have been ingested and repeated by countless women as advice to their own sex.[11]

In each of these instances what is complained of is the power to damage human life implicit in the rhetoric of ordinary Christian theology. It is, incidentally, evidence, if evidence be needed, of the continuing vitality of speaking of the death of Christ as sacrifice.

The thought is that one offers one's life to God, 'I appeal to you therefore, brothers and sisters' (so Paul in politically correct, but all the more ambivalent translation), 'by the mercies of God, to present your bodies as a living sacrifice, holy and acceptable to God, which is your spiritual worship' (Rom. 12:1). Or again, from Jesus himself, his disciples are explicitly told to 'deny themselves and take up their cross and follow' him (Mark 8:34–5). Those who offer their lives for the sake of Jesus and his gospel will save themselves. A whole spirituality has grown out of the project of being a participator in Christ's resurrection by partaking in his sufferings (1 Peter 4:12–13).

A somewhat fuller treatment of sacrifice and power will be offered in Chapter 6 of this book. But for the moment it is relevant to note that, in the view of more than one anthropologist, sacrifice is essentially about how divine or supernatural power is harnessed or averted.[12] There is nothing, therefore, unusual or surprising about considering the subject of power from the standpoint of Christ's death and resurrection. The precise manner of Christ's dying, crucified on a gallows, was, to be sure, anything but glorious. It was calculated to be the epitome of shame and degradation, as well as exceptionally slow and agonizing. 'Death on a cross' was the lowest point of humiliation; but Paul (quoting perhaps an earlier source) makes it the pattern of humility for Christian disciples, each of whom should strive to reckon others to be better than themselves (Phil. 2:1–11). For it is precisely that life which is glorious. A later writer in Paul's tradition bluntly teaches: 'Humble yourselves therefore under the mighty hand of God, so that he may exalt you in due time' (1 Peter 5:6). By patterning one's life upon the suffering of Christ, his sacrifice, one is releasing divine power whose fruit is the eschatological reversal, exaltation 'in due time'.

In enquiring about the extent of Christian responsibility for the success of the Nazi *Machtergreiffung*, it is more than tempting to engage in exculpations or to be wise after the event. But the purpose of this exercise is not the making of retrospective moral judgements. It is rather to understand a fact, namely, that millions of ordinary Christian people condoned an act and a regime subsequently responsible for crimes and wickedness on a massive scale. That alone would be a proper ground for the study of power and Christian theology. Indeed in some ways a certain abhorrence of 'power' and all its works derives from the bitter memory of the totalitarian regimes of the twentieth century. The fuller picture, however, is more complex, as our brief discussion of the crucifixion of Christ has shown. Christian theology has a larger and more ambivalent investment in this discussion than might initially have been supposed. The complete range of that involvement must now be illustrated.

III

Conventionally Christian theology is sub-divided into topics or *loci*. There is no agreement as to how many *loci* there are, or how they should be designated. That is traditionally left to the ingenuity of the individual theologian. Sometimes the content of theology is organized into three articles on a trinitarian pattern, in doctrines of God the Father and Creator, of God the Son and Redeemer, and of God the Holy Spirit and Sanctifier. Sometimes the articles of the creed are treated as the basis, and the sequence of the history of salvation is made the groundplan for the exposition. Different ways of organizing the total content of Christian theology have different implications, whose advantages or weaknesses are variously evaluated. But there is something to be said for having in mind a certain structure of the whole when considering any one aspect of theology. In what has been said so far it has been obvious that power impinges upon Christian theology in relation to the life and the death of Jesus Christ. *The doctrine of redemption* is the locus of theology in which, by convention, the implications of Christ's life and death are considered. At the same time it becomes clear, in Jesus' answer to Pilate, that Pilate's powers are exercised only by God's own gift. Human government is not autonomous, nor is 'this world' all that is the case. In other words, *the doctrine of creation* is involved in the consideration of power. Then again it has become obvious that narratives of the crucifixion include the eschatological element, the moment when the kingdom of God is revealed in a reversal of the pride and oppression of the present order. Thus the *doctrine of the last things* has a necessary place in the exposition of power. Creation, redemption and last things are, so to speak, the beginning, middle and end of God's story. They are each involved in any attempt to do justice to the range of the power of God. Redemption, we may say, is the focus of that power; beginnings and endings are its horizons.

At the moment we are speaking only of the power of God. But, of course, the narrative of the crucifixion involves human agencies and structures. Judas Iscariot is an essential part of that narrative, as are Pontius Pilate, Herod (Antipas) and Caiaphas, the High Priest. Inseparable from each of these individuals are the pressures, loyalties and fears of various groups, the disciples themselves, the Roman Empire and administration through procurator and tetrarchs, the Jewish people with its traditions, internal rivalries and diverse groupings. We have only to consider the deposition of Annas (High Priest until AD 15) by the then procurator, Valerius Gratus, or the fate meted out to 2,000 Jewish males crucified by Varus, Roman governor of Syria, in a revolt in 4 BC, according to Josephus, to realize the communal pressures upon the High Priest, Caiaphas.[13] The story of Jesus' crucifixion is unintelligible apart from these communal and social forces. Christian theology concerns both these specific persons and groups, and also the whole of creation. It is a unique, indeed bewildering combination of the absolutely particular and the most general. The claim made by the early Christian communities was that they were bearing testimony to the life, death and resurrection, not of a popular prophet, but of God's only Son (Mark 12:1–11; Matt. 27:54; Luke 20:70; John 1:1–10). The Gospel of John was written on the basis of the conviction that the ancient cosmic battle of light and darkness had come, in Jesus, to decisive issue (John 1:4). The Gospel of Matthew states that for three hours, while Jesus hung on the cross, there was darkness over all the land; at his death there was an earthquake (Matt. 25:45–51). The whole created order is seen as involved in the death of God's Son, who is, as the Fourth Gospel puts it, the Word through whom all things came into being (John 1:3).

Christian theology involves an acute dramatization of the ordinary. As well as living with the powerful memory of the death and resurrection of Christ, Christians more or less consciously set their lives within the context of a struggle between the light and the darkness. This gives meaning and depth to the trivial events and encounters of the everyday, poised, as it were, between memory and hope. In order to appreciate the full potential of this dramatization, we have distinguished between what one might call three theatres: the cosmic, the societal and the personal. In each of these, but superimposed upon each other, the drama of redemption is being enacted, within the horizons of creation and last things. Schematically one might lay the matter out as follows:[14]

1 There is a theatre comprised by the *whole of creation*, in which God is active to create, to redeem and to bring all things to their final goal.

1.1 We shall want to take into account God's power as *creator* in bringing the world out of nothing, and of sustaining it by his providence against mere chance. The traditional Christian language is embodied in the myth of creation; by the (powerful) Word of the Lord were the heavens created (Ps. 33:6). But modern theologies of creation have to give another account of the creative and sustaining powers involved.

1.2 There is the drama of the *redemption of the whole created order*. In traditional theology, it is told in relation to the kingdom of God, in its cosmic conflict with the powers of darkness, as we have seen. The natural order, in Christian faith, is not deified. Human beings as part of the whole created order have a role to play in understanding and co-operating with its powers to preserve it from disintegration and enhance its potential. There is a redemptive theology of creation.

1.3 In the horizon of the last things there is clearly presented the vision and hope of *a new heaven and a new earth*. This does not come about by human agency or remedial measures. Christian eschatology presents here a discontinuity with the old, and its remaking is the new context for the kingdom of heaven. What can be achieved in the present created order is both inspired, but also disciplined by the goal of a new order. The predication of cosmic catastrophe in modern science is not, for Christians, the end of the matter. In presenting the totality of creation as a theatre for the power of God, we are deliberately attempting to avoid the anthropocentrism of what is sometimes called 'salvation history'. The power of God in creation is not a matter of mere speculative curiosity; it is traditionally one of the grounds of worship. It is doubtless true that the praise of God in the created order, detached from his historic, liberating acts on behalf of the poor and oppressed, is in danger of legitimating the established order of things. To ignore the cosmic context of the power of God, however, would be a disastrous narrowing of horizons, with serious practical consequences for ecological responsibility.

2 There is, secondly, the theatre of the *societal.* In it, too, God is active to bring about, to raise and restore, and to perfect the corporate life of human beings.

2.1 The *creation* of human society is by means of order, embodied in human law, achieving victory over arbitrary violence and the oppression of the weak by the strong. Again Christians do not believe that the social order is divine; rather that the power of God to create human good is visible in a just and peaceful society. The commandments embody a vision of God's order; the love of God and of one's neighbour as oneself is foundational to that order. Human law may be modelled upon God's order, and where it is successfully achieved God's creative power is at work in human society.

2.2 But the whole of human society is in need of God's *redemptive activity,* which is visible in the life of the Church as it challenges false gods and lives as an authentic liberated community. God brings both Israel and the Church into history to embody his redemptive love. It is the sign and effective instrument of God's grace. In its historic existence the Church is not the sole theatre of God's activity; nor is it perfect. But to the extent that it actualizes God's forgiveness in what it teaches and does, the Church participates in God's power to redeem human societies.

2.3 The Church looks forward to a future in which the whole communion of the saints will be gathered together in God's kingdom. This gathering involves a resurrection to judgement for all humanity, guaranteed by the resurrection of Jesus Christ, the new Adam. It is promised that the gates of hell will not triumph over Christ's Church. In the new heaven and the new earth, there will be a new society of harmony and peace. That too will be brought about by the power of God. The theatre of the societal is, so to speak, superimposed upon that of the whole of creation. The physical order is not separate from the social; nor is the social from the personal, to which we now turn.

3 The theatre of the *personal* involves human self-awareness, the consciousness of being a centre of diverging forces.
   3.1 The drama of *creation* involves the power of reasoned thought over madness and illusion. The power of God is present in the triumph of truth over skilfully organized deceptions, and in the acknowledgement of what is the case. Reason is not supreme in the sense that it is unconstrained. On the contrary, its power lies in its humble openness to the truth, and its readiness to acknowledge the reality of what stands over against the inquiring intellect. The power of God is also present in the care of, and healing for, those afflicted by disordered thought.
   3.2 But all human beings are sinners in thought, word and deed. The power of God in *redemption* is present when grace, forgiveness and love triumph over deadly sin. Traditional theology speaks of expiation for sin being made by Jesus in his self-sacrifice. The atonement is God's power to restore humankind to intimate fellowship. The death of Christ is, thus, paradoxically, the victory over sin.
   3.3 And the resurrection of Christ is the power of God *to raise the dead to life*, and thus to enable human beings to live in hope, rather than in despair and meaninglessness. Death does not annihilate and make vacuous all the achievement of personal goodness. The investment of persons in each other, the way in which personhood is constructed and develops in relationships, does not come to an end with death. Nor do the memories of past misunderstandings, wrong or tragedy tyrannize over the present. God's power is yet able to draw human beings in closer fellowship with himself, and so with one another. The theatre of the personal holds out the promise of deeper friendship, the experience of mutual forgiveness, and the enjoyment of a complementarity of gifts. It is particularly, but not exclusively, associated in Christian theology with the Holy Spirit, the personal grace of God living in human hearts, nourishing and sustaining persons in love and mutuality.

The point of mapwork of this kind is not to achieve some kind of total viewpoint upon the mysteries of life and death. It is rather to illustrate the range and depth of issues which arise, and to give one a kind of foothold on the complexities of the topic. The map or checklist can prevent one from being obsessed with a particular aspect of the problem, for example the social or political dimensions of power. It can also encourage one not to overlook interconnections, nor covertly to shift difficulties from one area without noticing that they reoccur in another. We shall see, for example, that by an apparently slight adjustment of perspective, the importance of eschatology can be minimized in such a way as to encourage the Church to claim too much for its historic encounter with paganism.

Secondly, we should observe that one use of the map is to enable one to see what might be called 'the logic of opposition'. In each of the theatres a serious conflict is in hand whose outcome is only identified eschatologically. The logic of the triumph of the power of God is that the counteracting powers have to be taken seriously. It is *because* the theatre of the world witnesses the triumph of the redemptive power of the kingdom of heaven, that the powers of darkness are endowed with serious force. The terms of the drama require that one attributes power to the opposition, and it is always open to judgement at any one time in history how much counteracting power is being exercised. Needless to say this has serious implications for the attribution to God of 'omnipotence'.

'Co-operation' is also a striking feature of the dramas, as we have presented them. In relation to the physical cosmos the doctrine of providence plays an important role in how the creation is understood by Christian theology. The 'powers' of the created order make for its stability. The 'powers' are not divinized; but neither are they merely natural. The category of createdness implies a co-operation between God's sustaining, providential activity, and the potential of what God has brought into being. This is also true of humankind. There is such a thing as personal creaturehood and of a created sociality which entails God's co-operative work. That the work is not simply that of progressive reformation, but actually of transformation, is the point of eschatology. It must be asked, of course, whether the understanding of the human situation is in any way advanced by speaking of the power of God; whether the 'dramatization' may not involve illusion and falsification. The truth or adequacy of the Christian's view of the world has to be referred to the human situation itself, and its capacity to illuminate it at depth. We may be certain that human beings are acutely conscious of the realities of power, of their own actual and potential power with its attractive and frightening possibilities, of vulnerability to the power of others over them, of the social actualities of institutional power with its benign and alienating aspects. We are conscious above all of sheer luck, fortune and happenstance, which dishes out to each a human lot, sickness or health, happiness or misery without any apparent relation to merit or demerit. The Christian faith evidently engages with this reality by interpreting it all as part of a giant struggle between good and evil, into the toils of which God has entered in Jesus Christ. The effect of living in that world so dramatized is, in the words of Amos Wilder, to secure 'a house of being' against chaos, unreason and despair.[15] In the process evil assumes, in its specifically Christian context, huge – indeed apocalyptic – dimensions. In the mythology of traditional Christian theology, evil is organized around a single figure, with whom and with whose cohorts, the final battle is to be fought. The seriousness of the battle is measured by nothing less than the power of death itself to reduce everything to futility. The death of Jesus alters everything in the way power is approached in Christian theology but it by no means eliminates variety of interpretation, as we shall now see.

3

The Affirmation of Power

The substance of this chapter concerns one of the major responses of the Christian church to the multiple challenges of power. This major response I shall call 'the affirmation of power' and it has two separable manifestations. First, Christians came to believe that the Church to which they belonged, that is, the visible organization embedded in the historical order, was an agent in the cosmic dramas which patterned their world. As an agency, this organization was capable of exerting itself so as to achieve significant effects. Moreover, the power which the Church possessed as an organization was related in some positive way to the power of God. The affirmation of power thus refers in the first place to that tradition of theology in which the power of God and the power of a human organization are positively correlated.

Secondly, similar positive affirmations were made of legitimately constituted civil power. Notable is the Pauline dictum, 'There is no authority except from God, and those authorities that exist have been instituted by God' (Rom. 13:1).[1] Christians were evidently capable of believing that the execution of civil justice was itself part of divine power. It required, therefore, to be correlated to the agency of the Church.

In both of these manifestations the phenomenon of human power is positively evaluated. The atmosphere, if one may put it so, is constructive and optimistic, not pessimistic or cynical. Power is a reality, but it is a serviceable one, not inherently corrupt.

This is not, of course, the only tradition known to the history of theology; but it is unquestionably a major one. In the following chapter we shall concern ourselves with the opposite tendency, namely the tradition which rejects power. Christian history knows of both a readiness to embrace and exercise power, in the name and in the service of divine government, and a tendency to be suspicious of, and to reject power, in the name and in the service of divine self-abnegation.

Now this distinction obviously does not constitute anything remotely like an adequate basis for a history of Christian attitudes towards power, which have varied enormously over the centuries. It would not be difficult to extend the typology, for example in the manner of H. Richard Niebuhr's celebrated analysis of Christ and culture, distinguishing five typical positions.[2] If we were to do this then we would need to include, in addition to Christ the affirmation of power, and Christ the negator of power, three intermediate types, Christ above power, Christ and power in polarity and tension, and Christ the transformer of power. But precisely in further pursuit of Niebuhr's typology we would also have to admit that these 'ideal types' are rarely to be found in any unambiguous form even in one thinker. Moreover it seems that the more refined the typology becomes, the more difficult it is to resist the suggestion that every significant theologian dealing with the topic must fit somewhere in the scheme. My intention is different. At this stage it is important to draw attention to different tendencies within the Christian tradition, pulling in opposite directions. The precise way in which any given Christian thinker resolved the problems was often nuanced and sophisticated. Here I want to focus on the plain fact that the theological resources of the Christian faith lent themselves to a radically different construal.

The question is this: How did the Church, in the persons of those who were regarded as its leading thinkers, react to the necessity of coming to terms with power? Christian faith began as a reform movement within Judaism. The reform took place at a time when Judaism was itself in the midst of uneasy adaptation to yet another alien domination.[3] The inherited Jewish traditions contained a variety of potential themes for formulating a response, and the contemporary solutions were various. While it would be an exaggeration to say that Jesus took no interest in the matter, neither his teaching nor that of his early disciples amounted to much more than an occasional sentence. What came to be spoken of as 'Christianity' (earlier, 'the way') was patently not a political philosophy, nor did it offer a blueprint for a new religious organization. The question therefore arises, How did Christians cope with having to formulate responses to power as the movement grew in size, complexity and responsibility?

I

Two preliminary remarks are worth making before we examine the first of the major types of response. In the map offered in the previous chapter, the last things were given an important place as an horizon for the redemption. Paul and his congregations believed that they were simply waiting for the Son of God to return from heaven (1 Thess. 1:10; 3:13). Another writer boldly stated: 'The end of all things is near' (1 Peter 4:7). No precise date had been assigned for these events – indeed Jesus was reported to have denied that anyone knew (Mark 13:32). But some groups and individuals felt it to be close enough for practical steps to be taken; others (misleadingly) said it had already arrived (see 2 Thess. 2:2 and 2 Tim. 2:18 for the view that the Resurrection was passed already). By the end of the New Testament period explicit comment is being offered on the delay of Christ's coming (2 Peter 3:4; see also *1 Clement* 23, *2 Clement* 11). Christians are indeed waiting for that day, but in the meantime must live exemplary lives of holiness and godliness. Three hundred years later all these passages and more were given the most careful attention by Augustine in the closing books of *The City of God.* But he had to take the trouble to counteract an opinion according to which the advent of Antichrist, heralding the beginning of the last things, would occur after ten persecutions. Augustine expatiates on the vanity of speculating about the date, and advised those who make such laborious calculations to give their fingers a rest.[4]

Plainly there is a difference between a community whose conduct is partly determined by the brief interval before the end, and a community that is forcefully instructed not to be impressed with any suggestion of its imminence. In the latter much more attention will be given to the existing conditions of society, to government, and to the long-term stability and coherence of the Church. And that is exactly what we find. It is not just the case that the Church was compelled by its very success as a proselytizing movement in the ancient world to consider the problems of power. This necessary process of adaptation also occurs at the same time as a shift in emphasis in eschatology. It has been frequently observed that a sacramental theology affirming the reality of the presence of the Saviour in the elements of bread and wine grows in importance as the horizon of the Saviour's return recedes.[5] The exercise of

God's saving power in the present and in the future are plainly interlinked. And this is of fundamental importance to the Church's own sense of its God-given role in time and history.

Secondly we must draw attention to the Church's definition and use of 'Scripture'. Both Jesus himself and the writers of the documents of the New Testament cite the Old Testament as authoritative. But because of Jesus' own differentiated treatment of traditions, the early communities had a serious hermeneutical problem. How was the Old Testament to be understood? The resolution of it was to handle the Scriptures in the light of the conviction that Jesus Christ was indeed the long-awaited Messiah. This was the standpoint they occupied, and it was, they claimed, itself inspired. Paul affirmed that the old way of reading the Scriptures was benighted; a veil obscures the minds of those who have not yet turned to Christ (2 Cor. 3:13–17). But with the gift of the Spirit to the Church comes freedom, exegetical freedom; as a result the real glory of the new Moses shines out, and the Christian disciple reflects it.

In the same period when the Church was coming to grips with the facts of power, it was also both identifying its own, new Scriptures and interpreting the old Scriptures with astonishing freedom. This was a process of very great importance for our topic because of the sheer quantity and variety of material relating to power in the Old Testament. This is particularly the case in respect both of the understanding of creation and the last things. In one sense it might be said that the doctrine of creation was taken over from the Old Testament unchanged; in another sense, it could be argued that to identify Jesus as the Logos through whom all things came into being or in whom all things were created, makes a total difference (John 1:1–5, Col. 1:13–20). The interpretative scope is considerable; and to make the matter still more complex, developments in Jewish thought vital to understanding early Christianity lie off the page of both Old and New Testaments.[6]

Not merely do the texts of the Old Testament play a role in relation to doctrines of creation and last things, the new Christian communities' sense of themselves as 'the people of God', living in obedience to a new covenant and acknowledging a new king, was deeply influenced by the narratives and experiences of 'old' Israel. These include, of course, remarkably different episodes: the migration of Abraham; slavery in and liberation from Egypt; a wilderness experience; the infiltration, conquest and settlement in Palestine; prophets and Kings; the Davidic dynasty; episodes of assimilation to and revulsion from local culture; invasion, subjugation and exile; restoration and rebuilding. In their idiosyncratic interpretation of the Old Testament, the early Christian communities inherited a vast resource of texts dealing with power in virtually all its forms: the power of God in creation and history; God's vulnerability to challenge; his support of warfare; his eschatological power; the power of theocratic government and its agents; the criticism of the abuse of wealth and the perversion of justice; concern for the oppressed, enslaved and marginalized; ambiguous relations with powerful nations and tyrants of various kinds; movements of withdrawal into poverty and ritual holiness; longings for a powerful deliverer of one kind or another; acceptance of comparative powerlessness. All these are reflected in the texts, and were available for Christian retrieval. Sometimes the interpretation was transformed by reflection upon Jesus Christ; at other times it was simply transplanted. Moreover the theory and practice of the authority of the Scriptures permitted the use of single sentences taken out of context, on a theory of divine inspiration. Armed with the key to what God really intended in the Old Testament, new readings, including actual changes in the transmitted text, were always possible. The scriptural arsenal for meeting the demands of new situations was generously stocked.

The book of Psalms which, because of its liturgical use, had already acquired multiple resonances in widely differing situations, now became a particularly fruitful source for Christian interpretation. Jesus was remembered as having used the opening words of Psalm 110 ('The Lord says to my lord, Sit at my right hand, until I make your enemies your footstool') in controversy with the scribes. This important text could be taken to refer to the eschatological triumph of one who was called both Son of David and Lord (Matt. 12:35–37. See also 1 Cor. 15:24–5 and Heb. 1:13). A new Christian exegesis of the Psalms opened up enormous possibilities for those who saw themselves as direct inheritors of the promises made to Israel, by being the people of the great Priest-King.[7] The crucifixion itself was interpreted through two psalms (22 and 31) detailing both intense suffering and rescue. The former indeed finishes with a song of triumph:

All the ends of the earth shall remember
and turn to the Lord;
And all the families of the nations
shall worship before him.
For dominion belongs to the Lord,
and he rules over the nations. (Ps. 22:28–29)

The celebration of the power of God in creation, redemption and in final restoration is constantly reinforced throughout this period by the liturgical use of the Psalms.[8]

We should not, therefore, be surprised by the strength of the tradition of the acceptance of power which we are to examine. First of all, we shall inspect three classic examples of positive accounts of power (from Eusebius, on the divine origins of imperial power; from Pope Gregory VII and Giles of Rome, on the relation of temporal and spiritual power; and from John Calvin, a different account of the same relation); then we shall consider certain over-simple explanations for this position; and finally we shall present Augustine's nuanced but enigmatic treatment of power in *The City of God* as an example of the kind of realism which is neither cynical nor pessimistic.

II

First in the list of fervent supporters must unquestionably be the Church historian and bishop, Eusebius of Caesarea. Variously regarded by modern historians as a shrewd and worldly adviser (Momigliano), the first of a long succession of ecclesiastical politicians (Cochrane) and 'the prototype of weak-kneed political bishops' (Altaner), his panegyrics upon Constantine qualify him abundantly as a classic exponent of the tradition of power-acceptance.[9] In the *Laus Constantini*, delivered on the thirtieth anniversary of Constantine's reign (335–336), Constantine is celebrated in the following way:

> Thus outfitted in the likeness of the Kingdom of heaven,
> he pilots affairs below with an upward gaze, to steer
> by the archetypal form. He grows strong in his model
> of monarchic rule, which the Ruler of All has given to the
> race of men alone of those on earth.[10]

This, and other like expressions, constitute an overt adaptation of Hellenistic political metaphysics.

The correlation between monarchy and monotheism, already found in a popular pseudo-Aristotelian work of the middle of the first century, was taken over and transmitted by Philo to the Christian Church.[11] In the idea that rulership is a special gift of God, Christians would find no difficulty. But there are two markedly different ways in which this thought can be expressed. The first is exemplified in Clement of Rome or Tertullian who follow the New Testament precedent in insisting that Christians pray for the emperors to God who gave them their power, combining that intercession with a prayer for the delay of the parousia.[12] On the other hand, the position of the emperor can be held to be exactly analogous to that of the Logos. It is this latter idea, with its strongly subordinationist overtones, which from the time of Clement and Origen begins to play a considerable role in Christian thinking, and is picked up by Eusebius.[13] Imperial rule had already for some time been seen as providential. Melito of Sardis and Origen had already celebrated the empire by interpreting the simultaneous appearance of Christ and Augustus as an act of divine providence assisting the spread of the Christian gospel.[14] Eusebius now adds a further dimension to this view by asserting that, through his intermediary or viceroy, Constantine, the Logos (Christ's name is tactfully never mentioned) is at work exercising his divine sovereignty. The one monarch is the image of divine monarchy; his rule is a replica of God's, and his virtues (of *philanthropia* and *eusebeia*) are divine.[15] In him the promise to Abraham concerning the calling of the Gentiles has been fulfilled. As a religious legitimation of the power of a political regime the speeches of Eusebius could scarcely have been more complete. Their fundamental message matches and replaces the pagan metaphysical analogy between the tetrarchy of Diocletian and the fourfoldness of the scheme of things in the winds, seasons and elements.[16] Eusebius' philosophy of history became the foundation of Byzantine political theory which survived virtually unchallenged for over 1,000 years.

It is instructive to note, however, how much more reticent was the Western reception of Eusebius' ideas. In the case of Ambrose, Bishop of Milan (374–397), there were circumstances, notably a conflict over the ownership of basilicas, which prompted him to reassume the stance of persecuted dissident long familiar to the

Church. Then there was the famous rebuke meted out to the Christian Emperor Theodosius (emperor 379–395), the real founder of the orthodox Christian state. The emperor had ordered a reprisal massacre in Thessalonica in 390. The local bishops protested, and Ambrose successfully exacted public penance from the emperor. The event quickly passed into the Western Church's account of its standing over against the State, and limited the terms on which its theology accepted and celebrated even the Christian emperor's powers.[17]

The humility of Theodosius was a matter of importance to Augustine in his treatment of the felicity of Christian emperors, in Book 5 of *The City of God.* The tribute to Constantine is very moderately phrased. It is preceded by a striking passage of conditional clauses specifying under what circumstances a ruler might be called happy. It begins:

> We say that they are happy if they rule justly; if they are not lifted up by the talk of those who accord them sublime honours or pay their respects with an excessive humility, but remember that they are only men; if they make their power the handmaid of His majesty by using it spread His worship to the greatest possible extent . . .

It ends:

> . . . if they do not fail to offer to their true God, as a sacrifice for their sins, the oblation of humility, compassion, and if, for their sins, they do not neglect to offer to their one true God the sacrifice of humility and contrition and prayer.[18]

Whereas Constantine is given a brief accolade, his sons are passed over in silence. Theodosius plainly in Augustine's eyes had more closely fulfilled what is required of a Christian emperor. But even he, who occupied the 'loftiest summit of power', is soberly recalled. For:

> All the other things of this life, be they great or small, such as the world itself, light, air, earth, water, fruits, the soul and body of man himself, sensation, mind, life: all these things he bestows upon good and evil men alike. And among these things is

imperial sway itself, of whatever scope, which He dispenses according to His plan for the government of the ages.[19]

After the sack of Rome by the Goths in 410, Augustine's early elation over the 'Christian empire' had all but evaporated. The Christian accession to worldly power is not to be celebrated as the realization of God's own sovereignty. God's 'government of temporal affairs' is more mysterious than this; and the citizen of the heavenly city must learn to keep a prudent distance from crude triumphalism.

We shall consider the cautious and sophisticated views of Augustine further in this chapter. But there were other aspects to *The City of God*, and it was these which were developed in the Middle Ages, under very different circumstances. In modern times they were even given the descriptive label of 'political augustinianism';[20] and they, too, reflect a positive evaluation of the phenomena of power, though with some important distinctions and qualifications of their own.

The examples we shall briefly examine from this tradition concern not the power of the emperor, but the power of the spiritual government of the Church in relation to that of the emperor. An influential doctrine, which had the rhetorical merit of being vividly illustrated by an event from the passion of Christ, attempted to distinguish divine and spiritual powers. After the Passover Supper, according to Luke, Jesus told his disciples that for their new circumstances they would need purses, bags and a sword. The disciples replied, 'Lord, look here are two swords'. Jesus enigmatically responded, 'It is enough' (Luke 22:38). The two swords entered the allegorical tradition of Christian interpretation as two kinds of government.[21] In a letter to the Emperor Anastasius I, the late-fifth-century Pope Gelasius distinguished between 'the sacred authority (*auctoritas*) of bishops' and 'the royal power' (*potestas*). In matters touching his own salvation the emperor has to acknowledge the authority of those who administer the sacraments.[22]

It would be neat, of course, if the distinction of terms (*auctoritas* – *potestas*) heralded clarity of relations, but even Gelasius himself was not consistent in the use of them.[23] Moreover, a crucial ambiguity remained about how far the power of the sacraments extended. The category of sin plainly involved political injustice and wrong-doing, and it was within a priest's power to grant or withhold absolution to any Christian ruler. For this reason the boundary between the two spheres of interest was unstable and lent itself to aggressive claims and counter-claims. Gelasius himself paints an ideal picture of mutual co-operation:

> Christ . . . separated the offices of both powers (*potestas*) according to their proper activities and their special dignities . . . so that Christian emperors would have need of bishops in order to obtain eternal life and bishops would have recourse to imperial direction in the conduct of temporal affairs.[24]

This famous opinion contained a partially concealed premise, whose implications were far-reaching. It was Christ, the heavenly king, who had separated the offices; and the bishops were responsible for ensuring Christ's supreme authority over the whole world, secular rulers included.

Accordingly the view that the Church was itself supreme developed from the Gelasian separation. Where Gelasius had written that 'the world' is chiefly governed by bishops and princes, ecclesiastical records from the ninth century increasingly state that 'the Church' is divided into two persons, the sacerdotal and the royal. Hincmar, Archbishop of Rheims (845–882), wrote in commentary:

> The dignity of pontiffs is greater than that of kings, in that kings are consecrated to the summit of royalty by pontiffs, but pontiffs cannot be consecrated by kings: the charge of kings in human affairs is weightier than that of priests, in that the King of Kings has laid upon them the duty of promulgating laws and fighting for the honour, defence and peace of holy Church.[25]

The duty of promulgating and defending the Church, which was written into coronation rites from this time, might take singularly aggressive form, as in victories over the Saxons, Avars and Slavs. But the definition and recommendation of policy was in the hands of the bishops.

Indicative of the needs of this atmosphere is the (forged) Donation of Constantine (c.750), purporting to describe how Constantine decided to exalt the bishop of Rome above his own earthly throne, 'ascribing to it power and glorious majesty and strength and imperial honour'.[26] Perhaps more important than the claims of this document is the fact that Roman law and institutions had come to provide the Church with its means of self-interpretation. The attack of Pope Gregory VII (1073–1085) and the Gregorian reformers upon the pretensions of the 'pontifical kings' is in terms of the theory of jurisdiction. The authority of a lay person must, Gregory urges, be subject to that of the Church. Hence the Pope is empowered to depose Emperors, to absolve subjects of unjust rulers from their fealty, and to be judged by no one. Gregory, in a letter to Hermann, Bishop of Metz, laid special emphasis on the priestly and sacramental role of the Church. Kings need baptism, chrism and last absolution at the hands of priests; if they are evil (as they not infrequently are) and ruled by demons, then the power which exorcists possess confirms the superiority of the priesthood. 'Who can doubt that the priests of Christ are to be accounted fathers and judges of kings and princes and all the faithful?'[27]

A further example in the same positive vein derives from the early fourteenth century. The ferocious conflict between the pope and the French king was at its height, and there was already a long history of discussion of the relative spheres of papal and kingly power. It is in this context that Giles of Rome (c.1243–1316), pupil of Thomas Aquinas, canon lawyer and philosopher, with several works on both philosophy and theology to his credit, wrote a highly instructive tract, *On Ecclesiastical Power*, described by a commentator as 'the palmary example of papalist writing in its most grandiose and ambitious manifestation'.[28]

Giles refers to a traditional argument, found in Hugh of St. Victor already in the twelfth century, that 'the spiritual power must both institute the earthly power and judge it if it is not good'. The scriptural warrant for this is Jeremiah 1:10, where the prophet is set over nations and kingdoms both to destroy and to build. In addition to this Giles invokes the authority of Dionysius (the pseudo-Denis of later scholarship) in his depiction of a complete theory of hierarchical government:

> We can clearly show from the order of the universe that the Church is placed above nations and kingdoms. For according to Dionysius, in the *De angelica hierarchia*, it is the law of divinity to lead the lowest to the highest through the intermediate.[29]

Here the scriptural warrants are the passages from Rom. 13:1–2, deriving all authority from God, and Luke 22:38, the two swords incident. For Giles of Rome the fact of the divine origin of both swords, of spiritual and temporal power, implies, on the Dionysian assumption, that they must be ordered hierarchically: 'Therefore the temporal sword as being inferior is led by the spiritual sword as being superior'. He explicitly denies the possibility of any separation of spheres.

> If these things are ordained, then, the temporal sword must be under the spiritual, the kingdoms must be under the Vicar of Christ, and as of right – even though some may act against this in point of fact – the Vicar of Christ must have lordship over temporal things.[30]

The point of this argument rests entirely upon the legitimacy of power. Power which has not been conferred through the appropriate channels of divine government is simply usurpation. Giles of Rome cites Augustine's gloomy view of human affairs in Book 4 of *The City of God*, to the effect that, apart from divine justice, kingdoms are merely organized banditry (this, it should be added, is the traditional medieval interpretation of Augustine which harnesses his instinctive pessimism to the cause of theocratic government). So for Giles of Rome the ideology of papal theocracy rests upon the somewhat theoretical consideration that without the institution of priesthood to provide it with legitimacy, temporal power is more a band of robbers than a power.

Our third and final example is the reformer John Calvin. The return to Scripture, we should not be surprised to find, does not immediately imply a less positive view of power. There are, however, striking consequences. One relates directly to the understanding of the power of God. Nearly five hundred years of careful and intricate discussion of the question whether God can only do what he wills to do had led to the development of a distinction between 'absolute' power (*potentia absoluta*) and 'ordained' power (*potentia ordinata*). In truth the distinction was neither stable nor clarifying, though it was an attempt to wrestle with genuine difficulties. By the fourteenth and fifteenth centuries speculation particularly about God's absolute power had become exceedingly common amongst theologians of the nominalist persuasion.[31] Calvin, however, would have none of it, regarding the whole development as untenable. For him God's power is the power to act in accordance with God's own nature; God's power is always personal, never abstract; it is a power which is good, wise and righteous and could not be otherwise.[32] Part of the medieval discussion had been about the place of miracles in relation to God's power. Later Calvinist thought was to make ample room both for God's ordinary providence in nature, and also for extraordinary occurrences. In this way it created the intellectual space for the inquiries of science into nature's regularities. In our own day this has been reconceptualized in terms of God's power as a form of divine *kenosis.* Understandably, in Calvin's day, the created order was seen rather as the sphere of divine sovereignty, both in its origins and its final destiny.[33]

The combination of acceptance with modification of the tradition also features in Calvin's unequivocal affirmation of the supremacy of the spiritual realm over the temporal – but, of course, expressed in terms of the power of the Word of God, 'with which the pastors of the church ought to be endowed'. Once, however, endowed with the Word, pastors:

> May compel all worldly power, glory, wisdom, and exaltation to yield to and obey his majesty: supported by his power, may command all from the highest even to the last.[34]

Calvin has, moreover, a thoroughly positive account of the power of the Church in relation to doctrine, where it is governed by the Word;[35] of the need for law in the Church to foster peace and concord;[36] and of the power of jurisdiction in the discipline of church members.[37] Calvin's originality consists in providing the Church with institutional structures to preserve order (in place of a papacy), and in assigning an active discriminatory role to the whole church membership.[38]

The same positive disposition is encountered in his account of civil government, which he distinguished as a *regnum politicum* as contrasted (but not opposed) to the *regnum spirituale.* The political kingdom was, for Calvin, an agency of God in preventing public offences against religion, maintaining peace and property, and legislating for a moral social order.[39] The office of magistrate is that of acting as God's representative, and his exercise of force is entirely compatible with piety.[40] The Christian ought to obey the magistrate, even the unjust magistrate.[41] Following Augustine, Calvin taught that wicked rulers are to be regarded as divine judgement upon human sin.[42] However, at the very end of the section of the *Institutes* dealing with civil government, Calvin added that the magistracy may have a role in restraining the wilfulness of kings, and a single sentence in the final edition of 1559 hints that King Darius, in opposing God, had himself abrogated his power.[43]

Although Calvin himself did not draw revolutionary implications from this thought, there is a very good reason why it was coherent and understandable for his followers to do so. This was because of the destabilizing impact of Calvinist, more generally Reformed, teaching on the eucharist.[44] Late medieval eucharistic devotion, especially the celebration of the feast of Corpus Christi, amounted to an intense local manifestation of divine power which simultaneously legitimated and reinforced the social order surrounding it. To dispute the doctrine asserting that presence, as the reformers did through the medium of the printing press, had revolutionary potential. By simultaneously exalting the divine power of the ascended Christ and speaking of the sacrament as instrumental means in God's hands, Calvin created a distance between the divine and the mundane order, which, so to speak, he refilled with a congregational democracy. Gone were sacral kings and clerical intermediaries; in their place stood all those with faith in the ascended Redeemer. Though Calvin gave considerable significance to those occupying pastoral offices in the Church, the ecclesiastical equivalent of an aristocracy, his favoured mode of church polity was mixed, involving responsibilities for both pastors and faithful members of congregations.

This was nothing less than a new account of power, which despite Calvin's inherent conservatism had exceptionally important implications for European society.[45] But it was not, we should notice, an inherently negative or suspicious one. From medieval debate he took over the three main Latin terms for power, *imperium, auctoritas* and *potestas* as positive terms, using *puissance* indifferently in French as well as *authorité.* Although well aware that power could be abused in all forms of government, the best available remedy is good theology and self-restraint.[46] There can, therefore, be such a thing as a Christian polity in which both magistrates and pastors, deriving their authority ultimately from God's own absolute and unconditioned power, administer affairs to the benefit of all. Needless to say there was no easy resolution of the practical problems of such government in Calvin's Geneva.[47] Far from being any kind of ayatollah, Calvin had to struggle against encroachment for the relative independence of the pastoral office. In utterly new circumstances the old struggles of temporal and spiritual power reappear.

The three examples we have considered derive from remarkably different times, and the mere reference to them in such a brief and generalized form may very well give rise to serious objection on hermeneutical grounds. Could it be legitimate to abstract theological positions from all their particular associations in their own contexts and construct a 'tradition' out of them? This is not a question to which I propose to attempt an answer at this stage. Certainly, interpreting the justification for exercising power without observing the particular power struggles in which it occurred could hardly be a satisfactory method of procedure. On the other hand, the Christian faith *is* a tradition conveyed in rites and liturgies and sacred readings undergirded by social institutions. More than is the case in the history of thought we have the right to detect certain basic instincts and certain recurring problems. What may be claimed for our three examples is, then, that they express an instinct to evaluate positively the phenomenon of power in Church and state.

III

There exist a number of different ways of interpreting this well-known evidence. The first, and most radical, is that it constitutes a history of disastrous error. Human power (it is said) has nothing whatever to do with the gospel, which is a purely spiritual force. My kingship, said Jesus, is not of this world (John 18:26). But Christians, misled by the kingly vocabulary of the Scriptures, and tempted by the vision of imperial patronage opening out with the conversion of the emperor, entered into a disastrous alliance with the world. In its strictest form, as a complete separation of the Christian from politics, it is taught in Christian history by the Anabaptist articles of Schleitheim (1527), which we are to consider in Chapter 4. Calvin, who cites John 18:26, of course, and accepts the distinction between spiritual and political kingdoms, believes nonetheless that 'this distinction does not lead us to consider the whole nature of government a thing polluted, which has nothing to do with Christian men'.[48] On the contrary, when justifying the divine sanction of civil government, he goes so far as to affirm that in the authority of kings and other rulers, God Himself is to be seen as present with humanity, presiding over the making of laws and the exercising of equity in courts of justice.[49] Plainly it is neither the medieval Roman Catholic nor the Protestant Calvinist tradition which lies at the root of the radical protest against the acceptance of power.

The origin of the radical rejection of power seems to lie, rather, in a combination of a doctrine that true believers must live pure and holy lives, combined with a profound despair of the present order of the world. Not infrequently these beliefs are provoked or sharpened by persecution or other experience of profound dislocation, resulting in the sociological separation of the true Church from the rest of society. Historically Christianity has recurrently thrown up such convictions. Before the Anabaptists, we may point to that movement in the early Church, contemporary with Augustine, called 'Donatism' after its founder, Bishop Donatus. Both Donatists and Anabaptists insisted on a visible discontinuity between the Church and the compromises of the rest of the society. This, of course, is the classic profile of what has been called 'the sect' in sociological thought. On this way of thinking the Church made a disastrous mistake when, early in its history, it became entwined in the messy, compromised world of ordinary human power and rule.

What are we to make of this response? We shall have cause to consider the considerable variety of views to which the 'rejection of power' gives rise in the next chapter. But two preliminary remarks are in order, the first of which concerns the 'sectarian' origins of Christianity itself. The word 'sect' is very often used pejoratively in modern speech. But the persecution meted out to early Christians undoubtedly gave a sectarian character to some of their thinking, and it has grown less uncommon to identify at least some elements of the New Testament as having sect-like features. This is even true of the fourth gospel which has been described as sectarian and preaching a universal gospel.[50]

The second remark concerns the opposition frequently drawn in this tradition between 'spiritual' and 'worldly' views of power. Are these two different kinds of power, or perhaps two different entities altogether? The New Testament does not greatly help, since it fails to use a new Greek term for 'spiritual' power and leaves the relationship open to interpretation. The puzzle is assisted perhaps by recognizing that there is an analogy between ordinary power and the power of God, both taking place 'within the one public history which is the theatre of God's saving purposes and mankind's social undertakings'.[51] The language of power, indeed all political vocabulary, allows for a continuum of usages, some closer to, some more remote from God's 'kingdom'. What is called the 'sectarian' standpoint draws a sharper line at a point closer to the authentic heartlands of the faith than do other, more inclusive points of view.

Why did the Church opt so strongly for the latter, if, on the 'sectarian' account, that was a betrayal of its origins? The naïve reply, that it was tempted by the allure of worldly power and fell, is not the only way of construing this fact – if fact it be. The human condition, it could be argued, constantly faces human beings with the need to discriminate between what belongs to, and serves, God's kingdom, and what draws one away from it and undermines it. From time to time – occasionally on matters with massive consequences – the wrong choices have been made, for example in relation to the persecution of heretics. Usually, however, moderating or alternative voices can be heard in which a very different discrimination is being made. The history of the Church, on this account, is not one of massive defection from the original truth, but a genuine struggle for a right judgment without advance protection from the consequences of error.

A second evaluation of one part of the evidence we have presented, namely that relating to Eusebius, has been advanced in the twentieth century by a Roman Catholic theologian, Erik Peterson, in 1935, and independently by a young American church historian, George Hunston Williams.[52] Peterson's thesis, which was originally formulated with Hitler's *Machtübernahme* and its religious legitimation specifically in view, is to the effect that, properly understood, orthodox trinitarian theology of the fourth century makes the enterprise of 'political theology' impossible. In Peterson's account Eusebius is the chief evidence for the thesis that undifferentiated monotheism is intrinsically likely to lead to political theology; he unquestionably has in mind the lapse into non-trinitarian monotheism of Hitler's Liberal Protestant supporters, who found in the *Führer-prinzip* a significant expression of Germany's divine (and political) destiny. Eusebius, who traced the divine providential hand in the circumstances of empire, has, according to Peterson, transmuted religious eschatology into a political utopia to which the analogy of divine and earthly monarchy is applicable. By contrast belief in a triune God makes such an analogy impossible.

It is interesting to note that Peterson is a writer to whom Jürgen Moltmann, whose important contributions to this topic we shall examine in the next chapter, repeatedly refers. Moltmann's target is the association of Christian theology with what he calls 'power politics'.[53] Despite this support it must be said that the basic thesis is simply untenable. The metamorphosis of eschatology into a political utopia cannot be derived simply from a theologian's doctrine of God. Numerous motives contributed to the political character of Eusebius' theology, many of which are already in evidence earlier. Moreover, a whole variety of orthodox trinitarian theologians can be found to espouse the theses of political theology, among them Cyril of Alexandria (who, in a letter to Theodosius II spoke of the power of the emperor as an image of the heavenly kingdom), John Chrysostom, and Gregory of Nyssa. A reviewer of Peterson's book in 1936 pointed out an example from the end of the seventh century of the doctrine of the Trinity giving rise to a demand for a triumvirate.[54] According to the church historian, Theodoret, the principle of divine monarchy was used by the orthodox to defend Pope Liberius against the interference of the Emperor Constantius.

Nor does Williams's proposal fare much better. According to his theory, Arians considered Caesar to be the bishops' bishop, whereas Catholics included Caesar in the Church, the implication being that it was Arians who were the more strongly inclined to Caesaro-papism.[55] The evidence, however, suggests a different and more natural conclusion, namely that both orthodox and Arians provided a legitimating theory of imperial power when the Emperor was ready to act in their favour. Thus Athanasius' attitude to imperial authority changes between the writing of his *Apology to the Emperor Constantius* in 357 and the attack on Constante as an enemy of Christ a year later, in his *History of the Arians.*[56] A century later in the West, Pope Leo the Great is still ready to attribute to the emperor 'a semblance of sacerdotal power'.[57] In this respect he is more representative of the attitude of Western bishops, though later tradition chose to remember Ambrose's resistance to the Emperor Valentinus II.[58]

Neither Peterson's nor Williams's theory is adequate to account for the theory and practice of imperial power embodied in the Byzantine empire. Here the Eusebian theory lasted until the fall of Constantinople in 1453, and it survived for reasons that are deeply instructive.[59] The theocratic political theology which supported the role of the emperor was always capable of qualification by practice. Whatever the emperor symbolized, he was a mere man, who fought and judged and could not be a priest. Moreover his monarchy was limited, and no matter what the theory said he could be deposed if he became intolerable. Only if he conformed to the morally exalted specification of his role could he be taken as the Autocrat. Though the Patriarch was his subordinate and ought not to meddle in politics, a left-wing minority (especially in monasteries) might well pluck up enough courage to challenge his right to interfere in church affairs. Chrysostom's fervent support for, and later opposition to, the Emperor Eudoxias illustrates the possibilities which the Eusebian theory still left open.

A third, and very well-known thesis, is the direct converse of the previous two. Rather than regarding the political theology of the medieval church as a kind of deviation from or distortion of the Christian gospel, the distinguished medieval historian, the late Professor Walter Ullmann, presented it as its natural concomitant. Ullmann argued that there are two competing conceptions of law and government to be found in the middle ages, what he termed the 'ascending' and the 'descending' theses of government. The ascending theory is, in origin, the earlier of the two; it locates the power in the people itself, whose rulers have no powers other than those given them by the electing assembly. The alternative merely inverts the relation; all powers derive from God, and are delegated to a vicegerent on earth. The people have no power other than that given it from above, and the supreme officer is responsible to God alone. For Ullmann, 'the history of political ideas in the Middle Ages is to a very large extent a history of the conflicts between these two theories of government'.[60] Ullmann plainly regarded the ascending theory as the natural way of thinking, while the official theocratic-descending thesis had relatively little impact on the ordinary populace. Nonetheless he presented the descending thesis as having the direct backing of Christian theology, based on the teaching of Paul. By the middle of the fifth century, that is with the pontificate of Leo I, the basic elements of the descending theory of papal monarchy are all present; the direct succession to the powers and functions given by Christ to St. Peter, and plenitude of power in relation to the juristic government of the Church, subject to judgement by no one else on earth.

Precisely the same descending thesis was argued in respect of the powers of the emperor, and it is because these ideas belong to the same theoretical universe that they were bound to collide. The emperor, too, was understood to derive his power and authority directly from God. The crucial difference between papal and imperial sovereignty was formulated by Ullmann thus:

> Papal governmental ideology was the product of biblical and religious abstract reasoning and argumentation, though clothed in the only available language, that of the Roman law and constitution. The imperial governmental ideology was the product of historical argumentation which was reinforced by arguments from the Bible. In some ways, therefore, the picture was the reverse. The one started from the Bible and presented the conclusions with the help of Roman law. The other contrived a historic reality and buttressed the historical fact with an appeal to the Bible.[61]

Ullmann's thesis, though backed with an astonishing range of particular studies, has encountered serious criticism. Although Paul asserts that legitimately constituted power has a sacred character, this, as Calvin correctly perceived, is applicable to more than one kind of government, not merely to a monarchy.[62] Moreover, the New Testament texts from 1 Peter, 1 Timothy, Titus, John, 1 John and above all Revelation, which are more cautious than Paul (or even, in the case of Revelation 12 and 13, directly hostile to government), are evidence of a somewhat different tradition of reflection. Nor is it a tradition which comes abruptly to an end in the later Church, or even with Eusebius, as its influence on Augustine's *The City of God* abundantly demonstrates.

Neither of the last two theories we have examined measure up to the diversity and complexity of the evidence. The question we now have to confront is whether we can give an alternative explanation both for the tradition as we have presented it, and for the qualifications and limitations by which it is surrounded.

IV

Our starting-point will be the observation that this tradition has at least some basis in the texts of the New Testament. Of course, as we have already seen, there is a diversity of possibilities in the exegesis of the New Testament. Indeed, as so often in questions of systematic theology, the problem is *caused* by the diversity of the original traditions, and by the fact that they are already lodged in a history of tradition, reflecting different experiences at different times and in different places. But the radical surgery which demands that we excise all positive references to legitimate authority as imperial toadying has no basis in the texts, and little enough in common sense.

Paul had clearly stated in his letter to the Romans that everyone should be subject to the governing authorities; 'for there is no authority except from God, and those authorities that exist have been instituted by God' (Rom. 13:1–2). This passage, which deals both with political submission and the paying of taxes, revenues, respect and honour, is attached to teaching about the blessing of those who persecute Christians, and on not repaying evil with evil (Rom. 12:14–17). This is not original to Paul; Jesus himself had taught his disciples not to resist an evildoer, and to pay tax to whom tax was due (Matt. 6:39; Mark 12:14–17). As for the idea that the existing authorities have been instituted by God, it accords with Jesus' reply to Pilate that he owed to God's gift the power he was about to exercise in condemning Jesus to death (John 19:11). One might call it a commonplace of the Jewish tradition that individual human actions, including those of tyrants, could well be part of God's plan for human history.[63]

It could be held, of course, that Paul's attitude was conservative and prudential; that it was important at the time (the Emperor Nero was 21, a mere six years from the fire of Rome) for Christians not to be seen as politically revolutionary. This was the relativising argument of the humanist scholar, John Colet (1466–1519), in his 1498 lectures on St. Paul's Epistle to the Romans. The emperor – Colet believed the letter to have been written in the last years of Claudius' reign – was a man of 'changeable disposition' who might well have taken it into his head to destroy the Church.[64] Paul's caution is justified and opportune; but whether it articulates a fundamental principle of Christian politics (as Luther was to argue) is another matter.

Exegesis of this kind is, however, decidedly humanistic and modern in tone. As an authority in a patristic or medieval argument it has an altogether different impact. Here it may appear to commend passivity, on the one hand; alternatively on the other, it lends itself to deployment in commendation of theocratic government. In terms of the map of the previous chapter, Romans 13 seems to be an example of the triumph of law over anarchy, the implication of divine creation in the theatre of human society. Good government involves the operation of the power of God; 'it is God's servant for your good' and 'it is the servant of God to execute wrath on the wrong doer' (Rom. 13:3f.). A Christian ruler has a double opportunity of participating in divine sovereignty, first by personally acknowledging the kingdom of God, and secondly by enacting good laws and ruling with justice.

Chadwick is fully justified, therefore, in the view that 'the conversion of Constantine and the subsequent accession of a Christian emperor marks no great divide in the development of Christian thinking about government, power, coercion and war'.[65] Nevertheless Eusebius' employment of Hellenistic political metaphysics as an apologetic vehicle for his panegyric involved one acute danger, the loss of the Christian eschatological perspective. The reason why a Christian could concede that Pilate himself might be an agent in God's own plan of history had to do with the limited character and provisionality of Pilate's rule and judgement. Though there may be such a thing as good government, there is also flawed and evil government, and it will be subject to God's final judgement. The problem with the Hellenistic theological scheme is that it involved an altogether too complete realization of the presence and actions of the divine Logos in the person of the emperor.[66] The Church was itself to follow suit in its exaltation of hierocratic government, a 'real presence of Christ in the pontifical species' (as it has regrettably been spoken of, with overt reference to sacramental theology). The importance of eschatology, however, is to preserve the uniqueness of Christ's own judgement, and to allow a certain space for human ignorance, negligence and outright wickedness.

The mere fact that the emperor or other ruler is a Christian does not pose in itself a problem for Christian theology. In the fourth century the optimism engendered by the new political circumstances of the so-recently persecuted Church no doubt helped to eradicate vital elements of eschatological realism in its sense of future enemies to be overcome. In Eusebius' case it is significant, as Runciman has observed, that he was a Hellenized Syrian with little knowledge of Roman law, and thus unlikely to envisage how the Hellenistic king-doctrines could fit with the legal Roman accounts of authority.[67] The influence he seeks to exert is rooted, therefore, not in a legally articulated relation of corporations, but on the highly personal basis of favour. The account he gives to the emperor of his new opportunities and responsibilities is, accordingly, in the form of a panegyric. Even so, behind the inflated conventions of the rhetoric is concealed an admonition. It is the emperor who behaves in such a manner who will be commended; Augustine made the conditional clause explicit, having seen how a Christian ruler was capable of gross crime.

The verdict of *The City of God* upon power is enigmatic, as befits the writing of a huge work over 13 years by a person of restless intellect constantly involved in the interpretation of the Scriptures. J. N. Figgis was of the considered opinion that you could not present Augustine's political views on the basis of *The City of God* alone; that one needed the writings against the Donatists to balance and amplify (!) the picture.[68] But the tensions in the work are instructive enough. In a fine essay Reinhold Niebuhr encouraged modern people to take Augustine's realism seriously as a guide to the perplexities of its communities, from the family to the potential world community.[69]

Despite modern commendations one of the fundamental strands of the work is its interest in the activities of angels; indeed one could say that it is the character of its angelogy which makes the work generally positive about power. The early books of *The City of God* are principally concerned with the charge that it was Christian disrespect for and neglect of the Roman gods which was responsible for the sack of Rome. A great deal of space is devoted to the nature of those gods and their worship. According to St. Augustine these so-called gods are in fact malignant fiends and unclean spirits;[70] from their domination of the hearts and minds of multitudes, both deluders and the deluded alike, only the grace of God through Jesus Christ can deliver humankind.[71] It is not until Book XI that we are introduced to the fact that the rise of the two cities, the heavenly and the earthly, owes its origin to the two classes of angels. The citizens of the earthly city prefer their own gods, who are the fallen, evil angels, to the God of the good and holy gods, the good angels.[72] Indeed Augustine goes so far as to say that the holy angels constitute the greater part of the City of God, and were first created with God's creation of light.[73]

Against the background of the contrast and conflict of light and darkness Augustine sets human existence in a consciously dramatized way. He speaks, indeed, of the 'opposition of contraries' providing life with a kind of 'eloquence of things'.[74] But he will not allow there to be a dualism of equal forces. It is his fundamental denial that evil has an adverse source of its own which makes him a witness to the positive view of power we are expounding. There is no metaphysical dualism; this was Augustine's point of departure from the Manicheans. The whole universe, he insisted, is good and beautiful, enhanced as it were by touches of darkness in some places, vile though these may be when viewed in themselves.[75] At several points in *The City of God* there are magnificent passages in which Augustine celebrates the created order, including the created powers of humankind.[76] In each of these, explicit reference is made to God's omnipotence, and lesson are drawn from it, for example the inclusion even of empires of domination in the scope of God's providence, or the gravity of Adam's initial transgression. Augustine argues that it is solely within that providential order that particular Romans, such as Julius Caesar and Cato, were able to follow the path of virtue in striving for glory, honour and power. Even so their love of praise vitiated their achievements, and though God granted them the glory of an earthy empire, eternal life with the angels in the Heavenly City was denied them.[77]

The argument here is rather remarkable. Augustine knows that the love of earthly praise is not capable of being entirely eradicated from the hearts even of the faithful. They still need the stimulus of a better reward in the Eternal City. So the example of good Roman politicians is there to goad them on to higher things *a fortiori*; and the whole history of imperial conquest becomes a moral lesson for believers in how not to boast. This also covers the case of Christian rulers:

> But when those who are gifted with true godliness and live good lives also know the art of governing peoples, nothing could be more fortunate for human affairs than that, by the mercy of God, they should also have the power to do so.

Nonetheless the Heavenly City has the last word, as Augustine adds:

> At the same time, they understand how much they lack that perfection of righteousness which exists only in the fellowship of the holy angels, of which they strive to be worthy. Moreover however much we may praise and proclaim the virtue which serves the glory of men without true godliness, it is not for one moment to be compared with even the first and least virtue of the saints who have placed their hope in the grace and mercy of the true God.[78]

One might call this last passage a form of radical eschatological egalitarianism. Citizenship of the City of God involves participation with the holy angels in the true worship of God. God is worshipped in humility of heart; the theme of true sacrifice becomes crucial to the argument. All people, of whatever rank or station in human society, are called to that worship. Augustine writes about it with undisguised passion. The Holy City, he says:

> Has its form by subsisting in Him; its enlightenment by contemplating Him; its joy by abiding in Him. It is; it sees; it loves. Its strength is in the eternity of God; its light is in God's truth; in God's goodness is its joy.[79]

Like the prodigal son in Jesus' parable, the Christian longs to return home, to the single-minded undistracted worship of God. To do so is supremely to be; to fall away by deliberate choice is to tend towards non-being.

At this point in the argument we are given Augustine's most considered and characteristic statement about power, which he sees as a created, natural good. Greed, lust, boasting and pride do not, he maintains, imply a fault with gold, attractive bodies, human praise or power. The problem is rather the existence of defects in the human will, and all defection is a falling away from God to something of a lower degree of reality.

> Nor is pride the fault of him who gives power, or of power itself, but of the soul which perversely loves its own power, and despises a more righteous higher Power. Hence, he who perversely loves the good of any nature whatsoever is made evil through this very good as he attains it, and is made wretched because deprived of a greater good.[80]

All this is set within an argument about angels, and how it came about that some angels, good by nature, fell by their own evil will. Both they, and also, through the influence of the Devil, in due course Adam, slipped into open disobedience through pride and self-exaltation. This, then, is the fundamental difference between the two cities; in the one there is a community of good angels and devout people who humbly give the love of God first place; in the other a community of evil angels and the irreligious whose first love is for themselves.

It is this account which determines Augustine's idiosyncratic interpretation of justice in *The City of God*. A modern reader would want, and perhaps expect, Augustine to say that the due administration of justice was a good example of the observance of God's order for human beings, and thus a beneficient use of power. He seems to be making precisely that point when he begins his portrait of a good ruler with references to justice, mercy, impartiality and self-discipline.[81] It is, he maintains, a good of a certain rather limited kind, when in the inevitable wars and conflicts of the earthly city the cause that is more just triumphs.[82] The celebrated questions, 'Justice removed then, what are kingdoms but great bands of robbers? What are bands of robbers themselves but little kingdoms?', seems to align Augustine with a wholly positive view of law and order.[83]

But in fact Augustine is by turns startlingly post-modern and disturbingly theological on the subject of justice. He seriously considers that the proper definition of 'people' and 'commonwealth' is the neutral concept of 'an assembled multitude of rational creatures bound together by a common agreement as to objects of their love'.[84] But his preferred standpoint on 'justice' is that it can only exist when the true God is acknowledged and worshipped.[85] If a commonwealth were to be composed of pious people ruled by a godly sovereign there could not fail to be true justice in that sense. But as it was he knew only of mixed societies ruled by imperfect people. It might, therefore, have to be sufficient to aspire to a kingdom in which the wicked are held in check, and the righteous given space to live in peace.

We may well think this to be an evasion of a serious difficulty, and indeed Augustine seems to recognize as much. But the truth is that he was simply not able, as an interpreter of Scripture, either to spell out what social justice involved in detail, or to abandon it as a concept altogether. He is attempting to make sense of a variety of more or less contradictory biblical data: the lust for domination so powerful for males in certain societies, the virtually universal desire for peace and a readiness to settle for a relatively peaceful state of subordination, the ineradicable urge for glory, and an understanding of the depth of self-interest, combined with urgent appeals for respect for the law of God, for generosity towards the poor and outcast, and for humility of heart and mind. The result in *The City of God* is certainly no synthesis; but set in the dramatic context of a cosmic struggle between hosts of angels and demons the issues are given a rare depth. The response to power is fundamentally affirming, but there are more than hints of reservation. These principally concern the human – perhaps predominantly male – lust for domination, *libido dominandi.* And that is the starting-point for our next inquiry.

4

The Rejection of Power

Certain scriptural texts are a little like time bombs waiting to go off. Perhaps the image of a timing-device suggests altogether too predictable a reaction. It is as if the fuse is lit when certain apparently random atmospheric conditions are right. Words which until then have been seen in one way, are suddenly interpreted in another, with massive consequences. Or again 'suddenly' may turn out, with the wisdom of hindsight, to be an exaggeration. One may hardly say that in the sixteenth century it 'suddenly' became obvious that the Church's exercise of power involved serious abuses. The biblical texts to which appeal was made had not been newly discovered, even if they had been newly translated and made newly available in print. Most (but not all) of the interpretations of the text were familiar, even conventional, by the time they were advanced by Luther and sixteenth-century radicals. Reformations are often intensely conservative movements involving a return to classical sources, to documents whose authority is at least theoretically established beyond dispute. But they involve seeing old things in new ways.

In relation to power, the Old and New Testaments are an extraordinarily rich resource; and they are not lacking in materials upon which to build a case for the rejection of power in its mundane form. The last phrase adds an important qualification. The power of God in creation, redemption and final salvation is too well established in the biblical texts to be seriously challenged (or so an ordinary reader might think). Not so political power, or the exercise of power by the Church or in the Church. There are ample grounds on a plain reading of certain texts for caution, and it is these passages whose moment came with the reform movements of the sixteenth century, though fully prepared in earlier disputes and discussions.

I

When, in the Gospel of Mark, it is said that James and John asked for seats at the right hand of Christ in glory, the ten were indignant.

> So Jesus called them and said to them, 'You know that among the Gentiles those whom they recognize as their rulers lord it over them (*katakurieuousin autōn*), and their great ones are tyrants over them (*katexousiazousin autōn*). But it is not so among you; but whoever wishes to become great among you must be your servant (*diakonos*), and whoever wishes to be first among you must be slave (*doulos*) of all. For the Son of Man came not to be served but to serve, and to give his life a ransom for many.' (Mark 10:42–45)

The same story in virtually identical words occurs in Matthew who presumably copied it from Mark. The only change is that Matthew strives ineffectually to save James and John some embarrassment by putting the request for top places in their mother's mouth. In the Gospel of Luke, however, there is a somewhat different setting and form of the story. Immediately after the Last Supper itself:

> A dispute also arose among them, as to which one of them was to be regarded as the greatest. But he said to them, 'The kings of the Gentiles lord it (*kurieuousin autōn*) over them; and those in authority (*hoi exousiazontes autōn*) over them are called benefactors. But not so with you; rather the greatest among you must become like the youngest (*neoteros*), and the leader (*hegoumenos*) like one who serves (*diakonōn*). For who is greater, the one who is at the table or the one who serves? Is it not the one at the table? But I am among you as one who serves.' (Luke 22:24–27)

It is important to add that immediately Luke appends what one might call an eschatological compensation.

> You are those who have stood by me in my trials; and I confer on you, just as my Father has conferred on me, a kingdom, so that you may eat and drink at my table in my kingdom, and you will sit on thrones judging the twelve tribes of Israel. (Luke 22:28–30)

A further passage must be cited in this same connection, from the Last Supper in the Gospel of John, where Jesus washes his disciples' feet, and then asks:

> Do you know what I have done to you? You call me Teacher (*didaskolos*) and Lord (*kurios*); and you are right, that is what I am. So if I, your Lord and Teacher, have washed your feet, you also ought to wash one another's feet. For I have set you an example, that you also should do as I have done to you. Very truly, I tell you, servants (*doulos*) are not greater than their master (*kurios*); nor are messengers (*apostolos*) greater than the one who sent them. If you know these things, you are blessed if you do them. (John 13:12–17)

A final strand in the tradition we are to consider is comprised by Paul's agonized reflection on his status and authority as an apostle, which had plainly been challenged from within the church he founded in Corinth. With considerable eloquence he tells them that he originally preached the gospel among them without eloquence, so that its intrinsic power might be the more obvious. God has not chosen the powerful as his disciples, but the weak and despised, among whom he includes himself. Their faith, therefore, rests simply on the power (*dunamis*) of God. He himself, along with Apollos and any other leader claimed as the head of a church faction, are merely servants (*diakonoi*) under God. That is his only strength and boast. He, the powerless one, will have to come and sort out the arrogant people who are talking up their own position (1 Cor. 4:1, 10, 21).

The first letter plainly did not finish the dispute (2 Cor. 7:8). He has again to address the subject of his standing as an apostle, as someone exercising God's extraordinary power but through an inadequate vessel. He appeals to his church 'by the meekness and gentleness of Christ' (2 Cor. 10:1). If he boasts at all it will only be because of his afflictions and weakness. 'Power is made perfect in weakness' (2 Cor. 12:9). Christ indeed was crucified in weakness, but lives by the power of God; and that is how Paul will have to deal with them (2 Cor. 13:4).

None of these Pauline passages relate to the power of a Church as an organization, or the power of any of its leaders or ordinary members in relation to political life and government. They bear, rather, upon the exercise of power within the Church, on how leaders of the Church ought to conduct themselves. But because they refer explicitly to the teaching and example of Christ himself, they have the potential for being indirectly relevant to any form of the exercise of power. As a consequence the tradition we are to examine is anything but homogeneous. What justifies us in treating it as a type of response is the realization that power presents a problem; 'not so with you'. Jesus' words are heard as a challenge and criticism; some interpret them as applicable only to how the Church is to be governed, for others they concern how Christians are to comport themselves in public affairs. Vast acres of ambiguity yawn between the two positions.

Selective blindness to other aspects of the tradition is, of course, endemic in Christian apologetic. The Scriptures do not come with ready-made rules on how they are to be interpreted. It is human and understandable that we find embattled church leaders and their theological supporters reaching for texts and part-texts as legitimation for stances and courses of action pressed upon them by circumstances. But two forms of selectivity require some immediate comment. In the first place we should not overlook the fact that these scriptures were written in communities which were perfectly familiar with inequality of power. For all Paul's self-denigration as a weakling who inspired in people only disgust and contempt, he is (or claimed to be) their father (1 Cor. 4:15). As the planter of the church at Corinth, he feels entitled to deliver judgement in the name of Christ on a wrong-doer, and to offer an authoritative verdict on controversies. He also asserts his right to be financially supported. Distinguishing his claims from self-assertion, he legitimates his leadership among them by reference to Jesus Christ himself; he is sent as Christ's apostle and ambassador (2 Cor. 5:20).

Even the gospel passages make incidentally clear that the problem is not the mere fact that there are leaders in the community, but that the model of authority on display in public life is domineering, and radically inappropriate to life in the Church. The first letter of Peter makes this point, when the elders (*presbuteroi*) are told to be shepherds to God's flock,

> not under compulsion but willingly . . . , not for sordid gain but eagerly. Do not lord it (*katakurieuontes*) over those in your charge, but be examples to the flock. (1 Peter 5:2–3)

The youngest are to be subject to the elders, and all are to be clothed with humility towards each other, for (citing Proverbs) 'God opposes the proud, but gives grace to the humble'.

> Humble yourselves therefore under the mighty hand of God, so that he may exalt you in due time. (1 Peter 5:5–6)

The word used here of a domineering exercise of authority is the same as that used in Mark 10:42 to characterize the rule of those who are supposed (with, perhaps, a hint of irony) to rule over the Gentiles. There is no denial of the fact of inequality in the community; on the contrary there are elders in the congregation to whom the younger (the *neoteroi*) are to be subject or subordinate.

The Markan version of Jesus' saying, which likewise has a clear context in the life of the community transmitting it, sharply contrasts a domineering authority with servanthood and slavery. But even here the fact that there will be those who *wish to* be great or *wish to* be first is not denied or dismissed. The saying is not a rebuke to James and John for *asking* for the privilege of sitting at Jesus' right hand; rather it is directly against the terms on which the angry dispute between the disciples had been conducted.

The Lukan version, which appears to be a more radical rejection of authority in that there is no word corresponding to the word 'domineer', is not in reality less positive. There is no denial of the fact of greatness and leadership; rather those in authority are to become *as* the youngest (the subordinates), perhaps the young men used as waiters at feasts, and *as* those who serve. Though Jesus is among them 'as one who serves', the narrative setting of the story makes clear that he is presiding at the table. The Hellenistic world knew of masters who gave a feast to their slaves, and served them.

The Johannine version is even clearer in affirming that Jesus is teacher and lord, and that being a teacher and a *kurios* is entirely compatible with washing his disciples' feet and setting an example of humility.

Finally we should not overlook the realism of the eschatology. Whatever suffering service of the gospel may entail, there is a throne promised to those who have abandoned everything to follow Jesus. To have humility towards and to serve one another here and now is not incompatible with exaltation 'in due time'.

The second form of selectivity has to do with the way in which the passages relating to servanthood have recently been read. On the basis of an inadequate review of ancient non-Christian usage of the Greek words for 'servant' and 'service' combined with a desire to support the (wholly desirable) development of 'diaconal ministry' in the German Protestant Churches, it was claimed in an authoritative dictionary that *diakonia* meant 'active Christian love for the neighbour' and is an utterly distinctive usage in the ancient world.[1] Sustained by a number of other studies of a similar kind, a whole theological movement has developed which views the Church as 'the servant church' and its prime relationship to society as that of service. In order the more sharply to profile the revolutionary novelty of the standpoint, which has affected the Roman Catholic Church as much as the Protestant Churches, many writers formulate the difference with the slogan, 'Not power but service'.[2] In the same years a former Director of Management Research with American Telephone and Telegraph Company developed a view of institutional life which he published under the title *Servant Leadership, A Journey into the Nature of Legitimate Power and Greatness.*

In this chapter an effort will be made to understand why 'power' came to be seen as the opposite of 'service'. Of course Christian theology requires a serious treatment of the themes of humility and lowliness of mind. This internalized self-discipline was, though a formidable task, perfectly compatible with the exercise of substantial powers in both church and public life. Here the outstanding document was a treatise entitled the *Book of Pastoral Rule* (*Liber Regulae Pastoralis*), normally known in English as *Pastoral Care,* written in the last decade of the sixth century by Pope Gregory I ('The Great').[3] The point of calling it a *regula* or rule was to provide for secular clergy, especially bishops, the equivalent of a monastic rule. But it was destined to have a much greater influence than that, addressed as it was to *rectores,* in principle anyone exercising large powers of leadership, lay or ordained.[4] It was to have a remarkable career in England where it was translated into Old English by none other than King Alfred himself, in the late tenth century.[5] As we shall see in Chapter 7, the most notable feature of this work is its insight into both the insidious mechanisms connecting the exercise of authority to conceit, and the human proclivity for self-deception.

Armed with this teaching, those in positions of rulership might exercise their powers, if not safely then at least appropriately. But the medieval period was to throw up a very different critique of the exercise of power by clergy, with far-reaching implications for the shaping of the modern world.

II

The 'accursed Marsilius' (Marsiglio of Padua, c.1275–1342) set out the exegetical programme of the second of his discourses in the following terms:

> I shall first show, that Christ himself came into the world not to dominate men, nor to judge them by judgement in the third sense, nor to wield temporal rule, but rather to be subject as regards the status of the present life; and moreover, that he wanted to and did exclude himself, his apostles and disciples, and their successors, the bishops or priests, from all such coercive authority or worldly rule, both by his example and by his words of counsel or command. I shall also show that the leading apostles, as Christ's true imitators, did this same thing and taught their successors to do likewise; and moreover, that both Christ and the apostles wanted to be and were continuously subject in property and in person to the coercive jurisdiction of secular rulers, and that they taught and commanded all others, to whom they preached or wrote the law of truth, to do likewise, under pain of eternal damnation. Then I shall write a chapter on the power or authority of the keys which Christ gave to the apostles and their successors in office, bishops and priests, so that it may be clear what is the nature, quality and extent of such power, both of the Roman bishop and of the others.[6]

The references to Scripture and church theologians that follow are by way of supporting arguments. Discourse I of Marsilius' *The Defender of Peace* presented a demonstration, based on reason (and Aristotle), to show that government must pursue peace by lawful means, and cannot permit the intrusion of another jurisdiction. Marsilius intended radically to curtail the power of the pope – he was especially fierce on the claim for 'plenitude of power' – but he did not deny the sacramental power of ordination and priesthood. The crucial and revolutionary doctrine, which was indeed 'an imaginative leap', was Marsilius' contention that all coercive power is secular by definition. The role of priests is to serve 'by the example and command of Christ'.[7] And the scriptural proof of his thesis is drawn from a variety of passages, notably including those to which we have drawn attention. The work was completed in 1324, and condemned as heretical by Pope John XXII in 1327.

Two hundred years later Marsilius' arguments (except the case for popular sovereignty) were to prove irresistibly attractive in another context. The first English translator of Marsilius, the radical humanist William Marshall, received £12 from Thomas Cromwell, Vicar General to Henry VIII, as a loan to cover his costs. It was published in 1535, two years after the Act in Restraint of Appeals transferring the Church's jurisdiction to the English monarch. 'This realm of England', says Cromwell's Marsiglian preamble to the Act, 'is an empire . . . governed by one supreme head . . . who wields plenary, whole and entire power'. The popes, says Marshall in his preface, have always been 'proud and presumptuous usurpers'.[8]

The central question for Marsilius is the exercise of power within the Church. On the face of it there is nothing wrong with the concept of power in itself. Christian believers, says Marsilius, have no doubts that power and authority is truly possessed by Christ himself.[9] In the world to come (but not in this present world) Christ will administer coercive judgement upon sinners. But what Christ does here and now is to set his apostles the example of supreme poverty, in the sense that he acquired no ownership or *dominium* of any temporal thing or of its use.[10] His lordship, therefore, is to be understood as entirely spiritual. His disciples have no grounds, therefore, to go beyond teaching, admonishing and warning. All coercive acts are by definition this-worldly, and belong solely to secular authority. If one adds to the sharpness of the separation, the usual Augustinian doctrine concerning the *libido dominandi*, and the inveterate human tendency for strife, one is not far from the kind of 'realism' that was in due course to characterize the teaching of Machiavelli and Thomas Hobbes.[11]

Among the scriptural warrants for the exclusion of the Church from coercive judicial power figure are, not surprisingly, the passages from the Gospels recounting the disciples' quarrel about precedence. These are no longer understood as warnings about the difficulty of retaining the virtue of humility in the midst of great responsibilities; they are now a blunt prohibition from exercising any coercive power over anyone. Then to demonstrate the traditional character of this exegesis, Marsilius cites Origen, Chrysostom, Jerome and Bernard of Clairvaux – except that in the case of the first three he misquotes or falsifies the text to suit his own interpretation.[12] It is as if he is caught red-handed in the act of innovation.

The manipulation of these texts in the interest of separating spiritual persons from worldly issues did not, of course, deny to the Church all forms of leverage. Marsilius was quite clear that human societies still needed teachers (*doctores*), and influence is still a form of power. But something momentous was afoot as a widening circle of the governing and educated elites 'expressed a consciousness of secular power as separate in origin, purpose, scope and legitimation from the church'.[13] Machiavelli (1469–1527) was to abandon any attempt to circumscribe the exercise of secular power within the norms of Christian ethics. But he believed, or said he believed, in the desirability of their being a moral arbiter to supervise conflicts. The problem with the papacy of his day was that it had forfeited its right to be so regarded by its venal and self-interested political behaviour.[14]

The next voice we are to hear is Martin Luther's (1483–1546). Such was the dissemination of views developed in the late Middle Ages it did not greatly matter that Luther evidently had little precise knowledge of the history of medieval political theory.[15] His reputation, nonetheless, is 'to have done more than anyone else to promote princely authority'.[16] It is notorious that he thundered against 'the robbing and murdering hordes of peasants' in the middle of the Peasants' War (1525).[17] His – or what was supposed to be his – doctrine of non-resistance to tyranny became a pretext for passively enduring (or indeed colluding with) Nazism, and the separateness of the two kingdoms of which he spoke was invoked by theologians in support of Hitler's regime.[18]

The 'two kingdoms' of Luther have an obvious relationship to the 'two cities' of Augustine; they also share the complexity and the ambiguity of the distinction.[19] And there is a difference which lies in the still darker colours in which 'temporal authority' is painted. The German words which stand at the head of the most thorough of his frequent treatments of the theme speak of *weltlicher Oberkeit*. '*Weltlich*' is certainly 'of this world' and thus 'temporal'; but it also has some of the pejorative overtones of 'this-worldly'.[20] '*Oberkeit*' implies 'superordination', and is appropriate to someone who had no time for the view that all people were equal ('worldly kingdom cannot exist without an inequality of persons', he roundly told the peasants asking for freedom from serfdom).[21] Luther's German translation of Romans 13:1 ran: 'Let everyone be subject to authority (*Oberkeit*) and power (*Gewalt*), for there is no power (*Gewalt*) but from God'. *Gewalt* is a word used synonymously with 'power', but having also overtones of 'force'.[22] Immediately after quoting Romans 13 and 1 Peter 2 Luther speaks of 'the law of the temporal sword', his favoured emblem for this-worldly authority.[23] A commentator justifiably notes that 'it is not the Judge, but the Executioner who epitomizes ruling for Luther'.[24] Luther plainly enjoyed suggesting that any Christian with the necessary qualifications should not hesitate to volunteer to be a hangman, if one were lacking.[25]

So there is no question of Luther being the source and mainspring of the rejection of power, in the sense we shall shortly elucidate from a classic Anabaptist confession. But he was engaged in a deliberate sharpening of contrasts with a view to insisting that God's kingdom has nothing to do with temporal power. His initial understanding of government, indeed, is that it is only necessary for non-Christians. 'Savage wild beasts' need to be bound with chains and ropes.[26] Christians should not and would not use the sword among themselves; but 'the world is un-Christian'.[27] Christians should not and would not defend themselves if attacked; but they should go to the aid of their neighbour, and in this sense the governing authority and its sword are a divine service.[28]

However – and this was the whole point of a treatise designed to criticize rulers who had banned the reading and discussion of Luther's books – temporal government has no business encroaching on God's kingdom, and bishops have no right to coerce people on spiritual matters. Both groups are treated to a thorough reprimand; and in the process the tone adopted on the subject of power is markedly negative. An upright prince, Luther warns, is exceptionally rare, and one must only expect the worst from them. The wickedness of the world, generally speaking, matches the venality of the princes, but the world will not put up with their 'tyranny and wantonness' much longer.[29] What, then, of the bishops? Luther roundly says there should be no 'superiority' (*Oberkeit*) among them, because Christ has abolished it.

> Among Christians there is no superior except Christ alone. And how can there be superiority (*Oberkeit*) [or inferiority] when all are equal, and have the same right, power (*Macht*), goods, and honour? No one desires to be another's superior, for everyone wants to be the inferior of the rest.[30]

The government of bishops and priests is not a matter of authority or power, but a service and an office; this theme had already been expounded in the 1520 addresses, *To the Christian Nobility of the German Nations Concerning the Reform of the Christian Estate and The Babylonian Captivity of the Church.*

Likewise on the subject of power in relation to the spiritual life of the Church, no reader of Luther can miss the Pauline self-designation as a poor, weak and sinful specimen of humanity. He frequently quotes the paradoxical utterance, 'power is made perfect in weakness' (2 Cor. 12:9). He sees himself, in his office as teacher, as a radical egalitarian; 'a prince is the same to me as a peasant'.[31] But as in the case of Paul, the abnegation of one kind of power is compensated for by the claim that he speaks the word of God. In writing against the peasants, Luther is peremptory: 'I must instruct the rulers how they are to conduct themselves in these circumstances.'[32] The prophetic word he has to utter is that the peasants, in these last days, are doing the devil's work. They are to be put down by force; 'this is the time of the sword, not the day of grace'.[33] Shocking as these words are, they are the more objectionable as the command of someone who sees himself as 'powerless', and a 'servant'.

In quieter times service plays a major role in the attractive portrait Luther draws of a truly Christian ruler. This is a person who thinks of Christ, and remembers that Christ did not come to gain power, estate and honour, but to serve human need. So rulers should expunge from their hearts all thoughts of their own power and authority, and consider only the needs of their subjects, dealing with their concerns as though they were their own. A fine passage from his treatise, *On Secular Authority*, destined to be repeated in sentiment if not in performance by many in years to come, runs:

> I shall not seek my own advantage at my subjects' hands, but theirs, and I will serve them in my office, protect them, listen to them, defend them and govern them only for their benefit, not

> for mine. A prince should therefore dispense with his might and superiority, as far as his heart and mind are concerned, and attend to the needs of his subjects as if they were his own. For this is what Christ has done for us, and these are the real works of Christian love.[34]

Bearing in mind the fixed character of the inequalities of society in Luther's mind, one is bound to say that the limit of his ideas is a Christian ethical qualification of the ideology of aristocracy. But it is presented in the form, 'not power but service'. And precisely in that form it is a concealment of power, and it necessarily gives to the concept of power a certain negativity of association.

What, then, has changed? On the face of it, not much. Luther's views appear to be a version of the medieval doctrine of two swords, accentuating perhaps rather more sharply their independence; as Lohse concludes:

> He established and developed theologically the independence of the temporal arm. At the same time he accented and likewise theologically grounded the summons to the church to renounce temporal power: 'The sword' belonged to the kingdom of the world; the business of the church was 'the Word'.[35]

When it came to confronting armed rebellion, as it did in the Peasants' War, the theological theory of temporal power permitted decisive intervention. Luther's appeal to temporal power in the case of the Anabaptists is less easily justified; and what is at stake is not simply Luther's personal consistency. The issue is whether the Church's everyday involvement with temporal order permits the radical renunciation which Luther's programme required. There were contemporaries who insisted that something more far-reaching was required – the Anabaptists themselves.

From the same decade as Luther's major writings on political matters comes a rough grouping of radical voices with a very different view of the Church. Nicknamed 'Anabaptists' from their practice of re-baptizing as adults those true believers who repudiated their baptism as infants, they were in truth a heterogeneous collection of local movements.[36] Two features, however, they tended to have in common were: a commitment to grass-roots reformation with no delay and, concomitantly, a mistrust or outright rejection of a hierarchical conception of authority whether in secular or ecclesiastical life. Existing rulers might be asked to assist the necessary reformation, but if they did not do so they destroyed their own legitimacy. At this point the radicals divided. Some such as Thomas Müntzer advocated popular insurrection, launching into a vituperative attack on Luther (Doctor *Lügner*/Liar) himself.[37] Others taught radical separation and disengagement from the world.

The perceived threat to established order, including the carefully nurtured plans of the so-called 'magisterial' reformers (that is, those who worked co-operatively with the local magistracy) was out of all proportion to the numbers involved, except in the regions affected by the Peasants' War. The fact that the various groups of radicals made efforts to keep in touch with each other, and the degree of similarity in their proposals, made it easier for opponents to tar the whole movement with the more extreme excesses of any part of it.[38] Luther's own separation between the two kingdoms was the obvious source of some of the radicals' doctrines. The first of the ten articles of the peasants, for example, was a demand that a local community be allowed to appoint, and depose, its own pastor. Luther's initial reply had been that 'no ruler ought to prevent anyone from teaching or belie what he pleases, whether it is the gospel or lies', provided it is not seditious.[39] This was a conclusion which experience of the Peasants' War led him to withdraw.

Moreover the category of what amounted to sedition or rebellion was elastic. When, in Zurich, Anabaptist parents refused to bring their infants to baptism, believing it to be contrary to the New Testament, Zwingli saw that as a threat to social harmony. Still worse was their refusal to undertake military service of any kind, in literal conformity to the commandment, 'Thou shalt not kill'. By 1526 the situation in Zurich had deteriorated to the point that a mandate was issued threatening anyone who dared to rebaptize another with death by drowning.[40] The use of force against Anabaptists, coinciding with the Peasants' War (for which there was support from individuals associated with the movement), provoked a crisis. An assembly took place at Schleitheim on the Swiss–German border on 24 February 1527, which formulated the complete rejection of the use of force for the Christian cause. An outline confession of faith dealt with seven controverted points. This was widely circulated and elicited sharp replies from both Zwingli and Calvin.[41]

One must remember, of course, that this was the document of a persecuted church. Michael Sattler (c.1490–1527), its probable author, was captured, tortured and burnt as a heretic in Catholic Austria on 20 May of the same year.[42] But the message of these Anabaptists was one of radical withdrawal and separation from all contact, social, political or spiritual, with 'the evil which the devil has planted in the world'.[43] Specifically asserted in justification of that separation is the consequence of being finally liberated from 'the devilish weapons of force . . . such as sword, armour and the like, and all their uses on behalf of friends or against enemies'.[44]

The sixth article deals with 'the sword', to which Paul makes specific reference in Romans 13. It is, says the Schleitheim confession, 'ordained of God outside the perfection of Christ'. By this curious phrase is evidently meant that the Church is exclusively the sphere of divine righteousness. To have entered the Church by baptism means to have left the world behind. Therefore no Christian could take up the weapons of the world's justice again. The sword cannot be used, even against the wicked. Neither can Christians be judges or magistrates in worldly disputes. Temporal authority (Luther's word *Oberkeit* is used) and all it deals with is earthly, but the Christians' citizenship is in heaven. 'Worldly people are armed with spikes and iron, but Christians are armed with the armor of God – with truth, with justice, with peace, faith and salvation, and with the Word of God.' In support of this radicalism a variety of obvious and less obvious scriptural support is alleged. But we are not surprised to find the text from Matthew 'but not so with you', among them, introduced with the interpretative comment, 'Christ himself forbids the violence (*Gewalt*) of the sword.'[45]

The Anabaptist tradition has contemporary defenders who are right to remind the modern world of the cost at which testimony to the principle of voluntary association was bought. Moreover the exegetical arguments in favour of interpreting the early Jesus movement as entailing a radical rejection of violence in the service of the kingdom of God have greatly strengthened. A distinguished Mennonite biblical scholar, John Yoder, has subjected Romans 13 to critical scrutiny, and concludes that the passage, far from legitimating force, specifically requires non-resistance to tyranny.[46] Because the rulers of Paul's day gave no voice to the governed the text cannot mean that Christians ought to do military or police service. The phrase 'bearing the sword' simply describes the fact that Christians, like everyone else, are subject to the juridical and police functions of government, not including the death penalty or warfare. Yoder claims that the requirements of Romans 13 and of the teaching of the Sermon on the Mount are not in tension with each other, let alone formally contradictory. They both instruct Christians to be non-resistant in all their relationships, including the social. They *both* call on disciples of Jesus to renounce participation in the interplay of egotisms which this world calls 'vengeance' or 'justice'.[47]

At the same time, it is important to see that Yoder insists that 'non-resistance' is not a withdrawal from politics. It is, indeed, a political stance. Yoder distances himself from the tradition of the Schleitheim confession by explicitly denouncing the view which refuses contact with worldly structures on the grounds of their impure association with coercion and violence.[48] On the contrary, for Yoder the destructive 'powers' of this world are defeated 'within the structures of creaturely orderliness' by the presence of Jesus and his Church, herself 'a structure and a power within society'.[49] Not merely is this a more positive view of the Church's relation to power than that of the sixteenth-century Anabaptists; it is also significantly different from Luther himself. Fundamental to it is the distinction between power and violence; the latter is rejected, but the former has constructive potential. But it is the negative implied in Luther's ideal statement of 'not power but service' which has made a profound and lasting impression upon theology, as our next examples demonstrate.

III

The theme, 'not power but service' is prominent in the writings of two major modern theologians, Père Yves Congar (1904–1995), and Professor Jürgen Moltmann (b. 1926). The experience of the Nazi seizure of power and of the Second World War must certainly be reckoned as formative in both cases. Congar was imprisoned as a French military chaplain in Colditz. Moltmann was drafted in the last years of the war, taken prisoner and incarcerated in England. Both show a profound consciousness of the need for structural reform within the life of the Church, and share a respect for Martin Luther.

Whereas appreciation for the magisterial German reformer might be expected of a contemporary German Protestant, it could not be taken for granted in a French Dominican. But Congar's ecumenical interests were exceptionally broad, and from his early readings in Catholic Modernism he was concerned with the problem of true and false reform in the Church. *Vrai et fausse réforme dans l'Eglise* is the title of a work which he published in 1950, during a period when he was subject to active disciplinary measures.[50] His scholarly concern for the interpretation of Luther culminated in the production of a small volume devoted to the reformer's life and work (1983).[51] But Congar is chiefly valued for the quality and range of his works on medieval ecclesiology, in which some important perspectives on the relation of the Church to power came explicitly into view. These were expressed in popular form in 1963 in a work entitled, in French, *Pour une Eglise servante et pauvre*, given the English title, *Power and Poverty in the Church.*[52]

Here, in his treatment of authority in the Church, Congar's principal theme is 'the notion that the hierarchy consists essentially in service'.[53] For this thought Congar refers us to the article in Kittel's Theological Dictionary, whose formative influence on a whole generation of scholars we have already noted.[54] He does not deny that posts of authority properly exist in the Church, and that jurisdictional power is a justifiable reality. But he wants to insist that this power exists 'only within the structure of the fundamental religious relationship of the Gospel, as an organizational element within the life given to men by Christ, the one Lord and one Head of his Body'.[55]

The metaphor here is spatial, one reality existing *within* another, enveloping reality. A variant of the same picture is to assert that the idea of authority has been 'transposed . . . to another plane of reality'.[56] Elsewhere the point is made numerically. The secret of the New Testament concept of authority as service consists in the fact that authority is not put forward 'as the primary datum'; rather, the Christian life itself is the 'primary datum', and that is essentially, organically and ontologically a service, because derived from the grace of God.[57]

Congar's conception of the Church is radically christocentric. He will not, therefore, allow that what the New Testament documents have in mind is merely the spirit of personal unselfishness and service (important though this might be). The 'radical transformation' of 'the whole character and even the nature of authority' which Jesus has in mind has to do with the ending of all dominion and power in the eschatological condition of what Congar calls 'perfect interiority', the state when God will be all in all. Of this ultimate state the Church, which is the Body of Christ, is to be the anticipation or sign. The gifts given to this body are designed for the good of all. Hierarchical office is supposed to organize the service of each to all, and thus its very nature is rooted in service. Service is not only an *ideal* for the leader to follow, it constituted the basic *idea* of leadership. Thus Congar claims that the New Testament does not merely speak of the *use* of authority, as though leaders were under a moral obligation to exercise it in a spirit of service; rather:

> We must . . . sacrifice, abandon our human relationships in the form in which we receive them from the physical world of our first birth, which consist of two terms only: man and woman, master and servant; and we must receive them afresh from the Father as *Christian* relationships . . . of the very love with which God and Christ love [humanity].[58]

Parallel to this radical constructive position, and elucidating it, is Congar's depiction of the stages of a serious decline in the historical development of authority.[59] In the early Church we find a combination of a strong insistence upon authority, with an emphasis upon the intimate union of hierarchy and community, and a claim for the direct inspiration of the Holy Spirit. From the mid-fourth century, despite the dangers of the post-Constantinian settlement, the episcopate continued to represent 'an essentially moral view of authority', and authority was still exercised in conjunction with the community.[60] Increasingly, however, the clergy began to constitute a class apart within the *ecclesia* or Christian society, which was governed by both royal and priestly authorities. With the reforms of Gregory VIII, which Congar regarded as a watershed in Christian history, the hierarchy began to adopt for itself a powerful mystique of authority, 'invested with legal principles and a genuine political theology'.[61] The expression *Vicarius Christi* acquired a dominantly horizontal and jurisdictional sense. A legalistic interpretation of authority began to attach more importance to the possession of a valid title than to the actual intervention of God's grace. The terms the 'Church' came to refer to the clerics, and 'priesthood' to a mode of government. The papacy adopted the insignia, ceremonial, style and ideology of the imperial court. Despite both protest movements and the more balanced theology of Thomas Aquinas and Bonaventure, the medieval period testifies to a regression from a more primitive standard.

On the post-Tridentine developments Congar is especially severe. Questions of authority dominated the doctrine of the Church to such an extent that ecclesiology virtually became hierarchology. Centralization and a complete identification of the will of God with the institutional form of authority diminished the role of informed lay appraisal virtually to nothing. Speculation occurred on the 'real presence of Christ under the pontifical species'.[62] Despite a substantial modern return to an understanding of the pastoral and apostolic character of ministry, Roman Catholic ecclesiology is still 'too juridical, too remote from spiritual anthropology [and] continues to give a somewhat external character to the aims of authority'. (Congar was writing in 1961 before the Second Vatican Council convened, but after its preparatory work had begun.)

Certain features of Congar's work are immediately striking. The first is the emphasis he lays upon the categories 'religious' and 'spiritual', and the contrast he sees between these and legalism or moralism. He speaks warmly of 'wholly evangelical ways of exercising authority', which are plainly related to his central notion of the mystery of Christ.[63] What he speaks of as the 'vertical' relationship with a God of grace profoundly changes the 'horizontal' order of things, including the relationship between superiors and subordinates.[64] That order continues; Congar sees no tension between an episcopal hierarchy and a Spirit-filled community. He does not ask whether one of the functions of 'spiritual anthropology' is to dampen down the conflicts to which inequalities in the 'horizontal order' give rise. It is apparently presupposed that if the Church were to substitute a spiritual anthropology for its law-dominated understanding of hierarchy, a proper balance will have been achieved. Bearing in mind the major influence Congar had upon the documents of the Second Vatican Council, which had precisely that programme, one can appreciate the reasons for the element of disappointment in his response to the manifold conflicts of the post-Vatican II period.[65]

Secondly we must note the use of the word 'sociological'. Despite the fact that he is writing on a subject to which a number of distinguished French sociological and political philosophers have made important contributions, there are no references to any such writing.[66] Instead, the word 'sociological' has a pejorative connotation. Thus it is regretted that ecclesiology still bears a character that is sociological rather than interior or spiritual.[67] Despite the emphasis Congar lays on the fact of power in the Church, the word 'sociology' carries the connotation of an inferior level of reality. *Pure* reality, indeed, is, for Congar, the state of perfect interiority, in which all power relations have been abolished.

This observation leads to my criticism. Because he has dispensed with the need to work through the question of a sociological understanding of power, Congar's references to power betray an inconsistency. For the most part his respect for his own tradition compels him to recognize the role which it plays in the Church.[68] Loving service, he acknowledges, cannot simply eliminate power. But because, on the other hand, he is heir to a tradition which tends to identify power with domination, he occasionally seems to want to dissociate himself from it entirely. It is as if he envisages a Church, which, because it is indwelt by the Holy Spirit, has somehow transformed the relationships which obtain between those who enjoy unequal access to the sources of power, as a hierarchical Church must. He seems, consequently, to fall foul of a fellow Catholic theologian's criticism of 'blueprint ecclesiologies'. These are accounts of the Church in which a disjunction appears between ideal ecclesiology and the realities of the concrete church.

> They undervalue the theological significance of the genuine struggles of the church's membership to live as disciples in the less-than-perfect church and within societies that are often unwilling to overlook the church's flaws. As a consequence, blueprint ecclesiologies frequently display a curious inability to acknowledge the complexities of ecclesial life in its pilgrim state.[69]

In particular, with his integrative and evangelical instinct, he gives the strong impression that conflict has no part to play in the avoidance of domination. For a man who himself bore the scars of a bruising conflict with ecclesiastical authority, his insistence on the possibility of combining a command–obedience relationship to the hierarch with that of loving obedience to Christ and mutual service is truly remarkable. Yet one must ask the uncomfortable question whether there is not some danger in an authority cloaking itself with the ideology of service, and still, by skilful manipulation, silencing critics and setting them on the margins. The question of what the meaning of the word 'domineer' might be, and how it might be distinguished from power of a constructive kind, remains.

IV

There are three major theological writers who have strongly influenced Professor Jürgen Moltmann (in addition to other well-known philosophical conversation-partners), and it is their mutual incompatibility which make for the remarkable tensions in his works. To Luther should be ascribed his use of the *theologia crucis*, not merely as one doctrinal theme among many, but as a basic epistemological doctrine. Luther's distinctive understanding of the humility of Christ in his very being as Son of God is invoked at crucial moments in the discussion of christological problems.[70] To Luther one can also trace a characteristic antipathy to the exercise of power *in* the Church.[71]

In the second place it is obvious from Moltmann's discussion of problems of the meaning of the word 'God', how much he owes to Hegel. Hegel's deployment of Luther's ideas about 'the death of death' in the phrase 'the negation of negation' is profoundly sympathetic to Moltmann, who, like Hegel, regards himself as a staunch defender of Trinitarian theology. Moreover history, for Moltmann, as for Hegel, is 'in' God, and it is this influence which explains the combination of a radical doctrine of divine condescension and of human elevation.[72]

Finally, since Moltmann, unlike either Luther or Hegel, is a convinced, somewhat left-wing, democrat, we need a third source, which I believe we must find in Karl Barth, via Otto Weber, Moltmann's theological teacher. From Barth, also, Moltmann inherits a profound distrust of human religiosity and of the doctrine of the *analogia entis*, and a primary insistence that the being of the Church should be construed from the gospel, and not seen as merely another human institution.

Four works in particular deal with our topic, *The Theology of Hope*, *The Crucified God*, *The Church in the Power of the Spirit* and *The Trinity and the Kingdom of God*. These are permeated from start to finish by a running battle fought over the issue of power in relation to Christian theology.[73] Two themes, the eschatological and the trinitarian, have dominated Moltmann's entire output since 1964. A trinitarian doctrine of the kingdom, the subject of a final chapter in the last of these works, has a certain claim to be regarded as a summary of his theological reflection to date, and so it turns out. The summary depends on a sharp contrast drawn between monotheism, which he terms 'monarchism', and a genuine doctrine of the Trinity. 'The notion of a divine monarchy in heaven and on earth . . . generally provides the justification for earthly domination – religious, moral, patriarchal or political domination – and makes it a hierarchy, a "holy rule".' The dependency which is the corollary of this idea' according to Moltmann, everywhere requires 'abject servitude'.[74]

By contrast, the doctrine of the Trinity, properly conceived, overcomes monarchism and its attendant helplessness. Where political monotheism has been used to legitimate a whole range of forms of tyranny, the doctrine of the Trinity can be developed as a 'theological doctrine of freedom' pointing towards 'a community of men and women without supremacy and without subjection'.[75] There are, therefore, two major departures from the trinitarian position which have to be firmly opposed: political monotheism in the doctrine of God and clerical monotheism in the doctrine of the Church.

By 'political monotheism' Moltmann means the doctrine of a hierarchical world order, which we outlined in the previous chapter. As applied to the Christian emperor, the theory is more absolutist even than those based on Aristotle or the Stoics. The emperor is not merely the regent; 'he is the actual lord and possessor of the imperium'.[76] Moltmann refers the reader to Peterson's discussion of the matter, oddly citing also the study refuting Peterson's thesis, published in 1978, and adding certain qualifications.[77] Thus, though it appears that Peterson is mistaken in thinking that the concept of the divine monarchy is merely the reflection of an earthly monarchy, Moltmann has a much more radical thesis to argue than Peterson's. According to Moltmann even orthodox trinitarian theology did not really challenge 'the notion of a universal monarchy'. Neither of the two major tendencies of trinitarian theology, which conceive God as supreme substance or as absolute subject, overcome the difficulty.

> It is only when the doctrine of the Trinity vanquishes the monotheistic notion of the great universal monarch in heaven, and his divine patriarchs in the world, that earthly rulers, dictators and tyrants cease to find any justifying religious archetypes any more.[78]

By 'clerical monotheism' Moltmann means the counterpart to the divine monarchy in the church's hierarchy, especially the monarchical episcopate and the papacy.[79] The sequence, one church – one pope (or bishop) – one Peter – one Christ – one God, provides a legitimation for authority which permits subjugation. Here again Moltmann separates himself from Peterson, the Roman Catholic, who, despite his excellent analysis of political monotheism, 'overlooked the simultaneous clerical monotheism of the Catholic church of the time'.[80]

In place of monotheism, Moltmann desires a genuine doctrine of the Trinity, a doctrine to the demands of which neither the patristic, medieval nor modern versions of orthodoxy have so far risen. In this doctrine a unity is constituted out of the Father, Son and Spirit. But it is not a unity providing 'an archetype of the mighty ones of this world'. God is the Father of one who was crucified and raised for humanity; 'he is almighty because he exposes himself to the experience of suffering, pain, helplessness and death'. His glory is not that of crowns but of crucifixion. The Spirit does not proceed from the 'absolute practice of lordship', but by conferring on humanity the future and hope.[81]

What corresponds to such a doctrine of the Trinity is not the monarchy of a ruler, but 'the community of men and women, without privileges and without subjugation'.[82] This sense of community is the direct counterpart of the equal community of the Persons of the Trinity, their sociality. 'The Christian doctrine of the Trinity compels us to develop social personalism or personal socialism.'[83] Similarly in the Christian Church, the relations of authority and obedience characteristic of the theology of sacred dominion, have to be replaced by 'dialogue, consensus and harmony'.[84] In a genuine brotherhood and sisterhood, it is the presbyterial and synodal church order, rather than an episcopal or papal hierarchy, which corresponds best to trinitarian thought. 'The trinitarian principle replaces the principle of power by the principle of concord.'[85]

Moltmann's final word is to insist that it is this understanding of the Trinity which undergirds the quest for human freedom. Here he introduces a brief discussion of the function of Joachim of Fiore's doctrine of a three-fold world order, in which the kingdom of the Spirit becomes the *intelligentia spiritualis*, the day of liberty in which humanity has become no longer servants, nor even children, but friends of God. The concept of freedom itself has passed through several stages; by being defined in relation to competitive power (hence the pair, slavery and freedom), in relation to community and fellowship, and in relation to a future dream. He writes:

> Freedom as the lordship of man over objects and subjects is a function of property. Freedom as community between people is a social function. Freedom as a passion for the future is a creative function. We might sum it up by saying that the first means having, the second being, and the third becoming.[86]

It is this third sphere which, Moltmann believes, is the vitally required doctrine of participation in the creative spirit of God. Using the same three-fold division as we deployed in the first chapter, of creation, redemption and future consummation, he correlates the three doctrines to the Persons of the Trinity. There is a kingdom of the Father, who creates creatures who are dependent; there is a kingdom of the Son, who redeems and adopts humanity as his children, a family community of equal brothers and sisters; but there is a third kingdom, that of the Spirit, in which 'the servants of the Lord and the children of the Father become God's friends'.[87]

These kingdoms are to be seen as stages on a road, strata in the concept of freedom. With a final reference to both Barth and Hegel, Moltmann concludes that friendship abolishes the distance enjoyed by sovereignty, and constitutes the 'concrete concept of freedom'.[88]

Certain interpretative comments are called for. First, it is generally obvious when one reads Moltmann that he is dependent upon Paul, as would be entirely consistent for an admirer of Luther. It is the doctrine of the cross which is 'the criticism of and liberation from philosophical and political monotheism'.[89] Although he acknowledges that Paul's is not the only doctrine of order in the Church, what he terms 'the messianic gospel' which he has just expounded from Paul's epistles, is openly said to be the presupposition for any modern understanding of what is required.[90] The growth of a hierarchy from the days of Ignatius (and presumably beforehand) is simply a mistake; whatever pragmatic reasons may be in its favour it is theologically wrong.

> The development of the monarchical episcopate led to a quenching of the Spirit and was an impediment to the charismatic church . . . It broke up the genetic relationship between the commissioned church and its special commissions in a way that was totally one-sided.[91]

Although Moltmann nowhere refers to Hans Urs von Campenhausen's major work, *Ecclesiastical Authority and Spiritual Power*, precisely the same judgement is to be read there.[92] Paul, on this account, is the one upon whose writing any theology of the Church order must be based. The difficulty for this tradition is simply that it is innocent of any attempt to interpret Paul's situation in sociological terms, and to relate the theology of authority to the actual situation in which Paul's authority is subject to challenge.[93] Moreover, even if one could actually run a Church community on the lines Paul lays down (which is, in itself, open to serious question), one could not run the same community on the same lines after Paul's death. The study of Paul's letters shows him to be a man wielding immense power – such power that he anticipates that an assembly of the Church to excommunicate a person guilty of sexual immorality with his stepmother, with himself present in spirit and pronouncing the verdict, will result in the man's death (1Cor. 5:1–5).[94] Passages of this kind Moltmann nowhere considers. Without Paul's leadership, such a Church would experience a chronic power vacuum. Merely to contrast what happened subsequently with the Pauline theology of the church community, is to confuse the relation of theology and practice.

A second interpretative comment must relate to Moltmann's use of Hegel. So insistent is Moltmann upon the significance of the cross in undermining the absolutist implications of the divine monarchy, one naturally wants to know what he makes of the power of God in relation to the resurrection of Christ. The resurrection, he says, is neither a revivification of the dead Jesus, nor a resurrection into the kerygma (Bultmann). Rather – and the language is admittedly obscure – Jesus was 'raised into God's future and was seen and belied as the present representative of this future, of the free, new mankind and the new creation'.[95] But by 'seen' Moltmann plainly does not mean that the raised Jesus was physically visible. Rather, Jesus comes to be incorporated as a representative figure in the belief system constituted by Jewish apocalyptic. This system contains the symbol, 'resurrection of the dead', which refers to God's demonstration of his power over death at the end of time. The Christian *claim* is that 'this future of the new world of the righteousness and presence of God has already dawned in this one person in the midst of our history of death'.[96] Thus the meaning, for Moltmann, of the Spirit is precisely the acceptance of this claim. In *The Church in the Power of the Spirit*, a book which, despite its title, contains no analysis of what might be meant by the word 'power' in this context, it seems that the Spirit actually *is* a perception, a transition in the midst of believers which turns ordinary history into history moving towards its eschatological goal; and the work or power of the Spirit is exhibited in what happens if and when people embrace that idea.[97] The embracing of the idea is itself the victory over death.

This constellation of thoughts is inexplicable apart from Hegel, and the doctrine of the 'life of mind' expounded in the *Phenomenology*. Mind, said Hegel in a passage cited by Moltmann, is this power to endure death and in death to maintain its being, 'not by being a positive which turns away from the negative . . . but only by looking the negative in the face and dwelling with it'.[98] Moltmann's understanding of the Christian life is, accordingly, inclined to emphasize knowledge and acceptance, rather than conquest and victory. There is no such thing as 'life after death', but there is hope and courage in the face of misery and evil.

Reading Moltmann in the somewhat more confidently theistic atmosphere of English Christianity, one constantly has to remind oneself of the extent to which orthodox terminology has been harnessed to Hegelian metaphysics. But Moltmann does not see himself as a theist. 'Theism', he says, 'thinks of God at man's expense as an all-powerful, perfect and infinite being'; it is the direct result of the conquest of Caesar in the Church.[99] But neither is he an atheist, at least not in his own estimation. He desires a standpoint beyond theism and atheism, that of his own version of a trinitarian theology of the cross.

A third comment must be made, on a curious tension which emerges in Moltmann's writings. As we have seen his dissatisfaction with the role which power has played in theology, especially the doctrine of the 'omnipotent' God, and in theology's support for the governing elites, is not in any doubt. The finger is constantly pointed at the turn which the Church took in the fourth century, the monarchical and hierarchical God backing the 'power politics' of the Constantinian settlement. In late twentieth-century so-called 'first world' politics the 'structures of power' are constantly implicated in social, economic, racial and sexual oppression. It is not difficult to find passages where 'power' is simply equated with 'domination', or is regarded as the unacceptable alternative to friendship, love or service. On the other hand, Moltmann had to face squarely the issue whether or not non-violent protest was the only permissible form of intervention in contexts of political oppression. In the 1970s and 80s this matter was of central importance in Southern Africa and South America. In his essay, 'Racism and the Right to Resist', he distinguishes carefully between 'violence', 'power' and 'domination'.[100] Politics necessarily involves the exercise of power, and there is a just use of force in society. There is a clear distinction between a justifiable use of such force in domestic and foreign contexts, and brutal and unlawful acts of violence. 'The principle of "non-violence" does not exclude the struggle for power when this struggle is involved in binding power to justice.'[101]

While it is absolutely clear that Moltmann opposes the sacralization of the state, it is less clear whether he perceives the danger in the sacralization of the minority politics to which he is most naturally drawn. A critic identifies the social location of Moltmann's politics as that of the upper middle class 'knowledge and élite', characterized by anti-bourgeois 'adversary culture'.[102] In principle no-one is immune from the suspicious question as to the interests which their theological writing serves.[103] By identifying the movements of liberation as movements of the Spirit of Christ, Moltmann is in danger of propounding a new form of Constantinianism, that of a left-wing social democracy.

The critique is more than a little unjust, but highlights the interesting extent to which Moltmann has embraced the view of the radical reformation.[104] He certainly shares its hostility to Constantine and all his works. He is fully in favour of a free Church in a free

5

Sociology and Theology

I

The argument of this book to this point has been that the Scriptures of the Old and New Testaments present their interpreter, not with a single unified viewpoint, but with diverging tendencies. One of these is to be positive and affirming about the phenomenon of power; the other is to be hesitant, suspicious or downright hostile. The focus of each tendency is understandably different. Those who are positive about power orientate themselves to the biblical doctrines of the power of God, especially, but not solely, in the Old Testament. On the other hand, negative ideas of power arise most naturally from the narratives about potential or actual abuse of power, and from the paradox of the crucifixion of one called the Son of God.

To resolve this tension within a unified framework, it is conventional to distinguish between 'worldly' and 'spiritual' power, respectively the negative and positive poles of the diverging tendencies. The problem with this distinction, however, is it is exceptionally difficult to discern in any given example of Christian activity leading to discernible effects in the public arena which aspects are 'worldly' and which 'spiritual'. The instability and limited usefulness of this distinction has been exacerbated by the rise of the discipline of sociology. The argument of this chapter is to the effect that the study of sociology enhances and deepens a theological understanding of power. But we shall not arrive easily at that conclusion. First it will be necessary to observe the formulation of an influential and clearly anti-theological portrait of sociological study, as an enlightened, rational discipline liberating itself from the confines of religion and metaphysics. Then we shall examine the causes internal to the history of Christian theology for the accumulation of negative connotations in the concept of power. We shall see how profound is the conventional derivation of a sociological understanding of power from self-consciously non-Christian or anti-Christian sources. And we shall observe how difficult it has been for Christian theology to deal with this way of conceptualizing the subject, which, like popular psychology, has penetrated deeply into Western culture. Only then will we be in a position to reassess the situation between theology and sociology on the basis of more hopeful and constructive suggestions.

We shall, of course, be in difficulties if we see ourselves as engaged in lining up 'theology' at one end of the pitch and 'sociology' at the other and inviting them to play a game, preferably the same game. It will become clear that some sociologists simply refuse to play, on the grounds of the total incompatibility of the rules to which both sides are accustomed. A more promising suggestion proposes that though the terrain of study is the same, namely human societies, the type of map is different.[1] The games are, as it were, internal to the two sides, but on necessarily overlapping territory. Either side is free to pause for a moment and observe what is going on with the other. No-one is precluded from saying that the activities of the other are instructive and illuminating.

This way of approaching the subject has both similaries to, and differences from, a recent work. In *Theology and Social Theory* John Milbank produced in 1990 a quite exceptional analysis of the intellectual ancestry of modern, secular social theory, which covers in much greater range and detail the subject-matter of this chapter. Milbank's argument, which he announces in the Introduction to the book, is to the effect that supposedly 'scientific' social theories are in fact 'theologies or antitheologies in disguise'.[2] By tracing them back to their roots one can show that they derive either from theological heresies or forms of paganism. This latter is especially the case with Machiavelli and Nietzsche, both of whom have decisively influenced the way in which social theory constructs the human situation. It does so, according to Milbank, in terms of an 'ontology of violence', a pagan myth which has no greater claim to rational grounding than the Christian insistence on infinite peace. Christian theology, therefore, has no business colluding or compromising with sociology;

> I wish to challenge both the idea that there is a significant sociological 'reading' of religion and Christianity, which theology must 'take account of', and the idea that theology must borrow its diagnoses of social ills and recommendations of social solutions entirely from Marxist (or usually sub-Marxist) analysis, with some sociological admixture.[3]

A chapter of the book, entitled 'Policing the Sublime', is devoted to contemporary sociology of religion, arguing that because it can take no cognizance of transcendence on principle, it simply fails to offer anything by way of explanation of the phenomena it (re)describes.

There is a great deal in Milbank's thesis with which I am in sympathy, notably the impact on contemporary social theory of the theories of Machiavelli, Hobbes and Nietzsche. As we shall see, being 'realistic' about power has come to mean, in ordinary discourse, accepting something very like their analyses of the human situation. These are, however, as Milbank insists, theories or even myths, whose status or ways of constructing or shaping human experience are eminently challengeable. The argument of this chapter is that Christian faith has resources in its tradition to meet this so-called 'realism', and to set it in a different theoretical context or narrative.

I am not, however, persuaded that the situation is correctly characterized as one of complete separation from all the fruits of sociological inquiry. Experience of the life of the Church suggests to me that there is a good deal for theology to learn about how the Church works as an organization, including ways of penetrating the disguises which theology sometimes throws up when powers are being exercised.[4] To be on one's guard against the abuses of power, and at least to that extent to welcome the development of 'suspicion', is by no means to capitulate to a quasi-theological scheme of 'original violence'. The argument of this book is, indeed, that Christians both need and have the resources to understand and cope with power in many forms, other than violence.[5] To recognize these forms and *not* to see in them disguised violence of any kind is vital to responding to their constructive and negative potential. To neglect the analytic opportunity of sociology is wasteful, though (as Milbank justly contends) one must resist the imperialistic suggestion that sociological observation provides a complete explanation of the phenomena it describes, replacing the need for theological interpretation.

The view has already been propounded in Chapter 4 that the comparability between sociology and theology lies in the unavoidable element of moral evaluation in both disciplines. Though this conclusion is controversial in sociology, an argument has been, and can be advanced in support of the thesis. From the side of theology the case is hardly in doubt. To believe in God as Christians do is to live within the context of a (claimed) transformation of life, with obvious moral content. The Christian view of the human situation and of its potential for change for the better, is morally charged. The theologian may well hold that the existence and activity of God in redeeming humanity cannot be conveniently eliminated from the picture to yield a merely moral vision of human relations. But acceptance of belief in God is not a prerequisite for recognizing the element of moral evaluation in the Christian account of society. Quite apart from other considerations, such a view would contradict what research shows to be the heterogeneous sources of early Christian morality.[6]

Just as early Christians had drawn on a variety of pagan and secular sources in order to articulate their convictions about social and personal conduct, so external borrowings became a feature of Christian theology as it developed. The situation is clear in respect of human psychology. It became swiftly obvious to Christian theologians that the Scriptures offered nothing comparable to the detail and subtlety of Greek philosophy. By the end of the fourth century a Syrian philosopher-bishop named Nemesius of Emesa had written a theological treatise, *On Human Nature*, which developed Christian teaching about the soul with the help of a variety of philosophical sources, mainly Platonic in inspiration.[7] It was a work which, in Latin revisions, was much used in the Middle Ages, for example by Thomas Aquinas. 'What has Athens to do with Jerusalem?' was the rhetorical question of a teacher who had reasons for distancing himself from the uncritical assimilation of philosophical influences.[8] But the truth is that consciously and discerningly used, analyses of human psychology from sources external to Christian doctrine have stimulated outstanding achievements in Christian theology. The principal testimony to this fact lies in the work of Thomas Aquinas, who skilfully deployed both Plato and Aristotle as aids in the interpretation of the Christian drama of salvation. But neither in the case of Nemesius, nor of Thomas, does the willingness to learn imply forfeiting an independence of judgement.

What is the case as regards sociology? Here we are on somewhat different territory, and not merely because 'the study of human social life, groups and societies',[9] a convenient modern definition of the subject-matter, is a late arrival. The pastoral practice of the Church was based upon traditional understandings of communal care, and did not absolutely require philosophical–psychological justification or interpretation. But the Church had quickly to solve some rather pressing problems of a plainly sociological kind, first in relation to its own government, and subsequently in relation to the power structures of the empire. The practice came first, and the theory followed later.

In the field of church government and leadership the challenges were so immediate and pressing that accounts and legitimations of episcopacy, a novel pattern of leadership for the ancient world, are in evidence from the first.[10] But the situation was other in respect of what has been well termed a 'social cosmology', the account of how a whole society fitted together.

> Primitive Christian communities could not defend the empire; raise taxes; protect shipping from pirates, or mule trains and camel trains from bandits; organize the commissary for the army and bureaucracy; maintain literacy required by a religion of the book; or meet many other essential pre-conditions of Christian life. Christ said little about these matters, and the early fellowship did not produce a social cosmology. Although they said important and socially true things about the universal condition of humanity, and reinforced them with a small community structure containing simple, satisfying rituals, they said little about macrosocial organization and social differentiation. The first followers of Christ had to produce solutions from their *own* resources, the stock of beliefs and practices that come from Roman citizenship, gender, stratification position, and ethnic community.[11]

Precisely because the Christian movement implied a revolution in the ethnic consciousness and commitments of Judaism there was new work to do, for which the sources only provided the starting-points. But even if the sheer diversity of solutions we have noted in the previous two chapters be admitted, and even if sociology be acknowledged a latecomer to the academic community, there is in principle no reason to view sociology in any different light than the way in which we view philosophical psychology. Players on the same pitch do well to observe with care what others are doing. A theologian has much to gain from a conscious and discerning knowledge of sociology, not least in respect of power.

II

On the definition of sociology which sets it as 'the study of human social life, groups and societies', both Aristotle's *Politics* and Plato's *Republic* must count as sociology. But despite reflections and refractions of both these massive treatises, nothing in the medieval period poses even distant comparison with them. Augustine's *City of God*, though it might well be thought to contain at least an outline of a social cosmology, is neither clear nor detailed enough to amount to a 'study' of the subject, in the sense that Nemesius' treatise is a study of human nature. When, then, do we start to speak of the origins of sociological 'study'? The word 'sociology' was apparently invented by Auguste Comte (1789–1857), and it stood for a specific method of analysis of human conduct, one which has left theology and metaphysics behind and has embraced a 'positive philosophy' with the same logical form as that characteristic of other sciences. 'Social physics' was Comte's alternative name for the discipline.[12]

However influential Comte's view may have been, 'studies' that undoubtedly count as sociology can be identified at least a hundred years earlier. *A History of Sociological Analysis* begins with a chapter on 'Sociological Thought in the Eighteenth Century'.[13] The tendency of the author is not in doubt. He makes clear that the Enlightenment attack on religion was the essential precondition for the development of independent thought about the world ('the replacement of the supernatural by the natural, of religion by science, of divine decree by natural law, and of priests by philosophers').[14] One of the earliest authentic sociologists is said to be Montesquieu (1689–1755), precisely because he 'excluded the supernatural from the explanation of human societies and advanced the comparative method for the study of social institutions'.[15] It is ignored that there is a responsible argument for the view that one of the conditions for the development of science include specific theological or metaphysical doctrines about the world. Glossed or ignored too is the fact that a substantial number of the earliest practitioners of sociology were themselves religious people. Giovanni Battista Vico (1668–1744), for example, whose *Scienza Nuovo* ('Principles of a New Science Concerning the Common Nature of the Nations', 1725; third edition, 1744) is in truth a sociological work of first rate importance, could not be regarded as hostile to religion.[16] But the standard genealogy of sociology has already turned its relationship to theology into a problem.

The impact of the derivation of sociology from the liberating initiatives of the European Enlightenment is especially plain in relation to the understanding of power. As we have seen the open and heated discussion of papal or spiritual and regal worldly power is a commonplace of medieval, Renaissance and Reformation political thought. By the latter years of the twentieth century, power has become so associated with violence, as to be a matter of grave difficulty for an ethical discussion. In her classic work *On Violence*, Hannah Arendt reviews a series of contributions to the discussion and definitions of power from Voltaire onwards, and concludes:

> If the essence of power is the effectiveness of command, then there is no greater power than that which grows out of the barrel of a gun, and it would be difficult to say in 'which way the order given by a policeman is different from that given by a gunman'.[17]

How does it come about that 'power' acquired so negative a connotation, bearing in mind the centuries of positive usage to which we have referred?

We can pause a little to ask what kind of question that is. We are trying, on the face of it, to offer an explanation for a change of atmosphere in European thought comparing, say, the fourteenth century with the eighteenth, covering four hundred years of exceptionally rapid and radical change, economically and politically as well as in philosophy or theology. And, again, we are asking why an admittedly imprecise word acquires, with time, a nuance in the literatures not merely of different centuries, but of different types.

Moreover, there is a prior question to consider, namely whether Arendt's examples of the problem of power genuinely encompasses the literature from Voltaire to the present, or is composed, rather, of her private selection of authors. We shall see there is more than a grain of truth in the latter suspicion.

Even so, and despite the difficulties, there is something to be said on the subject of how power acquired its negative connotations. We have already noted the sharpening of Augustine's sober view of humanity in the writings of Luther, and the impact of Lutheranism in political thought was considerable.[18] It would be undoubtedly convenient if the finger could simply be pointed at 'Machiavellianism', an anti-Christian theory representing force as the fundamental, implicit sanction in all 'realistic' accounts of government.[19] Or again the French Revolution, with its violent severing of the connection between traditional authority and political power, is bound to have had a massive and negative impact upon inherited attitudes. But in truth the Christian Church has to accept much greater responsibility for the diminished reputation of power. In particular two further factors must be mentioned, the notorious justification offered for the physical coercion of schismatics by Augustine, and the growth of a doctrine which accorded 'plentitude of power' to the Pope.

Subsequent centuries have not found it difficult to indulge in bouts of liberal indignation when it comes to Augustine's views on the 'correction' of recalcitrants; and more recently there have been some notably more sympathetic accounts.[20] But in truth the caveats and the attempts to enter into Augustine's mind and situation are characteristically modern procedures. For centuries it was enough that the great Augustine had declared that 'it was better for a few abandoned people to perish than that innumerable souls, whose way to salvation they impede, should burn with them forever in Hell'.[21] But he had not come to such a view without a struggle, because it contradicted – or at the very least was in tension with – a mildness and gentleness he read in the Scriptures. When, indeed, he reflected on that inheritance he heard two voices, one which was strict and punitive, and that was mostly in the Old Testament.[22] But Augustine's view was not that the Scriptures of the Old Covenant were simply superseded. In a vivid image in the *Confessions* he likened the requisite judgement to the knowledge that it was inappropriate to do in the dining room what might be proper behind the stables.[23] One simply must know where one is. Faced with human indolence, with force of habit, and with occasional displays of Donatist violence in the countryside; and bolstered by well-established precedent of appeal to authority's interest in good order, he came slowly to think it possible and right that the empire should legislate against schismatics and enforce these laws.

Augustine knew perfectly well that forced conversions frequently made bad Christians.[24] But not inevitably; and his doctrine of predestination in any case meant that God would have sorted out the true from the feigned from the start. And were there not at least some features of the New Testament which might justify compulsion? What, for example, of the exorcisms, or of Jesus casting out the money-changers from the temple?[25] And was not Paul's conversion accompanied by a power which blinded him and threw him to the ground? The justifications did not all rest on the text 'Compel them to come in'; but that too was harnessed to the cause.[26] To speak of Augustine's attitude to coercion as merely the invoking and acceptance of the powers of compulsion exercised by the empire is not, however, to do justice to one important feature of his case. What was spoken of as *cohercitio* had been exercised against paganism by Christian emperors for many decades. But Augustine's words for what he wanted were different; *correptio* (rebuke) and *correctio* (setting right). He desired the corrective treatment from imperial authority to be not a brutal suppression, but a kind of discipline with moral aims in view.[27] Fear was only justified if it could be replaced, cast out by love.

Augustine also understood all too well the fickleness of humankind, and the 'mysterious solidarities' in which human beings could be engulfed.[28] He knew what Machiavelli also later recognized, that the memory of a single demonstration of well-timed force lingers within a new normality. One does not need to be brutal all the time for violence to make its point.[29] All that was needed was a Christianly sufficient reason for one pre-emptive strike; and Augustine already inherited that in the doctrine of divine judgement. If it was morally certain that heretics would be everlastingly damned, then the restricting of their social world through coercion could be justified as an act of mercy. Though the bishop would not himself use coercive violence, he might encourage or even instruct a ruler to do so. This was the explicit view of St. Bernard in didactic letters to Pope Eugenius III in 1150. Both the spiritual and the material sword belong to the Church. The latter, though in the hand of the soldier, is to be used 'at the bidding of the priest and the order of the emperor'.[30]

Through such a doctrine the idea of moral qualifications to the use of physical force was seriously compromised. That physical constraints have to be used at certain times is obvious from ordinary human experience with small children, with mentally disabled or sick adults, or with criminals and aggressors. In all such cases a moral justification has to be offered, relating the reason for using what English common law knows as 'reasonable force' to the way in which those persons are held within the community. In the case of prisoners, for example, sight cannot be lost of the objective of restoring the person to society, as a morally responsible adult member. Such an argument eliminates the use of prison torture or terror. The threat of physically (or for that matter mentally) damaging a prisoner is not, or ought not to be, the 'final' sanction. For Christians to advocate the use of physical coercion upon heretics undermines the way in which those persons are subsequently to be held within the community of the Church. This argument is valid irrespective of the outcome of a campaign of terror or persecution in the short or long term. No one should be compelled to confess Christ, who would subsequently be taught to see all other Christians as equally brothers and sisters. Canon law forbade forcible baptisms. Luther recognized that you could not compel interior assent. But both Catholics and Protestants persecuted heretics, having either redefined heresy as sedition, or taken Augustine's view that coercion was the lesser evil.

A variety of motives might persuade the Christian that coercion was justified. In Augustine's case he believed himself to be acting mercifully in the heretic's best eternal interests. So far as the Church was concerned Augustine operated on the principle of what one commentators has described as a 'higher utilitarianism';[31] coercion could be justified if it brought about genuine conversion. And it did – or at least Augustine persuaded himself that it did: 'some now say . . . thanks be to God, who has stirred us from our negligence with the goad of terror'.[32] Precisely the same calculation could be made in other circumstances. Augustine had held, appropriately enough, that a Christian ruler's power was well used in propagating the worship of God far and wide. Eventually, however, it came to be thought that this might be achieved by holy warfare against pagans.[33] Christians are in no position to blame Machiavelli for a 'realism' about power which already had centuries of theological justification attached to it.

A second reason from the side of Christian history for the negativity attaching to the concept of power has to do with the development of justifications for the 'plentitude' of papal power. The involvement of the papacy in temporal power, especially in the struggles of the city republics of North Italy, was complete both as to fact and to theory. By the end of the thirteenth century the Papacy commanded a large area of central Italy. In the Papal Bull, *Unam Sanctam*, of 1302, Pope Boniface VIII maintained that both the temporal sword and the spiritual sword were committed by Christ to the Church. Supported by the arguments of his theologians, notably Giles of Rome, he 'produced a hierocratic dossier of unprecedented proportions and ingenuity, whose general trend was to assail or abandon every moderating or qualifying tenet about papal omnipotence suggested by past theory and experience'.[34] This was, of course, an ideological weapon in an unequal struggle, bearing in mind the vastly superior armies of the King of France, who by way of answer, proposed to put the pope on trial before a general council.

The doctrine of 'plentitude of power' had developed from referring to the superior jurisdictional competence of the pope, as compared with that of a single diocesan bishop, to the assertion that the pope is not bound by the laws because he made them. The whole history of hierocratic doctrine was powered by what has been aptly described as 'a Christological political logic'.[35] All power (*potestas*) has been committed to Christ according to the Gospel of Matthew; therefore it must legitimately be exercised only in subjection to the Vicar of Christ, the Bishop of Rome. In what Congar described as 'the most extreme formula', Thomas Aquinas (reputed but not certain author of *de Regno*) had stated that to the pope, 'the vicar of Christ, all kings of the Christian people should be subject, as if to our Lord Jesus Christ himself'.[36]

According to Giles of Rome, no power was legitimately exercised unless it was subjected to the pope, who held *dominium* or lordship over all things. Infidels could neither own legitimate property nor exercise legitimate authority.

> All men and all possessions are under the governance (*sub dominio*) of the Church, because the whole world and all who live in it, belong to the Church.[37]

The doctrine in a certain sense was theoretical or ideological. It met with fierce criticism at the time and later, not least as we have seen from Marsilius of Padua, and from Dante, who pertinently insisted that Christ's intention had been to save human beings from the pride and corruption involved in concentrating spiritual and temporal power in one person.[38] The conciliar movement of the late fourteenth and early fifteenth centuries challenged the assertion of papal control over the life of the church, and within the struggles of the Italian city states new doctrines of liberty and representation were developing.

But the official doctrine of the Church was not in doubt and it was hierocratic. The authority given to the pope, though given to a man, is divine, and the pope can be judged by no one. 'We declare, state, define and pronounce that it is altogether necessary to salvation for every creature to be subject to the Roman Pontiff.'[39] It did not help that *Unam Sanctam* was repromulgated on the eve of the Reformation at the Fifth Lateran Council; nor that it was used by a seventeenth-century Spaniard to justify the military annexation of the Americas.

We may ask how we are to account for this (now) astonishing doctrine? It was justified in the exigencies of the struggle for independence from over-weaning imperial authority, and on the grounds of the sins of rulers. One notes, for example, that those who objected most strenuously to a *plenitudo potestatis* for the pope were inclined, like Marsilius, to subordinate the pope to the secular government. Henry VIII was such a ruler, and to accommodate the text of Marsilius to his monarchical vanity, suitable excisions of communitarian passages were made.[40] Faced with the growing territorial ambitions of rulers an assertion of 'plenitude of power' is at least understandable. It might even be argued that the rivalry of conflicting ambitions served the cause of freedom in the long run. But what is not defensible are the corruptions which accompanied the claim for 'plenitude of power'. One may not believe all that the passionate critics, such as Marsilius, Dante and Luther stated to be the case; the approval of Machiavelli is, if anything, a more devastating endictment.

> Alexander VI did nothing else, he thought about nothing else, except to deceive men, and he always found occasion to do this . . . Nevertheless his tricks always succeeded perfectly since he was well acquainted with this aspect of the world.[41]

Against such a background it is understandable that the formula 'not power but service' advanced by both Marsilius and Luther should be so attractive.

III

When we turn to contemporary views of power within sociological literature the general reader is immediately struck with two features of the situation: the sheer quantity of the literature, and the lack of unanimity about the subject. In this section an attempt will be made to do some justice to the reasons for this variety, to construct a narrative about the history of the subject, and then to locate the modern variety of theological responses to that narrative. Only in this way shall we be able to take proper account of what it might mean to relate critically and independently to elements in our culture, as first-century Christians did in theirs.

We note, in the first place, the public acknowledgement that there is no unity of treatment of power in the sociology of the last three decades. To readers of Steven Lukes' masterly brief history of the topic it will be swiftly apparent that we encounter 'unending disagreement as to how power and authority are to be conceptualised and how they relate to one another'.[42] And though that review article was published in 1979, it is already clear that important perspectives are lacking from it and that the story needs amplification and correction. Nor will it be otherwise in the future, so long as sociologists continue to take the view that power is a central (some hold it to be *the* central) concept in sociology, and so long as organizational theorists have the practical stimulus of helping managers manage.

When sociologists account for the vast extent of the modern literature on the subject, they tend to trace the impetus to a specific group of philosophers and social theories, including Machiavelli, Thomas Hobbes, Nietzsche, Marx and (pre-eminently) Max Weber. We have already remarked on the distance between the sixteenth- and seventeenth-century authors with which this list begins

(Machiavelli and Hobbes) and the equally vast *theological* literature on power of the previous centuries. The originality of Machiavelli's notorious advice on how to govern, the treatise *The Prince* of 1513, later dedicated 'to the magnificent Lorenzo de Medici', lay precisely in the necessity he saw of a ruler having to embrace not a conventional Christian morality of leadership (as earlier humanist treatises had urged), but a morality adapted to the game of dog-eat-dog politics, where the very survival of an even half-decent ruler was a matter of continuous vigilance and forethought. Consistent with this context, his view of humanity is phrased in terms of Augustinian gloom: 'This may be said of men generally,' he says, 'they are ungrateful, fickle, feigners and dissemblers, avoiders of danger, eager for gain. While you benefit them they are all devoted to you . . . but when you are hard pressed, they turn away.'[43] To govern with success in such a context requires an unflinching commitment to the use of power in all its forms, including occasional actions of coercion and violence. The novelty of his views of the art of government lies in his blunt assertion that 'a ruler who wishes to maintain his power must be prepared to act immorally when this becomes necessary'.[44]

Hobbes (1588–1679) was also an adviser to a ruler, though in his case the ruler was Charles II, in the immediate aftermath of civil war in a kingdom confronting the urgent question of the locus of sovereignty.[45] Hobbes' theory, propounded in his systematic work *Leviathan* (1651), was at once empirical, metaphysical and, in a certain sense, mythical. Noting that the desires of human beings, left to themselves, necessarily conflict, he devised an account of the state powerful enough to ensure order, but not so invasive as to deny individual human satisfactions. Hobbes' concern above all was to legislate for a rational order of things, on the assumption that without such a system the life of humanity is all too likely to be (in his celebrated phrase) 'solitary, poor, nasty, brutish, and short'.[46] Therefore there is need for a sovereign power combined with a covenant, such that all the people invest their individual power in a person or body which protects them from violent death.

For Lukes, Hobbes stands at the head of a long tradition of social and political thought which 'sees authority as conventional and power as asymmetric, indeed coercive'. The conceptualization of power undergirding his theory of government is absolutely fundamental to its character. Leviathan itself is an ungovernable sea-monster, whose power is celebrated in the book of Job, and described 'a king over all the children of pride' (Job 41:34). The sovereignty expressed in this metaphor is the mirror image of the absence of the power of God. Though Hobbes had the reputation for atheism, and was indeed in practice an atheist, he never formally denied the existence of God.[47] But he removed God to such a distance from the world, diminishing any idea of revelation and abandoning the doctrine of the Holy Trinity, that quite casually he could speak of 'the secret working of God' as the same as what people call Good Luck.[48] God has no moral qualities – or if he does, we have no knowledge of them. But he remains the term to which the notion of absolute, indeed arbitrary, power is attached – 'the right of afflicting men at his pleasure, belongeth naturally to God Almighty; not as Creator, and Gracious; but as Omnipotent'.[49] When Job asks why the innocent should suffer, God's answer is with arguments drawn from his power. It is precisely this notion of irresistible dominion which constitutes the rational idea of sovereignty, and which human beings need to make a society work. It has no intrinsic moral quality; human beings, astonishingly, are valued at the worth attached to their power.[50] Though the role ascribed to sovereign government is hedged about with limits, they are derived from prudential considerations not moral doctrines. Hobbes is, indeed, a radical relativist.[51]

From a contemporary point of view Hobbes' defence of what amounts to a separation of spiritual and worldly power remains fascinating. Abandoning both royalism and the Anglican and the Presbyterian forms of establishment, Hobbes finally justified a certain kind of independency.[52] The state had no business interfering in the realm of beliefs essentially private to individuals, always assuming that such individuals had also consented to the contract maintaining the state's own sovereignty. Nor had the Church any business claiming to exercise powers other than the power to preach and teach. A long chapter of *Leviathan* deals with 'Power Ecclesiastical' and outlines a theory of how both Scriptural Canon and Office developed in the early Church. Hobbes then consistently asserts that the absolute sovereignty of the civil power cannot be halted at the appointment, or even ordination of pastors, if civil peace demands it. He writes, of course, in the light of experience of the English Civil War.[53]

Hobbes was deeply interested in contemporary science, and developed his schema on the basis of a materialist psychology and of the principle of mechanics. As a consequence *Leviathan* offers a demythologized model of rational order for human beings, in which power is explicitly identified with causality. Although its particular practical recommendations did not commend themselves to Hobbes' immediate audience, the impulse given to social *science* has proved irresistible. Correspondingly the post-modern abandonment of the idea of a rational, guiding principle of all action has seen precisely in Hobbes' scheme the origins of a discredited project obsessed with a mythical notion of sovereignty. Writers in the same tradition see rather in Machiavelli's acute observation of the flux of politics a more realistic interpretation of the power in which the 'myths concerning moral action become gamesplayers' resources rather than a topic which frames what the game should be'. The difference between the two theorists has been put thus:

> While Hobbes would propose to legislate for a social contract, Machiavelli would interpret a strategy; where Hobbes founds a discursive framework for analysis of power as motion, causality, agency and action, Machiavelli instead describes an ethnographic research method for uncovering the rules of the game.[54]

Machiavelli's ideas were denounced from the start by Christian writers, beginning with Cardinal Reginal Pole (in 1539) and Roger Ascham (1554).[55] Both Protestant and Catholic writers on government profess themselves revolted by his apparent commendation of the infamous Cesare Borgia, son of Pope Alexander VI (1492–1503). In fact there is a great deal more than 'Machiavellianism' in Machiavelli's political thought. He is strongly critical of the Roman Church, and especially of recent popes, for having forfeited spiritual authority by deviousness and military involvement in Italian politics. But though he esteems highly the role of religion in civic government, his method of using classical models for guidance and instruction gives his writing an almost Durkheimian quality.[56] Machiavelli's 'objectivism' and 'realism' have appealed strongly to modern theorists, tending to reinforce the gulf between earlier Christian condemnation and the self-consciously modern type of interpretation.[57] Hobbes' ideas had a more ambiguous fate in theology, but in the long run the impulse he gave to the development of the liberalism of civil society has proved a reality with which theology has had to come to terms. But it is unmistakable that these particular thinkers of the sixteenth and seventeenth centuries are chosen as leading examples of the origins of the modern study of power partly because of their clear independence from the constraints of conventional Christian piety.

The self-conscious critical distancing from the Christian tradition is conspicuous also in the thought of both Nietzsche (1844–1900) and Marx (1818–1883). Nietzsche's contribution was strongly to reinforce Hobbes' realistic portrait of the human psychological investment in power, as a basic drive.[58] The notion of a 'will to power', given in notes written between 1883 and 1888, and published posthumously in 1901 and 1906, grew in part from his forthright opposition to a Darwinism understood as a packet of adaptive strategies for human survival.[59] The vital thing about humanity, on the contrary, is the human will to impose itself upon the environment, 'the tremendous force which shapes, creates from within' to incorporate and subdue what is external.[60] As such, of course, the will to power must be positively evaluated since it is life-sustaining. His attack on Christianity focused on its supposed tendency to celebrate the feeble, not least for their implicit envy of the strong and forceful, and their attempts, through the support of equal rights, universal suffrage and parliamentary government (for which he had nothing but scorn), to impose mediocrity on a civilization, 'an instinctive conspiracy of the whole herd' to preserve and elevate 'the oppressed, the mediocre, the hard-done-by, the half-failed'.[61]

The influence of Nietzsche upon subsequent psychology and sociology was profound. Although in the Anglo-Saxon world Nietzsche's reputation was unnecessarily tarnished by propagandist distortions connected with the World Wars (both in anti-Germanism and in Nazism), his indirect impact upon Freudian thought and especially through Weberian sociology is widely acknowledged.[62] Through Nietzsche's influence there is a marked tendency to sharpen, even to exaggerate, the degree to which social life must be regarded as the area of unrelenting and irresolvable power struggles, and to privilege a pessimistic denial of the possibility of a co-operative use of power in the realizing of genuine communal harmony.

Marx's remarkable analysis of modern capitalist society with its roots in a particular mode of production developed out of his critical examination of Hegel's philosophy of civil society. Where Hegel had identified the motion of absolute spirit as the inner dynamic of modern stages, Marx claimed it was 'political economy', the forces of production needed to transform nature. Power has a variety of historical forms corresponding to the relation between property and production. Power is, therefore, pre-eminently class power, exercised within and reinforcing the constraints imposed by, the mode of production.[63] Authority is also a form of power, exercised in devious or open ways by the ruling class, which determine the 'ruling ideas' of a given society. It is also effective through various non-violent means in the family, in education, in law and the labour market; but it is backed by coercion and naked force in the state. This view has been greatly developed in subsequent Marxist thinking on 'hegemony' in the work of Antonio Gramsci (1891–1937), who argued that intellectuals need to engage in long-term educational work in order to produce the consensus or 'collective national will' making government without overt coercion a possibility.[64]

The theory that behind the consciousness of human agents lies a system of ideas, imposed from above and disguising their real situation of enslavement, generally known as 'ideology', has played a highly significant role in modern liberation theology. Only actual social intervention to change the dominant class structures would achieve the necessary clarification of ideas. Hence the primacy of the *practice* of liberation over its theoretical formulation or promulgation. But the struggle over ideology has its importance in so far as 'Christian' values have been harnessed to the dominant ideology. In the unmasking of all attempts to ideologize the gospel, the Christian theologian is to play the role of 'organic intellectual' elaborated by Gramsci, and to rewrite theology 'from the underside of history'.[65]

A number of central ideas in what has been called the 'dominant ideology thesis' have been called into question. It is not, for instance, clear whether, as Marx and Engels believed, the classless society would be one in which all power and authority would have been eliminated. The status and interests of the 'organic intellectual' are notoriously ambiguous, if it is thought that his or her own interests are epistemologically privileged, and exempt from ideological scrutiny. Questions of a factual nature have been asked about the degree to which subordinate classes genuinely are incorporated within the so-called 'dominant ideology', and whether the actual situation is not more complex and pluralist than the theory supposes. The capacity of any political system to generate resistances of various degrees of strength capable of rising to ascendancy under a number of different conditions needs more differentiated analysis. From the Christian point of view it is striking that the eschatological conviction that Christ will deliver the kingdom into his father's hands 'after he has destroyed every ruler (*archê*), and every authority (*exousia*) and power (*dynamis*) (1 Cor. 15:24), is transposed in Marxism into an analysis of an historical process, Thus for Gustavo Gutierrez, one of the most influential of Latin American theologians, a Peruvian Catholic, 'it is and ever shall be the poor who are the makers of history'.[66]

Stimulated by, but also opposed to, many of Marx's most characteristic theses was the massive contribution of Max Weber (1864–1920), 'the "realist" who offered the subtlest and richest account of power and authority in the whole history of social and political theorizing'.[67] Weber, moreover, specifically considered the question of authority in religion and wrote extensively upon the sociology of religion. But it was his achievement, together with that of Georg Simmel (1858–1918) and Ferdinand Tonnies (1855–1935), to create a tradition of analytical, 'scientific' sociology which has greatly contributed to the understanding of the main features of the modern world. In addition to his study of the great world religions of China, India, Judaism, Christianity and Islam, Weber wrote fundamental statements on the relations between politics and morality, politics and science, law and economics, art and technology, and science and art. His first major work, combining economic, religious and moral sociological analysis, *The Protestant Ethic and the Spirit of Capitalism* created a new method for interpreting the impact of religion upon modern society and has remained controversial both as to form and substance ever since.[68]

Equally controversial is his attitude towards what he later proclaimed to be the 'value-free' status of sociology (its *Wertfreiheit*). It is understandable that much was made of this during the 'committed' 1960s, when many universities in the Western world were convulsed by conflicts taking their inspiration from Marxist or radical models of society. Weber's defence of rationality and his exposition of an irreducible value pluralism proved an apparently secure 'scientific' ground for a discipline under siege. More recently, however, closer study of Weber's complex response to the circumstances of his own culture has qualified this portrait of him as the founding father of 'positive' sociology. What Weber rejected was that sociology could establish a rationally guaranteed hierarchy of values, on the basis of which society could be constructed or reconstructed. At the same time he insisted that modern science and rationality had the inescapable duty of eliminating illusion from public life, including the illusion of totalitarian explanation, whether Marxist, religious or from whatever source. He thus stressed the *limits* of academic sociology, while upholding personal and individual responsibility for life-values.[69]

At the same time, and specifically with reference to this major contribution to understanding power in society, the framework is implicitly Nietzschean, as Anthony Giddens among others has pointed out.[70] The central concept of *Herrschaft* (or 'domination', though the appropriate English translation has varied)[71] inherently implies the threat of coercion in all relations between the rulers and the ruled. Weber was quite consciously responding to what he called the 'disenchantment' of the modern world, that is the impossibility (as he saw it) of construing public life and social relations in terms of divine or supernatural forces or authorities. *Herrschaft* or domination also characterized religions; the main difference between them and politics is that the sanctions they could mobilize in their internal struggles for power only included what he called 'psychological compulsions', not the threat of force or violence. But violence was the bottom line in all human politics; and a state is characterized as a territory on which a given order has successfully monopolized the use of force.[72]

But it is an observable feature of the tradition stemming from Hobbes, and including Marx and Weber, that it is assumed that the interests of individuals conflict, and that more power for one agent or group will inevitably mean less for another. Authority is needed to prevent societies from falling apart, and is ultimately based on coercion, however that coercive potential be legitimated. This 'realism' about power has not gone unchallenged, especially by those who hold that social order is constituted by shared belief, and that this shared belief identifies who has the right to exercise power in the last resort. The 1950s saw an intense debate in the United States of America initiated by a sociologist who insisted that small power elites in the world of business, politics and the armed forces, dominated American life, to the detriment of others.[73] Identifying this as a classic case of 'zero-sum' power analysis (more for one necessarily means proportionally less for others) Talcott Parsons, who had received his graduate education in German and been instrumental in translating much of Weber's work into English, objected. Power, according to Parsons, is comparable to money. When a society agrees on collective goals, the amount of it can be increased in the social system. Conflict, therefore, is not central to the analysis of power. Hobbes' *Leviathan* is flawed, Parsons held, through its basic concern with coercion. Turning rather to Durkheim and the notion of a set of common norms or values, a *conscience collective*, Parsons focuses on the 'generalized capacity of a social system to get things done in the interest of collective goals'.[74] This will certainly involve inequalities, which are excusable in the collective interest. It has been observed that Parsons, unlike most of the sociologists we have considered, begins with an assumption that power is fundamentally benign and legitimate.[75]

Explicitly respectful of Nietzsche, but scornful of the pretension of the human 'sciences', Michel Foucault (1926–1984) plainly but paradoxically belongs to the canon of major sociological writers on power. His work over 20 years centred on the histories of certain 'discourses', psychology and psychiatry on mental illness, medicine in general, the 'knowledge' claimed by modern science, prisons and penal theory, and finally a three-volume work on *The History of Sexuality*. These brilliant studies offer a kaleidoscopic variety of insights into, and proposals about, the nature of power, which in many ways is the linking thread in his works. Foucault believes that he has identified a non-sovereign type of power, that is a power that is not the result of any individual's will to dominate a society. This is the 'power of normalization', relations which bind people without their knowing it, an emprisoning network of which they are the unwitting agents and victims. One of the main elements in this network are the claims of various kinds of knowledge, which merely contribute to the construction of a normative, constraining social world. The origins of sociology are, startlingly, said to be doctor's knowledge.[76] Prisons are places where power is naked. Much is made of Bentham's proposal for a prison building called Panopticon, which would ensure surveillance at all times. Normalization is a society's capacity for surveillance, reaching down into the minutest particulars of human conduct, especially sexuality.

Foucault's claims for the truth of his observations (if true, how could they escape from his own strictures upon science?), and its recipe for deliverance from domination are less easy to elucidate. To a very large degree his works trade upon the negative connotations of the idea of power, which is occasionally used to mean domination. Liberation from domination, and thus power, appears to be the motivation for the identification of the omnipresence of the strands of the web. The intellectual is apparently assigned the task of struggling against being an instrument of power.[77] Another strand of the argument, however, is the impossibility of eliminating power from the picture, and the unsatisfactoriness of only seeing power as repression.[78] This Foucault sees as a baleful consequence of focusing upon royal power, as old as the Middle Ages, and upon sovereignty, as did Hobbes. Power does not emanate from the top downwards. His method of cultural analysis, which he terms 'genealogy' attends to the outer fringes of social life, and illustrates the networks in all their profusion and complexity.

Foucault is extremely difficult to 'domesticate' to 'normal' sociology, except by challenging one or more of his central contentions. He is evidently a kind of anarchist, whose positive proposals for human society and individual conduct are aesthetic; only in this way can he escape the implications of recommending ethical norms.[79] Without becoming disciples, Christian theologians have good reason for responding positively to a number of strands in Foucault's thought-world, notably in the critique of power as sovereignty. The plurality of powers and their omnipresence, the impossibility of evading the implications of power and its exercise, the negative potential of apparently benign forms of power – none of these are inimical to Christian theology.[80]

Furthermore there are other positive aspects to the remarkable outpouring of effort in delineation of the sociological field of study covered by power and authority. Despite the fact that the discipline of sociology has been formed in virtually conscious opposition to what are supposed to be the concerns and interests of theology, it can be properly claimed that what in fact has occurred has enhanced and deepened a theological understanding of power.

In the first place it appears that the use of terms such as 'power', 'might', 'domination' and 'authority' is overlapping and variable. As we have seen, it was not otherwise in the New Testament. But there is no necessary connection between the terms 'power' and 'force', such that the phrases 'the power of God' or 'the power of the gospel' are incapable of use.

Secondly all exercises of power are accompanied by contrary power or resistance. No human agencies control all resources, and the notion of a monopoly of power is mythological.

Not all forms of power, thirdly, reside in agencies or are manifest in specific acts. Structures also embody and exercise significant amounts of power and require careful analysis in relation to human agency.

Fourthly, in a variety of ways it is evident that the production (or manipulation) of consent to governmental and other societal practices constitutes a form of power, though not necessarily a sovereign or controlling one.

Finally, analyses of power are capable of identifying that moral or religious ideas play a role in the complex interrelations of forms of power, but they (the analyses) do not specify what these moral or religious ideas should be. The concept of power itself is morally ambivalent.

These points are not presented as 'assured results' of what remains a vigorously contested intellectual scene. But they have sufficient currency in the various arguments to justify being highlighted. None of them are in the least discouraging to Christian theology; it remains, therefore, to attempt to explain why the Christian response has hitherto been so partial and fragmentary.

IV

Certain features of the hesitating character of Christian response to the modern discussion of power have already been mentioned. It has, of course, been observed that there is a marked circularity in the fact that the modern discussion traces itself from the time when, and the authors by whom, the Christian framework was first discarded. In such historiography (though not in Lukes' admirable survey) it is not mentioned that Edmund Burke (1729–97), Joseph de Maistre (1754–1821), Louis de Bonald (1754–1840) and Karl Ludwig von Haller (1768–1854) wrote in explicit defence of what they understood to be the point of view of tradition. Their political conservatism has evidently much to do with their relegation from the genealogy of modern social thought. In the case of De Bonald, writing in the context of the French Revolution, the restoration of authority, opposition to enlightenment individualism, and affirmation of the importance of intermediate associations as a way of minimizing the impact of unitary political sovereignty, were principal themes of a major treatise, entitled *Theorie du pouvoir politique et religieux* (1796), occupying 700 pages of his collected works.[81] Another way of interpreting the history of sociology is to see it precisely as the story of opposition between social authority (rooted in tradition and community) and political power (based on individual will and coercion), stemming from the French Revolution.[82] But the dominant (*nota bene*) narrative is the radical and realist one which has been outlined, and a great deal of Christian thought has followed it, albeit uneasily. It has done so for specific and identifiable reasons.

In the first place it must be said that both historical research and the history of Europe in the twentieth century has given abundant cause for concern and vigilance about the totalitarian abuse of power. Repeatedly, Christian apologists for conservative regimes have been found to have closed their eyes to conditions of abject poverty and desperation in societies which were theoretically supposed to be harmonious and stable. Then, the rival religious legitimations of German and British military and propagandist activities in 1914–1918 were exposed to view, in a technological warfare shorn of heroism. Neither Protestants nor Catholics were exempt from the contamination of suspicion; and in the face of the rise of fascism, the Catholic Church's grasp of, and commitment to a liberal social order proved too weak, and the Protestant churches intellectually too flexible, to provide solid institutional resistance.

The post-War division of Europe into communist regimes and liberal democracies was decisive for the Western churches' intellectual life. Marxist or neo-Marxist analyses of power focused attention on the supposedly devious ways in which the governing class kept the masses content, by subverting the thought and activities of churches, schools, the mass media and even trade unions, and by promoting and encouraging conformist intellectuals. Christian theology was uneasily caught between a committedly atheistic sociology which implicated the churches in collusion with injustice, and a value-neutral positivism which declared Christianity to be no more than one moral view among many. On the whole, the major investment of intellectual energy went into the study of, and dialogue with, Marxism, a stance which fully coincided with the Christian involvement in certain deeply troubled parts of the world, notably South and North America and South Africa. The civil rights movement in the United States of America claimed support from leading Christian theologians, white and black. In 1968 a conference of Latin American Roman Catholic bishops included among its documents a significant analysis of institutional violence.[83] In the following year James Cone published a manifesto on Black Power.[84] In Germany a 'theology of revolution' was widely canvassed in the heady atmosphere of university protest. The Christian world was sharply divided between those who accepted a liberationist method which identified much Christian orthodoxy with the hegemonic thinking of the dominating classes, and defenders of various types of liberal pluralism. The strongly growing feminist protest further divided even the latter, as the long-standing Christian defence of patriarchalism came under severe attack.

The notion of freedom from slavery, of course, had a long biblical tradition in the Exodus narrative. The Prophetic Books and the Psalms contained denunciation of injustice and concern for 'the poor'. But despite certain themes in the Gospels, the absence from the New Testament of a social cosmology and the presence of conformist attitudes towards slavery and patriarchal structures complicated the Christian theological response towards the basic analysis of so-called 'structures of injustice'. Moreover it was unclear whether the end-state, after liberation, would be one in which there was no power and authority, despite the use of coercive, revolutionary means to achieve it. As a consequence some liberationist writing betrays a more deeply rooted objection to authority and power in all its ecclesiastical manifestations than others. At the root of the uncertainty, however, lay understandable weakness in the analysis of power itself.

This was exacerbated by the importance to modern theology of two central christological motifs, those of *kenosis* and *diakonia*. The humility of Christ, the servant, had been a major theme of Luther's own theology, and it was Lutheranism which gave rise in the nineteenth century to a new type of 'kenotic' christology. Divine self-limitation, in the pioneering work of the mid-nineteenth-century Lutheran theologian, Gottfried Thomasius, was the only condition upon which it was possible to give a coherent account of the incarnation, in the context of the newly stressed humanity of Christ, as revealed in the Synoptic Gospels, prime sources for the incipient 'Jesus of History' research.[85] Self-limitation was applied to the divine attribute of omnipotence specifically because it was held to be a 'physical' not a 'moral' attribute of deity. Thus the divine power of Christ was said to be withdrawn from actuality to a state of potentiality, and to be held, so to speak, in reserve.

The cautious, moderate and strongly trinitarian character of this theology contrasts markedly with the subsequent history of Kenoticism. Beyond the constraints of orthodox Lutheranism, which insisted upon a real communication of properties between the divine and human natures of Christ, the way was open for a less guarded affirmation of the complete 'abandonment' by Christ of divine prerogatives to a state of powerlessness.[86] Combined with the reformers' antagonism to the abuse of power in the 'spiritual' offices of the ordained clergy, and their willingness to free themselves from hierarchical church government, a 'powerless' servant Christ became a recurrent motif in a variety of theological contexts, not least outside Protestantism. It lent specific support to the liberationist contrast between the 'worldly' powers, in the meshes of whose devices the church had become entrapped, and the 'powerlessness' of the poor with whom the church was urged to identify.

Whatever merits this stance has in exegesis or systematic theology, the treatment of 'power' as a theme was often uncertain and unconvincing. For example in *Church: Charism and Power*, Leonardo Boff strives to articulate a dialectical understanding of the Church as sacrament of the presence of Christ, according to which it both represents Christ among the faithful (the identity of Christ and the Church) and also has its own status, structures and logic like any other human power structure (the non-identity of Christ and the Church). Boff asserts that Christianity is not against power. But at the same time he constantly uses power as a negative term (the 'model of power', the 'perspective of power'), contrasting 'power/domination' with weakness, service and *diakonia*.[87] Sociology is referred to in order to unmask strategies of legitimation from 'the institution'. But there is no systematic attempt to analyse the implications for the organization of needing a power structure, nor of the modes of communication he himself employs powerfully enough to provoke the future Pope Benedict XVI, Joseph Cardinal Ratzinger, prefect of the Sacred Congregation for the Doctrine of the Faith, to summon Boff to Rome for an interview.[88] Claims for powerlessness plainly cannot be taken literally. In many contexts they are a rhetorical device which is intended to draw upon the resource of moral values present within a community. Only if power were to be identified with physical coercion could such a mode of speech count as other than itself a power ploy. It is part of the problem we are to examine that such analytic inadequacy has become common currency within the theological response.

The one-sidedness of the idea that the Christian gospel is inherently antagonistic to power is evident from the evidence of a completely opposite response, in contemporary evangelical circles, stressing the importance of 'signs and wonders' in evangelism. On the basis of exceptional success a pastor of a church in Southern California, John Wimber has focused specifically on the issue of power in two works entitled, *Power Evangelism* and *Power Healing*. In these the claim is made that we are living in the midst of a battle with Satan, in which our resources are the power of the Holy Spirit, in the gifts of the Spirit. There are particular occasions, which Wimber entitles 'power encounters', when a specific and visible episode demonstrates the fact that Jesus Christ is more powerful than the false gods or spirits worshipped or feared by others. Accordingly exorcisms, healing and definite revelations about future events play a vital role in evangelism. 'In power evangelism, resistance to the gospel is overcome by the demonstration of God's power in supernatural events, and receptivity to Christ's claims is usually very high'.[89] Drawing upon passages such as Matthew 28:18–20, Mark 16:15–18 (the ending supplied to the gospel in the second century), John 14:12, and 1 Corinthians 12–14, Wimber attempts to show that just as early Christians had an openness to the power of the Spirit which resulted in signs and wonders and church growth, we too need to be open to the Spirit's power. Receptivity to those ideas is very widespread and needs to be taken more seriously than apparently it is in theological circles. But its very existence is eloquent testimony to the fact that power is frequently spoken of in the New Testament in a positive way, and that careful theological and sociological work needs to be undertaken in order to interpret it.[90]

But Weber had not made it easy to deploy his sociological analysis in relation to the New Testament. He himself drew on the biblical data for the early Jesus movement in illustration both of what he called 'charismatic authority' (exemplified by Jesus) and the 'routinization of charisma' (already in evidence in Pauline churches).[91] A personal friend of Weber, Ernst Troeltsch (1865–1923), outlined a sociological theory in his classic work, *Die Soziallehren der christlichen Kirchen und Gruppen* (1912; a title misleadingly rendered in English as 'The Social Teachings of the Christian Church'). But Troeltsch saw the development of Catholic Christianity as a deviation from Jesus' own principles,[92] and Weber had embedded in his conceptuality a basic obstacle to using his method for constructive purposes. Power (*Macht*) was, as we have seen, Weber's most general term. But the special instance of power, for which Weber used the term *Herrschaft*, was understood in German, as well as in its usual English translation 'domination', to imply something overbearing. 'Domination' is said to rest upon two bases, either by virtue of a constellation of interests or upon 'authority'; and 'authority' itself has three sub-types according to their mode of legitimacy, namely 'legal-rational', 'charismatic' and 'traditional'.[93] The startling effect of all this is to make charismatic authority, of which Jesus is one of Weber's examplars, a type of 'domination'. But, of course, in popular usage (and in Marxist theory) 'domination' is an *im*proper use of power. When Jesus said to his disciples, 'Follow me' and they obeyed his command, are we to regard this as an instance of 'domination'? On Weber's definition of *Herrschaft* it was. Perhaps in terms of a Marxist view of religion it might be. But for ordinary Christian usage 'domination' is a totally inappropriate word in this context. It is hardly surprising, therefore, that the major German Protestant theological work on the growth of the church office in the early Christian centuries, Hans Urs von Campenhausen's *Ecclesiastical Authority and Spiritual Power in the Church of the First Three Centuries*, contains a single dismissive footnote relating to Weber.[94]

Recent sociological study of the New Testament has closely mirrored the variety of methods and proposals characteristic of the discipline as a whole. But in addition to the kind of sociological theory we have briefly considered two other related disciplines have played a considerable role, social anthropology and social history. The reason for this is not far to seek. The early Jesus movements took place in a social context very unlike the technological and industrial societies which are the implicit subject of modern sociological theory. Weber's understanding of the 'ideal type' of charismatic authority, for example, was subjected to an effective criticism by a student of a millenarian movement in Melanesia.[95] He suggested that the origins of Christianity lay in millenarian belief, which performed a particular social function for an oppressed group. Functionalism, the idea that social events can be best explained in terms of the contribution they make to the continuity of a society, has provided a fruitful theoretical perspective for more than one sociological interpretation of early Christianity. Particularly notable has been the work of Gerd Theissen, in drawing attention to the activities of 'wandering charismatics', itinerant preachers who left their homes to proclaim the immanent rule of God as an answer to the crisis of aggression within Palestinian society.[96]

A sharply contrasting perspective is offered by Richard Horsley in a series of studies, who explicitly criticizes functionalism for its lack of interest in historical developments, its underestimation of serious conflict and its conservative bias towards stability and social balance.[97] Instead Horsley draws upon studies of social stratification and the politics of aristocratic empires to give him a perspective on the fundamental conflicts between the rulers and ruled in Jesus' day.[98] Far from alleviating such conflicts, the Jesus movement exacerbated them by drawing attention to the exploitation involved in heavy taxation with resultant indebtedness and poverty. At the same time, however, Horsley is critical of certain versions of conflict theory, which fail to account for the existence in Jewish biblical tradition of authoritative texts, highly critical of established authorities. Attention to particular historical features in first-century Palestine corrects the historical tendency of much sociological theory.

Pauline studies have also been deeply influenced by new approaches deriving from the social sciences. Here the influence of Peter Berger and Thomas Luckman's idea of the way in which 'social worlds' are constructed has been very marked.[99] Wayne Meeks, for example, published in 1983 a ground-breaking study entitled, *The First Urban Christians: The Social World of the Apostle Paul.*[100] Two years later the same principles were applied to the social structures and relations in Paul's dealings with the slave, Onesimus.[101] Both of these studies owed a substantial debt to the work of a social anthropologist, Victor Turner, especially to his study of the relation between structure and anti-structure in the processes involved in ritual. In early Christianity the rituals of both baptism and eucharist relate to the crucifixion, death and resurrection of Christ. Applied to the circumstances of the believer passage through these rituals was intentionally life-transforming. Comparisons with other rituals in other circumstances alerted interpreters of Paul to features of his writings which had escaped remark. Of course it is true that there is no absolute difference between sociological and good historical interpretation of the texts;[102] the theoretical bag and baggage of sociology is no substitute for the mastery of resources from the social history of the period. But discerningly used it is undoubtedly a form of enrichment.

The 1970s also saw new developments in the sociological interpretation of Paul's exercises of authority in relation to his communities.[103] It was noted that Nietzsche had accused Paul of wanting power for himself, using Christian doctrine as the means for tyrannizing over the masses.[104] A suspicious reading of his rhetoric, accusing him of manipulative strategies was published.[105] The social effect of the rhetorical power was made the focus of an inquiry into the Pauline passages on imitation, which explicitly drew upon Foucault's theoretical perspective.[106] In a sense the cat may now be said to have entirely been let out of the bag. Far from Paul being an example of meek powerlessness, he is revealed as an architect *par excellence* of what Foucault terms 'pastoral power', a form of power whose ultimate aim is to ensure individual salvation in the next world.[107] He is engaged, moreover, in an exercise of radical 'normalization', the suppression of variety and the imposition of an internalized power of invitation. The Pauline, indeed early Christian, drive towards a particular understanding of truth 'reinscribes the relations of power in early Christian communities and renders impossible competing interpretations of power and truth'.[108] The truth which sets you free is also a power which binds you. But perhaps that would be no great surprise to a church familiar with the phrase 'whose service is perfect freedom'.

For all the difficulties of using Foucault as an authority on interpretation (he once said he would ideally like his books to self-destruct after use, like a Molotov cocktail),[109] and if one takes his professed irrationalism with a pinch of salt, one returns without a sense of paradox to the biblical phrase 'the power of the gospel'. The gain from the recent history of sociological writing, including that of Foucault, is the loss of naïve innocence in the use of such a phrase. To understand the gospel as real power implies having to face the danger of the dominative use of the gospel, a gospel misappropriated and misused sometimes through a form of wilful self-deception. It requires, of course, an effort of imagination to read Paul's letters as the rhetoric of power. It also requires a certain human sympathy not to dismiss him as a gross manipulator of his audience, who had little by way of Christian experience or teaching upon which to draw. He had few enough strings to pull, and those he had he tugged for all he was worth. He was, as his musings about power and weakness show, a charismatic with a guilty conscience. There have been plenty of charismatics in the Christian churches since Paul's day who have had no conscience at all. If we are to be denied naïveté on the subject of charismatic gifts, we have less difficulty in being denied interpretative naïveté on the reading of Paul.[110]

V

Sociology offers one further enrichment of the history of theology, on this occasion relating to the distinction we have drawn between a tendency to accept and celebrate power, and a tendency to reject or be suspicious of it. Modern sociological thought, as we have seen, knows of a somewhat similar tension. In his 1957 study of class conflict in industrial society, Dahrendorf asserted that there have been two divergent views of society throughout the whole history of Western political thought. The one, which he termed the Rationalist view, regards society as cohering only by means of force or constraint, one group achieving domination over another, or others, by various techniques of subjugation. The second theory, the Utopian, holds by contrast that order exists in society by means of a general agreement or consensus. Social conflict is conceived differently by the two types of theory. In the Rationalist view it provides the key to the disclosure of the identity of the dominant group; on the Utopian hypothesis it constitutes merely an unavoidable strain on the social system. Similarly, the analysis of power characteristically differs. Rationalists see power as mobilized for sectional interest and therefore distributed unequally, thus giving rise to conflict; for Utopians, on the other hand, power, when it is given any open consideration, is conceived as a facility for achieving the common good, and is a secondary feature dependent upon shared norms and values.[111]

A somewhat similar distinction is made by Lukes between what he terms asymmetrical and collective conceptions of power. By 'asymmetrical' Lukes means those in which there is an imbalance of power, and the concept implies domination of one individual or group over another. Its historic roots lie with Hobbes, who assumes that in a state of nature human beings have irreducibly conflicting interests. Liberal theories or authority stemming from Locke share the same characteristic; and for the Marxists class domination is essential to their analysis of capitalism and its precursors. But it is with Pareto, Weber and the elite theorists of the twentieth century that asymmetric analysis acquires its distinctive realist flavour, the first of these holding that consent is always manipulated, and authority imposed by power.[112]

Collective conceptions of power are embodied in the ancient world in both the republican and the imperial models, which stress the benign and integrating character of the exercise of authority. According to Lukes (though here the picture deserves to be somewhat more fully discussed), the hierarchical views of the medieval period also stress the collective aspect. In modern times the tradition is represented in the functionalism of Durkheim and Talcott Parsons, both of whom insist on the importance to the collectivity of common values. For Parsons, indeed, power is 'the generalized capacity of a social system to get things done in the interest of collective goals'.[113]

Both Dahrendorf and Lukes hold that these analyses are complementary, rather than competitive. Dahrendorf sharply remarks on the fact that inclination to one analysis rather than the other may itself be an expression of class interest. Thus, he observes that factory workers, who have an obvious interest in unmasking a dominant group's techniques for acquiring and retaining control, incline to the Rationalist view of power; whereas the middle classes, who have no less obvious an interest in maintaining a consensus defined largely by themselves, incline to the Utopian view.[114] The application of this insight to appeals to the *consensus omnium* in the Christian Church is obvious enough.

Moreover, social movements instigated from subordinate groups have the habit of presenting themselves as power-movements (thus student-power, black-power, female-power), and of justifying the use of the slogan by a general theory of social conflict based on dominating interests. Academics, moreover, are perceptibly more inclined to favour the underdog, except where their support for the prevailing system is a more or less open expression of their instinct to preserve structures supportive of their own institutions.

If we apply this distinction to the diverging tendencies we have observed in Christian theology the distinction works itself out somewhat in the following way. As Lukes observes, a hierocracy has an interest in a collective or Utopian view of power; whereas a Rationalist will be inclined to emphasize the negative possibilities of even properly exercised authority, and be on guard against abuses. There is, however, another way of interpreting the contrast and relating the two modes of approach. Lukes suggests that if one confines one's focus to a given collectivity abstracted from its relationships with other collectivities, then an analysis in terms of co-operation in a common achievement may yield illuminating results. In other words, a given community may be internally cohesive without the necessity of dominative power, whilst at the same time be engaged in an external struggle with rival communities, in a manner which also yields possibilities in terms of the asymmetric analysis.

The precise converse of this situation may also be possible. Thus a given system, such as capitalism, may only be capable of analysis in terms of its internal power conflicts; whilst at the same time the whole of the system itself possesses and embodies certain collective capacities, such as its productive power. In other words, a given system may be internally conflictual, whilst at the same time be engaged in the production of co-operative benefits.

Without much difficulty a parallel application may be made to the Church itself. On the one hand, it would be feasible to argue, as mentioned already, that the Church is a collectivity internally cohesive in virtue of shared values, but in external conflict with rival powers. On the other hand, it would by no means be out of the question to observe that the Church is a system characterized by chronic internal power struggles, but at the same time engaged by virtue of these struggles, in its universal mission to humanity. In either case, what has to be stressed are the analytic possibilities of a particular conception of power. The Rationalist and the Utopian are only exclusive of each other if they deny the other's right to some explanatory significance. Both may have interpretative force when applied to particular circumstances in a particular way. But how are we to decide in what circumstances and in what way?

A simple, but important idea, itself the result of modern reflection on the deployment of power in politics, suggests itself at this point. Maurice Duverger in *The Idea of Politics: The Uses of Power in Society* draws attention to what he calls the ambivalence of politics, and the Janus-like character of power.[115] In its organized form, successfully wielded power inherently contains both an element of antagonism or conflict as well as an element of integration or harmony. One and the same political order may be seen, therefore, in either of two aspects: as the domination of the privileged, or as the integrating activity of an authentic order. Analytically, one and the same system lends itself to two interpretations, both of which are likely to be able to provide plausible argumentation in their favour, neither of which are likely to be exhaustively true to the exclusion of the other.

Two passages from the New Testament epistles indicate the sensitivity of these early writers to the ambivalence of the forms of power with which they were familiar. Paul's discussion of the authority of his own ministry in 2 Corinthians contains this surprising statement:

> We have renounced the shameful things that one hides; we refuse to practise cunning or falsify God's word; but by the open statement of the truth we commend ourselves to the conscience of everyone in the sight of God. (2 Cor. 4:2)

The reference is, presumably, to the false apostles with whom Paul is in conflict throughout the epistle. But the implication is that Paul had realized that some advantage, however temporary, might be gained by their secret methods of adulteration of the gospel, and had consciously decided to renounce them. Although Paul is, of course, accusing his opponents of disgraceful conduct, the statement contains an indirect recognition of the manipulative potential in preaching, a potential which Paul has laid on one side in order to proclaim what he believed to be the truth openly. His position, he is ready to affirm, may be judged by ordinary human moral insight. Paul is alert to, and recognizes, the ambivalence of the actual power which he wields.

The second passage is somewhat more obvious. In 1 Peter elders are exhorted not to domineer over those in their charge. At the same time the younger are instructed to be subjected to their elders. Here again the ambivalence of power is acknowledged. It takes very little imagination to think that the very same action could appear either an act of service to the unity of the community, or a piece of domineering presumption, depending on the standpoint from which the action was viewed.

The ambivalence of power is not mitigated merely by the invocation of service as the motive for its exercise. Here we must notice the phenomenon of camouflage, to which Duverger draws attention. Those who hold or are attempting to gain power are adept at sensing what are popularly regarded as respectable motives for wanting to be powerful. Within the Christian community the motif of service (*diakonia*) is so prominent a part of the basic theological interpretation of roles, that reference to it is obligatory on every occasion when powers are being conferred.[116] Plainly, the mere statement that all the powers to be exercised are to be exercised as service by no means guarantees that what is eventually carried out will be in accordance with the divine will or even, for that matter, with the moral law. The invocation of service refers to the intention which lies behind the action. It does not describe the action itself, which might be illegal or monstrously unjust. Nor does it bear upon how the action will be experienced or interpreted by those affected by it. The agent, moreover, could lack insight into his own motivations, with the result that what is spoken of as service in the interest of others is, in fact, self-serving. Or, indeed, while the motivation could be genuine, the consequences of the action could also be deleterious to their interests. The mere invocation of service precludes none of these possibilities.

That the exercise of authority should be disciplined by the recollection of the motif of service is a central and valuable Christian tradition. But it ought not to be possible to invoke that tradition without also being conscious of the political phenomenon of camouflage and the toils of self-deception; and with such consciousness one returns again to the ambivalence of power. One of Nietzsche's more chilling aphorisms may be recalled. Under the heading 'Reaction of the Little People', he proposes the view that 'love gives the greatest feeling of power'. Should the Christian be as shocked as Nietzsche intends? Only if power and love are considered to be antithetical; only if the interpretation given to Christian faith is one which has attempted to eradicate the centrality of power to the understanding of its foundational event, the death of Christ.

6

Power and Sacrifice

It is not to be thought that this chapter is written as a kind of resolution to the problem we have identified in the earlier chapters. We have seen that the Christian tradition has given rise to diverging tendencies in its treatment of the complex issues of power. This chapter offers no synthesis. We have also observed from time to time certain developments within the Christian tradition, which have been deplored as harmful. This chapter proposes no remedies of guaranteed efficacy. On the contrary, it has to be admitted that for most of its history Christians have professed a doctrine of the sacrifice of Christ, which has hardly seemed connected to the issue of power, let alone been regarded as an antidote to the abuse of power.

What then is to be offered in this chapter? It will be argued, first, that there is an explicit acknowledgement of the plurality of powers in Christian theology, unified in the narrative or drama of creation, redemption and last things, whose central, pivotal event is the crucifixion. Sacrifice, especially the sacrifice of Christ, is about these powers and their relationship. They cease to be a random network in which human beings happen to be trapped at any one time, both prisoners and jailers. As these powers are orientated around and interpreted by the death and resurrection of Christ, their potential for good emerges, while (at least in the present life) their ambivalence never entirely vanishes.

In other words, it is going to be argued that Christians have a particular way of living in the world of the powers, to which the key concept is that of sacrifice. This by no means resolves the ambivalence of power. The ambivalence remains because, on the contrary, the essential resource for speaking of the sacrifice of Christ is the particular collection of narratives we possess in the New Testament. Again it cannot be claimed that the recollection of Christ's sacrifice in doctrine and ritual observance delivers members of the Christian religion from each and every temptation to abuse power. An elementary knowledge of Church history relieves the student of such simple-mindedness. Moreover, both the doctrine of sacrifice and ritual of eucharistic sacrifice lend themselves to abuse; because they participate in the world of power they share its ambivalence.

The exploration of sacrifice, therefore, is, in effect, a continuation of the study of power and Christian theology, not its attempted closure. On those terms I am hopeful again not to lose those readers who may have suspended disbelief to this point, on the grounds that they share with Christians an interest in the ethical outcome of a discussion of power. As we argued earlier, though it makes a difference to a discussion of power to take the putative power of God into account, it does not necessarily follow that the difference can only be seen as the difference between believing or not believing in God. Sacrifice enters the discussion in exactly the same way. To speak of the conflict of powers, in a Christian context, is to speak of the sacrifice of Christ, as the Son of God. But a way of seeing the difference that that makes to the understanding of power is to attend to the moral commitments that follow from (as Christians might put it) living within the narrative of the sacrifice of Christ.

It belongs to the way in which the different aspects of Christian theology hang together, and the terms on which themes from theology relate to the pressures of circumstance. It is impossible to guarantee that a person who believes x would be incapable of doing y, and would be bound to do z (where z might seem to be the natural concomitant of belief x, and y its opposite). Single elements of belief are always in complex relationship to other elements of the belief system, and the 'system' is rarely entertained as a whole. Moreover human beings have running internal dialogues between voices of belief and of custom, or prudence, or doubt. And church leaders and assemblies have other urgent considerations which bear upon their decisions and actions.

A twentieth-century Christian author belongs within this multiplicity of voices; it is a pretence to presume to surmount, survey and control their insistent demands. Nor is enmeshment within a bewildering network of power different for any other commentator or student. The facts about power impose the issue of ethical commitments, about how powers are going to be used. Discourse about power refers not merely to politics or relationships, but to the act of writing itself. This chapter, then, is admittedly a way of attempting to meet the demands of power from within the resources of Christian theology. Unless the history of Christian attempts to cope with this subject has been seriously misrepresented, this is an important matter; and not merely for Christians.

One of Nietzsche's thought experiments illustrates the nature of the moral commitments of Christianity with some sharpness. Nietzsche's view was that by moving the doctrine of selflessness and love into the foreground, Christianity has enhanced egoistic individualism (the desire for personal salvation) and set back the cause of the human species The species requires selection, and selection necessitates human sacrifice. But Christianity has made all souls equal before God, which in practice means a preference for the suffering and the underprivileged. This is nothing other than a hampering of the forces of selection.

'Genuine charity demands sacrifice for the good of the species – it is hard, it is full of self-overcoming, because it needs human sacrifice. And this pseudo-humaneness called Christianity wants it established that no-one should be sacrificed.'[1] With this astringent alternative in mind we turn to the form that sacrifice has taken in Christianity, which is by no means as Nietzsche conceived it.

In the mapwork offered in Chapter 2, Christian theology was said to be rooted in drama. The early Christian communities lived in a mental climate of high cosmic drama, which included the whole of human history as they knew it. The terms of this drama concerned specific significant effects, including events in their own history, in which the reality of divine power was, they believed, seen to be operating. Nor was the world in which they lived merely the theatre of divine power; Paul, it will be remembered, attributes the very death of Christ himself to the activity of those shadowy beings he calls the 'rulers of this present age' (1 Cor. 2:8).

In order to illustrate the complexity of this dramatization of the world, three theatres were distinguished, those of the world, of society and of the individual, and three dramatic actions of God were identified, those of creation, of redemption and of a hoped-for future consummation. The superimposition of the three enables one to say that the Christian participates in the victories of creation, redemption and final salvation, whilst at the same time he or she is conscious of being the subject of the creative, redemptive and consummating activity of God in human society and in the world itself. The importance of this comprehensive frame of reference is its securing for the Christian of 'a house of being' against chaos, unreason and non-being.[2]

It is important to observe, again, the logic of binary opposition. The dramatization of human experience is in terms of the sharpest contrast: creation–chaos, redemption–sin, and hope–annihilation. This has important consequences for the theme of the ambivalence of power which emerged from our treatment of the sociological literature. The fact that, in most of its human forms, the deployment of power lends itself to an analysis which identifies both a coercive and demonic, and a collective and benign character, appears to provoke the religious response of acute separation. It is because of the ambivalence of power that the religious response is sharply to demarcate the opposition between the two realms. But the logic of the opposition has the contrary effect of giving a form of permanence to the countervailing forces, at least until the eschaton. The importance of eschatology in Christian theology is that it represents an acknowledgement of the state of ambiguity in which Christian existence is here and now enmeshed. Slight shifts in eschatological perspective can lead, as we saw in our examination of the power-acceptance tradition, to the danger of an uncritical belief in the Church's realization of the divine power in history. In fact, eschatology is an oblique affirmation of the ambivalence of all exercise of power in the present. The Christian is, or ought to be, thoroughly at home with the conclusions from our examination of the sociological literature. It coheres both with the Christian's sense of being a power living in a world of conflicting powers, and, at the same time, of needing to acknowledge the ambiguous character of all exercises of power and the necessity of unmasking power-disguises, even in the treasured heart of the motives of service and of love.

From the Christian perspective, however, the powers are set within the framework of the power of God. The narrative which speaks of God's activity represents the events of the redemption and of the last things as a victory. Even creation itself is a triumph over the powers of darkness and chaos (Ps. 24:13–17). Its consummation results in the fulfilment of God-ruling. Moreover those who participate with Christ in the battle against evil will share his sovereignty. The saints, according to Paul, are to judge even the angels

(1 Cor. 6:3). At the very place where the Gospel of Luke introduces the most striking criticism of dominative modes of exercising power, as contrasted with service, there is a clear guarantee of eschatological compensation (Luke 22:28–30). The faithful will be garlanded with wreath or crown and robed in the white garments of an imperial victor (Rev. 7:7–14). Christian apocalyptic has thus taken over not merely the democratized royal enthronement as the reward of the righteous, but also its close connection with the kingship of Christ; as Christ has been enthroned with the Father, so will Christians be enthroned with Him. The first thing to say about Christian existence, therefore, *before* speaking of the ambivalence of the exercise of all power, is to affirm Christian participation in Christ's eschatological triumph. Christians are, in Paul's telling image, captives in Christ's triumphal procession (2 Cor. 2:14).

The means of this victory, moreover, is specifically located as the cross of Christ. The word of the cross is for Paul 'the power of God' (1 Cor. 1:18). Human helplessness and sin is the context in which the cross – and resurrection – is so powerful (2 Cor. 12:8–10). The love of God, exemplified in God's gift of his own Son for human salvation, is the guarantee of the unconquerable power of the love of Christ dwelling within the Christian (Rom. 8:38–39). That the cross itself can acquire the connotation of the victory of the resurrection, and become the comprehensive symbol of divine power, is a potential realized in the Johannine theme of raising or lifting up; 'I, when I am lifted up from the earth, will draw all people to myself' (John 12:32).

By the time of Justin Martyr, there was already a Christian interpolation into the text of Psalm 96. Added to the words 'Say among the nations, "The Lord reigns!"' is the phrase *apo tou xylou*, from the tree.[3] The kingship of Christ had been purchased by his suffering; as Justin himself asserts, it is 'the hidden power of God which is exhibited in the crucified Christ'.[4] In an imaginative interpretation of Isaiah 9:6, Justin applies the words 'and the government shall be upon his shoulders' to the pinning of Jesus' shoulders upon the cross.[5] When, in Psalm 24, the rulers of heaven are commanded to open the gates to the victorious Christ they do not recognize him because of his unattractive and mean appearance; they ask therefore, 'Who is the King of glory?' (Ps. 24:8) To which, says Justin, the Holy Spirit answers, 'The Lord of powers (*kyrios ton dynameon*). He is this King of glory'.[6]

It is thus for Christians the cross of Christ which is the agency of the divine victory. Commenting on the celebration of the 'breadth and length and height and depth of the love of God' contained in the letter to the Ephesians (Eph. 3:18), a fourth-century writer, reflecting traditions already 200 years old, affirms:

> Paul knows indeed that the Cross, divided into four branches from the central point, signifies the power (*dynamis*) and the providence which came from Him who is seen upon it, and which penetrates everything, and for this reason he gives each branch a special name [that is, length, breadth, height and depth]. . . . Now this signifies that there is nothing which is not under the empire of divine power, neither that which is above heaven, nor that which is under the earth, nor that which extends transversally to the limits of being.[7]

The cross here is not merely the mysterious divine event which atones for human sin and achieves the reconciliation of God and humanity; it is the expression of the universal providence of the divine *Logos*. As the cosmic cross, it has the attributes of God the creator, of consolidation, of distinction and of unification.

This material from the early history of Christian doctrine makes one very important theological point: that the victories to which the binary opposites refer are the consequences of the outpouring of the love of God for humanity, focused in the cross. The power of God, in other words, in *each* of the theatres of creation, redemption and future consummation is the power of the cross. The love of God which is evident in the drama of creation in the power of providence over chance, of law over anarchy and of reasoned thought over madness is not other than the love of God in the drama of redemption. The theology of the power of God is, as Karl Rahner insisted, a theology of the cross;[8] it is, I propose now to argue, a theology of sacrifice.

II

The relation between power and sacrifice is already a familiar topic in social anthropology. John Beattie has made precisely this relation the central issue in his typology of sacrificial rites. 'Almost always sacrifice is seen as being, mostly, about *power*, or *powers*.'[9]

Either this power is regarded as a more or less personalized spiritual being or beings, or it is held to be an impersonal and diffuse quality or force. Then the rite itself is regarded as either achieving a closer intimacy with the being or force, or is aimed at separation from it. The two distinctions create a four-fold classification which, Beattie holds, enables one to comprehend most, if not all, of the known sacrificial rituals.[10] Meyer Fortes somewhat similarly, though less schematically, argues that the long period of powerlessness and vulnerability experienced by human infants can plausibly be held to be the psychological origin of a range of 'rituals of defence', of which sacrifice is one.[11] External vulnerability to war, disease, hunger or social upheaval; internal vulnerability to mental disorder, lust, and anger; and finally vulnerability, above all, to death is the root of sacrifice. Even thanksgivings, according to Fortes, 'have an obvious prophylactic intention'.[12] The application of these insights to the sacrificial rituals of the Old Testament, complex though they are to interpret through the medium of the written traditions, is direct and immediate. Fortes, indeed, claims 'that the defensive character of the Old Testament sacrifice is apparent all through'.[13] The Old Testament scholar, Rogerson, likewise, though expressing caution about the extent to which the Old Testament actually provides a sufficiently comprehensive ethnographic record for satisfactory theory, has no doubt that anthropological works such as those of Leach and Douglas contribute importantly to an understanding of how the ancient Israelites structured their world.[14]

At this point we must take account of the stimulating and controversial proposal of Girard that 'violence is the heart and secret of the soul of the sacred'.[15] Arguing that the deflection of the violence endemic in every community is carried out by means of the selection of an agreed surrogate victim, he holds that human culture has known three main methods for eliminating the chronic problem of revenge. The first is the institution of sacrifice, which ritually diverts the spirit of revenge into other channels; the second is the curative technique of harnessing revenge in compensatory measures and trials of combat; and the third is the imposition of a judicial system.[16] Girard's theory is thus an attempt to account for the disappearance of sacrifice from culture. The reason why modern societies have given up rituals of sacrifice is that justice has broken the circle of private vengeance by limiting it to a single act of reprisal. The difficulty for modern society is that, having discovered that justice is merely the strict application of the principle of vengeance, the necessary transcendental aura surrounding it has been lost. Having unmasked the system of reciprocal reprisal, we discover that the vicious circle from which we believed we had escaped has tightened its grip on us.[17]

In a fascinating discussion of the passion narratives of the Gospels, Girard claims that theological interpreters, like their sceptical critics, have missed the central point: that the whole mechanism involved in scapegoating is being revealed.[18] On the evidence of the text itself, those who crucified Jesus do not consciously know what they are doing. Caiaphas believes it expedient that one man should die for the people (John 11:50); he wants to limit violence as much as possible, but is ready to permit its use on one whom the gospel has already identified as 'the Lamb of God'. 'Caiphas is the perfect sacrificer who puts victims to death to save those who live.'[19] His action is implicitly denounced by the Gospels as a total mistake, a denial which unmasks the nature of Western political thought. This is based, in either its conservative or radical forms, on 'partial and biased adaptations of the Gospel revelation'.[20] It is precisely when it is broken up that that revelation provides weapons to justify violence vastly superior to what would otherwise be available.

Christians, however, have failed to perceive the true originality of the text, which is that it demystifies 'the original murder that is found at the heart of all mythology'.[21] Because they fail to read the Gospels literally, theologians make sacred the violence that has been divested of its sacred character by the gospel text.[22] Once victorious Christianity in its turn became tyrannical oppressor and persecutor.[23] But Girard does not hold that liberation consists in accepting the view that Christianity is no more than another religious myth. On the contrary, Christianity is responsible for our understanding and only if we take the gospel story seriously will we see that it is a radical critique of violent religion.[24] On the basis of the texts on the Holy Spirit, the *Paraclete*, in the Gospel of John, Girard argues that 'the Spirit is working in history to reveal what Jesus has already revealed, the mechanism of the scapegoat, the genesis of all mythology, the non-existence of all gods of violence'.[25] The time has come, he concludes, for forgiveness. 'If we wait any longer there will not be time enough.'[26]

Girard's argument is a radical version of Fortes' less all-encompassing proposal concerning rituals of defence. One of its weaknesses is the breadth and ambiguity of its concept of violence, which includes not merely its obvious social and individual manifestations, but also incest and death, and the social threats constituted by contagious diseases, drought or flood; in effect, violence is a symbol for all human afflictions, hard to distinguish from evil, 'original sin' and even, as Beattie remarks in a critical review, power itself.[27]

Critics of Girard have amply commented upon the selectivity of the evidence for his sweeping claims, according to which the whole of human culture, religion and social institutions turn upon the operation of this single mechanism. Nonetheless there are points at which his treatment of sacrifice is illuminating for Christian theology, despite the explicitly atheistic expression of the argument. The importance of Girard's observations has to do specifically with violence and the cycle of revenge. As against those understandings of the victory of the cross in which the actual events of the crucifixion play a minimal role (where, for example, the cross is seen as a cosmic transaction dependent upon the worth of the divine sacrifice, or as a spectacle calculated to arouse pity), I want to lay prime emphasis upon the character of the violence done to Jesus, and his response.

In order to identify this violence with precision, it is, of course, necessary to rehearse the story of Jesus' way to death. If claims are to be made and sustained about the representative character of Jesus' death, *pro nobis* then we are dependent upon the observation of specific features of that narrative which mark it out as capable of bearing the sacramental principle that like stands for like.

Here certain presuppositions play a role which ought to be acknowledged. I propose to assume with a considerable quantity of recent theology (and now the support of Alastair MacIntyre) the central importance of the role of realistic narrative. As MacIntyre has put it: 'I can only answer the question "What am I to do?" if I can answer the prior question "of what story or stories do I find myself a part?"'[28]

Christian existence is, I shall presuppose, the drafting of persons into the all-embracing narrative of Jesus Christ. Secondly, the stories will be taken in the form in which they are found in the Gospels, rather then as they may be reconstructed in historical criticism. This is not because historical criticism is unimportant; on the contrary, in the last 150 years, it has performed the literally indispensable service of refuting the attempts to falsify the Gospels' basic historical truth claims. But for Christian existence it is the text of the Gospels as they stand which constitutes the core of the Church's spirituality and liturgy. It is, therefore, with the impression of Jesus derivable from a reading (or even a hearing) of the narratives that systematic theology must come to terms. The third presupposition is that narrative is indispensable to the understanding of the sacrifice of Christ. A sacrifice is a symbolic action generally taken to involve the slaying or destruction of a victim or a gift (though there are acute definitional difficulties into which we cannot now enter).[29] But for the Judaeo-Christian tradition it is a symbolic action in a narrative context, in which knowledge of the intentions of the actors is indispensable to construing the content of the action. To speak of the death of Christ as sacrifice is not, strictly speaking, to use a metaphor. The death of Christ *is* the sacrifice, the sacramental (in that sense, symbolic) action which effects what it signifies. If we are to explore what it is that that sacrifice effects, why this symbol has been thought capable of carrying the weight of the whole human experience of power and its ambivalence, then it is the specific interplay of violence and Jesus' response which will illuminate it, if anything will.

The three-fold exposition will treat, first, Jesus' way to death as an experience of injustice done to an *individual*. Then, secondly, we will see the same way to death as a form of *corporate* manipulation. And, finally, the *cosmic* disorder implicit in the passion narrative will be brought out.

III

(i) Violence in Jesus' way to death is experienced by him as *individual* oppression. The stories in the Gospels make absolutely clear that Jesus was unjustly treated. In Stephen's speech in Acts 7 the continuous story of individual injustice perpetrated upon the prophets is the background to the culminating episode involving Jesus. Stephen asks:

> 'Which of the prophets did your ancestors not persecute? They killed those who foretold the coming of the Righteous One, and now you have become his betrayers and murderers. You are the

ones that received the law as ordained by angels, and yet you have not kept it.' (Acts 7:52–53)

The passion narrative of Mark makes clear that the evidence against Jesus brought before the chief priests, elders and scribes was fabricated and contradictory. The substitution of Jesus for Barabbas by Pilate was a flagrant act of appeasement of a mob (Mark 15:11). In Matthew, Pilate goes through the ironic charade of washing his hands of Jesus' blood (Matt. 27:24); in Luke, one of the criminals crucified with Jesus and the centurion watching the last moments emphasize Jesus' complete innocence (Luke 23:47).

Luke-Acts lays particular emphasis on the prayer for the forgiveness of his assailants uttered by both Jesus (at least according to certain reputable manuscripts) and Stephen (Luke 23:34; Acts 7:40). Forgiveness has no meaning unless genuine guilt is attributed to those who not merely carried out the execution, but also those who planned and legitimated it. Indeed, the fact that Jesus' death was itself a judicial, but grossly unjust, civil act plainly limits the degree to which any subsequent Christian political metaphysic can plausibly be invoked to condone injustice. The central story of the gospel knows and disapproves of the bad exercise of lawful power. Acts goes still further in describing Herod's excruciating death as a consequence of his failing to deny an attribution of divine dignity (Acts 12:33).

The events following Jesus' betrayal in due course prompted the early communities to refer to Isaiah 53:8, citations or echoes of which occur in Luke-Acts, in Matthew and in 1 Peter. The version read by the Ethiopian eunuch contained the words, 'In his humiliation justice was denied him' (Acts 8:33); in 1 Peter the Isaianic phrase, 'although he had done no violence' is rendered 'he committed no sin' (1 Peter 2:22). The sinlessness of Jesus, the fact that by any scale of human desert he did not deserve his fate, becomes for the epistle to the Hebrews a cornerstone of the confidence felt in the high priestly intercession of Christ on behalf of sinners (Heb. 4:15–16).

The violence done to Jesus is, therefore, violence done to a guiltless victim; but, as Rowan Williams following Girard argued in *Resurrection*, Jesus' response to this violence, as portrayed in the New Testament, is neither one of revenge nor of complicity. Jesus persistently refuses the role of oppressor; 'when he suffered he did not threaten' (1 Peter 2:23). Thus there is 'no sense in which Jesus used counter-violence of a verbal or any other variety'.[30] He is one who is essentially and archetypally victim.

Williams' argument here takes us a stage further in that he specifically relates the quality of Jesus as pure victim to the problem of judgement, guilt and condemnation. As he indicates, the Fourth Gospel in particular offers an elaborate commentary on the concept of judgement. Though judgement is inseparable from the event of Jesus, nonetheless it is not the Father's will that anyone should be excluded, nor is Jesus come to judge, but to save the world (John 12:47). Williams' comment on this tradition is to the effect that it issues a divine proclamation to all earthly authorities of 'release from the pendulum swing of attack and revenge'. 'There is more to human interrelation than the opposition of the one who possesses coercive force or authority to condemn and the one who suffers it.'[31] This, moreover, is of application to the system of oppressor–victim which constitutes the very psychological atmosphere of all human relationships, not least those of family life. 'We are born into a world where there is *already* a history of oppression and victimization.'[32] Though we cannot dispense with the categories of moral responsibility or of conscious option for or against violence, there is a sense in which the whole of human life is scarred by a pervasive element of mutual diminution and deprivation. The discovery that all are victims is not by means of a bland generalization, but by uncovering our own past of oppression and collusion in self-diminution. This, says Williams, is entailed in 'belonging to the single human story'.[33]

The profundity and fruitfulness of this argument is plain enough. Jesus' response to individual oppression could be represented simply as fortitude; certainly Peter explicitly uses the example of Jesus as an encouragement to a persecuted Christian community to endure injustice (1 Peter 2:13–21). But mere fortitude yields to a deeper analysis when the complicity of the 'long-suffering' victim is exposed as a form of collusion in violence, with great potential for self-injury and subtle forms of tyranny. In this way it is apparent that individual release from entrapment within networks of violence is no easy matter. It is now unmistakable that it is spectacularly inappropriate to use the word 'sacrifice', at least in a Christian context, to designate death in battle. Mortal danger can, of course, elicit heroic and altruistic behaviour, which should be honoured as such. But to identify the sufferings of an army of conscripts with those of Jesus, in order that the former should be endowed with the aura of divine approval and the power of redemptive sacrifice, is an abuse of theology, as Wilfred Owen, a theologically educated poet and soldier, appreciated. He subverts the story of Abraham's defeated attempt to sacrifice his son Isaac, in obedience to God's command, by telling how the old man would not accept the substitute victim, the Ram of Pride, 'but slew his son,/And half the seed of Europe, one by one'.[34] The text is memorably set in Benjamin Britten's *War Requiem* against a background of boys singing the offertory versicle from the Mass: 'We offer to thee, O Lord, a sacrifice of prayer and praise: do thou receive them on behalf of those souls whom we commemorate this day.'

It is also an abuse of the theology of sacrifice not to perceive the danger in an approach to God involving an annihilation of self. A penetrating study of the damage inflicted by Simone Weil on herself, in her very self-identification with the sufferings of Christ, reveals what is at issue here. The desire for oblivion, for being consumed by God, which she expresses in her later prayers and writings, trapped her in the dialectic of domination, rather than freed her, as she hoped, for life at a higher level.[35] The feminist objection to presenting the death of Christ as sacrifice relates to the abandonment of pride as the supposedly archetypal human sin, as well as to female susceptibility to the demand for superhuman acts of self-denial.[36] From the standpoint of the problem of power with which we are concerned, feminist theology is fully justified in drawing attention to the doctrine of creation. A created being, male or female, has God-given powers which ought not to be depreciated, let alone denied. The story of Jesus' way to his own death is not one of the deliberate courting of self-annihilation. Those rulers who oppress and crucify Jesus are condemned for doing so; only the responsibility of those immediately carrying out orders is mitigated by the words, 'They do not know what they are doing' (Luke 23:34).

To understand created powers as good, but not to divinize them or to exempt them from the potentiality of misuse, calls for the exercise of judgement. When mistakes are made, or when more deliberate forms of abuse are disclosed for what they are, then the challenge is not to be fixated upon the past. In Christian thinking the death of Christ stands for the possibility that past error can be overcome; that ignorance, evil and tragedy do not have the last word. The network of powers in which human life is lived is itself framed by the power of God to rescue and redeem from futility.

(ii) Violence in Jesus' way to death is also experienced in the form of *corporate* manipulation. Essential, here, is the role of Judas, the link between the intimate fellowship of Jesus' disciples and the challenge to the corporate authority of chief priests and scribes inherent in Jesus' success as a teacher. Mark makes clear how Judas' personal motivation, which is left ambiguous, is subsumed into a larger entity, only to be engulfed in the still larger stakes of Roman *raisons d'etat* (Mark 15:11–15). Luke sharpens the focus of this latter context by emphasizing the tension between Herod and Pilate, and the irony of their reconciliation by means of Pilate's believed recognition of Herod's jurisdictional rights (Luke 23:7–12). John adds to the scene the self-condemnatory answer of the chief priests, 'We have no king but Caesar' (John 19:15).

Jesus, then, is the victim not merely of an individual injustice, but also of a society locked in a tense and ambiguous relationship with an occupying regime. The very fact of being subjugated is already anomalous enough, in the light of the conviction that God is the only true King of Israel. But from Jesus there is no tradition of the fomenting of rebellion; the test question concerning tax is handled with an adroitness that evokes amazement whatever its precise implication (Mark 12:14–17). Jesus' challenge is directed rather to the source of the distinction between Israel and the nations, namely the traditional teaching about purity. The extension of his mission, to embrace the Gentile world, if not based on his own teaching, is at least a consistent elaboration of it. The kingship of Christ is by implication universal, as the rending of the temple curtain and the response of the centurion, 'Truly this man was a Son of God' (Mark 15:39), are intended to demonstrate.

But to be caught up into the complex struggles of the governing authorities is by no means an unambiguous fate. On the basis of the gospel narratives themselves it could be said that Jesus provoked the authorities. Unrelenting in their insistence that Jesus knew that he was to be betrayed and crucified, the gospel writers present Jesus as 'setting his face to go to Jerusalem' (Luke 9:51). His behaviour in the temple in driving out those who sold and bought implies a self-assertiveness that is quite other than conciliatory (Matt.

21:12–13; Mark 11:15–17; Luke 19:45–46; John 2:13–17). Finally, and above all, Judas' intention is presented in all the Gospels as known to Jesus (Matt. 24:21; Mark 14:18; Luke 22:21–22; John 13:21–27). Indeed in the Fourth Gospel Judas is specifically instructed by Jesus to carry out his act of betrayal with speed (John 13:27). As many writers have noted, but especially Karl Barth, Jesus does not escape implication in the guilt of Judas, the willing agent of the corporate violence which eventually engulfed them both.[37]

We have already noted in Chapter 4 the eschatological context in which the gospel writers set Jesus' betrayal and trial. The powers involved are plural and diverse; there are angels, on the one hand, and the real but limited powers assigned to Pilate 'from above' (John 19:11). Encompassing all, however, is the conviction that the last judgement will disclose God's unique power to vindicate the cause of right. This is the background against which Jesus invokes that element of the tradition speaking of a reversal of failure for the poor and oppressed. The psalm (22) which contains the words from the cross, 'My God, my God, why have you forsaken me?' (v.1) also contains the words, 'For he did not despise or abhor the affliction of the afflicted; he did not hide his face from me, but heard when I cried to him' (v.24) and finishes with a song of victory, 'For dominion belongs to the Lord, and he rules over the nations' (v.28). The Jewish tradition of radical theocracy is an ideological weapon of very great power. Jesus' teaching of the kingdom and the reconstitution of communities in the light of the reality of God's rule is intended to relativize the claims and impact of the governing authorities. Jesus did not indicate, or support, a revolt of the peasants. But his movement was nonetheless deemed to be political in the sense of a hostile challenge to the governing authorities, who closed ranks to dispatch him.

With Girard we may see that the violent putting to death of Jesus is the communal selection of a scapegoat, a surrogate victim, in a situation threatening to implode. The difficulty of his treatment of the Gospels, which is in many ways brilliantly illuminating, is his lack of interest in the type of movement which Jesus initiated by his teaching and healing, and the continuation of that movement in the churches of the early missionaries, including Paul. The characteristic consequence of that movement was a specific type of community. That community was enmeshed within the network of powers of a given social salvation. Its function was not to preserve a set of documents for later decoding by brilliant literary critics, but to embody a certain style of relationships. In the face of hostility, oppression and violence, it is obliged to attempt to discriminate, as did Jesus, between real options in the world, and to accept the consequences of an honest pursuit of the good. The death of Christ, his self-sacrifice, is community-creating. The early communities as they reproduced themselves in the ancient world in a variety of new contexts saw the closest connection between Jesus' death and the attitudes needed to sustain these communities. They taught the absolute necessity of humility. There were to be no 'rabbis' or 'fathers' or 'teachers'. There was but one teacher, the Messiah, who conducted himself with humility (Matt. 23:8–12). Rivalry and personal vanity were to be given up. Christ's humility in accepting death by crucifixion was to inform their bearing towards one another (Phil. 2:5–11). The instruction had an entirely practical consequence for the conduct of their meetings. If they failed (as the church in Corinth, so Paul believed, had failed) to perceive the body of Christ – his crucified body, which body they indeed were – then, devastatingly, their meetings could do more harm than good (1 Cor. 11:17). The rich are not to shame the poor by self-indulgent consumption of food and drink; they are to wait for one another. They are to live as a corporate whole, filled and united by the Spirit, loving one another with a love which is patient, kind, courteous and generous-minded (1 Cor. 12–13).

The claim that the world of the powers can be altered by the creation of such a community was a political claim. It entailed not allowing the gross external circumstances of a particular context, whether of Palestine or then more widely of the Roman Empire, to create a particular mindset among both the ruled and the ruling elite. Contexts differ markedly. In the modern world one of the most extraordinary struggles for the realization of the political implications of Christian faith has taken place in South Africa. Here the churches have been obliged to abandon both irresponsibility and false innocence, and accept the implications of immersion in an ambiguous world, attempting to realize the good by means consistent with its internal life. In this and other places the churches have also sustained a corporate eschatological vision and hope which has included individual martyrdoms. It is true, of course, as the early Church discovered, that potential martyrs may have to be discouraged. The power of self-sacrifice is such as not to be free of ambiguity. But to give oneself wholly to the cause of freedom, justice and generosity is to court disappointment. The self-sacrifice of Christ, as celebrated by the Christian community on the day of his resurrection, has given Christians an unshakable conviction in the final victory of the good (1 Cor. 15:58).

(iii) Finally we must explore the possibility that the violence in Jesus' way to death takes the form of *cosmic disorder*. Of this it is, of course, the most difficult to write, at least convincingly. The gospel writers are clear enough. From midday to three in the afternoon a darkness fell over the whole land. Matthew asserts that at Jesus' death there was a violent earthquake. John records no cosmic portents such as are frequently found attending the deaths of great heroes; but he has already made clear that a more mundane darkness had enwrapped the traitor Judas as he left the disciples' meal table (John 13:30). The light will shine on in the dark, and the darkness will never master it (John 1:5). The whole New Testament deploys the symbolism of light and darkness in relation to the ministry of Jesus, which is light for those living in darkness and the shadow of death. So the death of Jesus is a moment when the 'world rulers of this present darkness' seem briefly to have triumphed.

The whole world is the sphere of God's rule; that at least is clear from the doctrine of creation. The powers of the created order are not, then, a neutral backdrop to the drama of human life. Neither Judaism, nor its offshoot, the Christian religion, is indifferent to what occurs in the natural world. There is an order in creation, or a potential order, which praises the creator. An integral part of God's faithfulness to his people is the order of sea and dry land (Psalms 89, 93, 96, 104). Praise emanates from the whole of creation, sun and moon, snow and ice, fruit trees and all cedars, creeping things and feathered fowls, together with (*nota bene*) kings and earthly rulers, princes and judges over the whole earth (Psalm 148, and the Benedicite). A human being is, as George Herbert put it, the secretary to articulate the praise of the creator on behalf of the inarticulate.[38] In a sense the tribute of the creation to the creator is contained in a single word, Glory! (Ps. 29:9).

It is precisely this tradition which collides with the story of the crucifixion; and the early communities interpreted what then happened in the light of a passage from Isaiah 53 describing a tortured servant, without beauty, majesty or grace to commend him, but who will bear the sins of many and after his suffering will be vindicated and bathed in light. John, indeed, goes further and insists that the crucifixion is the glorification of Jesus. The true glory of the Son consists in the complete accomplishment of the Father's will; hence the saying from the cross, 'It is finished' (John 19:30).

But it is Paul who develops with the greatest subtlety the range of this symbol. For him the whole creation is subjected to futility, waiting to be 'set free from its bondage to decay and obtain the glorious liberty of the children of God' (Rom. 8:21); no suffering in the present, therefore, can be compared with the glory to be revealed. Likewise, the sense of the whole ministry is rendered in the phrase 'the light of the gospel of the glory of Christ, who is the likeness of God' (2 Cor. 4:4). This glory is indeed that of the creator himself, who said 'Let light shine out of darkness' and has now shone in the believer's heart so that they too may reflect his glory (2 Cor. 4:6). This, moreover, is the ultimate source of the Christian's power, a power contained in earthen vessels (2 Cor. 4:7). Thus, though Christians carry around in their bodies the death of Jesus, their very same bodies are also filled with his life. Whilst the outer nature is subject to decay, the inner nature is constantly being renewed (2 Cor. 4:16).

It would be dangerously trite to say that the implication of Jesus' sacrificial death for the created order is, on the one hand, to deepen the enjoyment of its beauty with a recognition of the realities of suffering and death, and, on the other, to permeate the grimness of decay with the beauty of new life. Part of the discipline of pain and death is to let them be what they are, and not to falsify their reality by a specious prettiness. But the New Testament invites us not absolutely to attribute to death, specifically Jesus' death, a status separate from that of the glory of the creator in his creation. Luke, in the response of the centurion who witnessed Jesus' death, states that 'he gave thanks to God'; Paul vividly gives expression to the mistakes of the powers who bought about Jesus' crucifixion as a failure to recognize 'the Lord of glory'. Here too the sacrificial language is powerful and acutely dangerous, as attempts to follow Christ by offering both soul and body as a sacrifice of praise are exposed to the charges of masochism. But praise remains the characteristic note of Christian response to the creator. In the life which ended as Jesus' life did, in a complete act of self-oblation, there is that note of glory which belongs to creation itself. It is instinctively to poets that we turn for words to describe this 'inscape' of things revelatory of the power of God, and among English poets, to none more appropriately than Gerard Manley Hopkins, with his sense of the fire which breaks forth from the very buckling of the falcon 'a billion times told lovelier, more dangerous' and the potential in the routine of religious life to break open and reveal the beauty and power of Christ's sacrifice:

> No wonder of it: sheer plod makes plough down sillion
> Shine, and blue bleak embers, ah my dear,
> Fall, gall themselves, and gash gold-vermillion.

Laus deo semper.

7

Power in the Church

I

In his 'Reflections in Retirement' on the office of bishop, Archbishop Stuart Blanch cited a sentence, orally gleaned, he believed, from William Temple; 'the acute institutional stage of the Church may well be over'.[2] It is not a remark to which any particular analysis is appended. But it expresses a certain unease which a distinguished and devoted Bishop and Archbishop felt about the contemporary construction of those offices. He quoted a prominent Roman Catholic theologian on the tradition embodied in the Gospel and letters of St. John, marked by a pronounced lack of interest in precedence or status. Then he added:

> This does not at all sound like the Holy Catholic Church we are familiar with. It is to secular society that that Church owes much of its distinctive patterns – the decision-making, the hierarchies, the appeal to tradition, the attitude to dissidents, the judicial procedures, its defence mechanisms. Such knowledge as we have of the Johannine community must cause us to question our assumptions about the great ecclesiastical institutions we have come to take for granted. They may not be indispensable . . . 'Patterns of episcopacy' will be different. Bishops might be seen as 'apostles' once more, leaders of mission rather than servants of a great institution, close to the ground rather than enthroned on high, *primus inter pares* rather than potentates.[3]

The difficulty to which the Archbishop points is the plain fact that if an institution is large and influential, its leaders will be people of prominence whether they see themselves as 'potentates' or not. Or to put it another way, they will have standing in public life, whether or not they personally claim status for themselves. They may long for apostolic simplicity, but if they preside over large budgets, have pastoral care for large numbers of clergy, and are looked to by the public for spiritual and moral guidance, their lives will be full of irresolvable tensions.

Of course, the decline of the institution, the diminution of its public role, the shrinking of its budgets and staff – all of this will, perforce, entail retreat from 'greatness'. But none of that was what Stuart Blanch had in mind. And he knew well enough that the Church was not in charge of its own destiny. What secular society demands of the Church is important. The development of the episcopate in history demonstrated its capacity for adaptation to particular circumstances. In his reflections he tried to identify what for a bishop in the contemporary Church of England constituted the heart of the task, in administration, pastoral care, theological reflection and (especially) mission.

In the previous chapter I attempted to show how every form of personal, social and political relationship takes place within diverse networks of power, and argued that Christians should not be so paralysed by the ambiguities of such entanglements as to fail to achieve what is achievable in history. In this chapter I want to consider the special case of offices of leadership in the Church. Here, if anywhere, the maxim, 'not power but service' tends to hold sway. But here, too, the simple contrasting of the two concepts masks real complexities and the phenomenon of disguise needs to be seriously considered. And, as we argued earlier, there is no reason why the intention that an action should be done in service to others implies that no power or powers were used to bring it about.

But, first, one needs to acknowledge openly, what is widely known but rarely spoken of, namely the powers of a diocesan bishop. Two examples will suffice. The bishop of the diocese has very substantial powers of informal patronage. That is to say, he is in a strong position to exercise those comparative judgements which result in the recommendation of particular people for appointment and preferment. Though current legislation curtails his legal right to present a priest to a vacancy forthwith, what I am speaking of is a consequence of the bishop's wide knowledge of the diocese and of the trust placed in his capacity for discernment, exercised both negatively and positively. Powers of patronage are exceedingly familiar to sociologists of organizations. They consist in the opening and shutting of gates of opportunity or access. They can be overt or covert, and repose both in the written reports and unwritten comment. Inevitably they are exercised not just by the formal management, but by the bureaucrats and secretaries – and, if Anthony Trollope is to be believed (and he is, in my view), by the wives of bishops too.

A second example is even more familiar and concerns discipline. It was a duty inherent in the bishop's office from the first to prevent damage to the Church by error or misbehaviour. Modern legislation rightly protects those holding the bishop's licence from arbitrary persecution. But the powers of discipline exist, and must be exercised in non-arbitrary form, sometimes with very far-reaching consequences for those involved. These powers are also very similar to those of chief executives, even though the clergy are not, technically, employees. Again, the bringing of formal sanctions against a person is not the only way in which a bishop may quite properly discharge his responsibility for discipline.

No-one who carries such responsibilities could be unaware for a moment that abuse of these powers was a genuine possibility. When considering appointments in the relative privacy of the bishop's study, it was a manifest temptation to neglect the distinction between necessary discernment and an unnecessary denigration of a priest's character or the circulation of unverified gossip. It was also tempting to want to be liked by one's clergy, and to prefer (sometimes literally) those who gave the least indication of appreciation. It is not impossible to imagine that the necessary power of discipline might be accompanied by the temptation to enjoy dangling an errant priest over the threat of proceedings; or, more insidiously still, to derive some pleasure out of a magnanimous act. The tortuous route of disciplinary proceedings, moreover, could give ample space for preserving the appearance, but not the reality, of impartiality. And because bishops necessarily have a rather clear view of a church's systems of decision making, the opportunities for devious and covert forms of manipulation under cover of consultation and public expressions of humility, are not inconsiderable.

I speak, of course, of temptations to abuse power. But acknowledging that the powers exist is not the whole story. With the conferring of the powers goes a very large measure of trust – not least trust in the power of God to protect the bishop from the temptations of his office. If that trust turns out to be justified in practice, then what we tend to speak of as the 'authority' of the bishop, namely confidence in his self-disciplined use of his powers, actually grows. So the question, how ought an archbishop to use his power?, is by no means improper. It is undeniable that he has powers of various kinds; by the appropriate use of them we shall come increasingly to enjoy his authority.

II

Fortunately for Christian theology, this question and an answer to it are deeply embedded in the tradition. In the year 590 a new pope was acclaimed, one Gregory, Abbot of St Andrew's Monastery in Rome. Having sought with absolute sincerity to decline this honour, he wrote an extraordinary treatise, the *Liber Regulae Pastoralis*, literally the Book of Pastoral Rule, or *Pastoral Care* as it is normally known in English.[4] It is probable that he composed it for a friend, John, (arch)bishop of Ravenna who had rebuked him for attempting to evade what he deemed was his responsibility. The treatise is entitled a *Regula*, a rule, and seems to have been meant as the equivalent of a monastic rule, but for secular clergy. It was to have a remarkable career in English.[5] Brought to England by Augustine of Canterbury; whose mission began in June 596 and continued until his death in May 604, it was praised in the following words by Alcuin of York writing to Archbishop Eanbald in 734:

> Wherever you go, let the pastoral book of St Gregory be your companion. Read and re-read it often, that in it you may learn to know yourself and your work, that you may have before your eyes how you ought to live and teach. The book is a mirror of life of a bishop and a medicine for all the wounds inflicted by the Devil's deception.[6]

In the late tenth century a West Saxon translation was undertaken by King Alfred the Great, since when the treatise has been – until recently – exceptionally influential in alerting leaders both ecclesiastical and secular to the necessity and difficulty of the exercise of power. In what follows I want to offer a modern interpretation of this work, which I believe very acutely illustrates our problem when we consider issues of power in the Church.

In the first place the contemporary reader of *Pastoral Care* will be immediately struck by the writer's insight into the complexity of human motivation. The reason for the treatise, indeed, is given as the need for vigilance (I, introduction). Humility, and the very great difficulty of exercising this virtue consistently, is a leading theme. The burdens of major public office are so great and distracting, it is very difficult to sustain the effort of concentration needed to keep pride at bay (I, 4). People, Gregory recognizes, like to quote the text, 'If a man desire the office of a bishop, he desireth a good work' (1 Tim. 3:1), but forget the requirement of blamelessness which follows and the probability in the early Church that episcopal office would lead to severe suffering or even martyrdom. People regularly desire not the office, says Gregory, but the glory of the office;

> A man not only fails completely to love the office, but he is ignorant of it, if, yearning for supreme rule, he feasts on the subjection of others in the hidden reveries of his thought, is glad to hear his own praises, feels his heart surge with honour, and rejoices in the abundance of his affluence.[7]

Gregory is devastating in laying bare the triviality of the defences ordinarily marshalled against pride; the mind often lies to itself about itself and tells us we do not desire glory when we secretly do. Consequently, after a brief interval, spiritual intentions are often all forgotten along with the good works which were promised, if a position of superiority were to be attained.[8]

In a central chapter of *Pastoral Care*, Gregory uncovers the insidious mechanism which connects the exercise of authority to conceit. The passage deserves quotation in full:

> Often, however, a ruler by the very fact of his pre-eminence over others becomes conceited; and because everything is at his service, because his orders are quickly executed to suit his wishes, because all his subjects praise him for what he has done well, but have no authority to criticize what he has done amiss and because they usually praise what they ought to blame, his mind, led astray by those below him, is lifted above itself. While he is outwardly surrounded by abounding favours, the truth within him is made

> void. Forgetful of what he is, he is diverted by the commendations of others, and believes himself to be such as he is outwardly proclaimed to be, not such as he should inwardly judge himself.[9]

Behind this passage of great psychological insight, which applies no doubt to prime ministers as much as to archbishops, lies a very specific theological doctrine which Gregory had inherited from Augustine. This is the assertion of a distinction between ruling and helping based on a radical doctrine that all occupying the office of ruler are, in fact, the equals of their subjects in nature. 'All who are superiors should not regard in themselves the power of their rank (*potestas ordinis*), but the equality of their nature (*aequalitas condicionis*); and they should find their joy not in ruling over men, but in helping them.' Commentators rightly point out a similar sentiment with the same play on words (*prodesse* [help] – *prae esse* [rule over]) in the Rule of St. Benedict (ch. 64). But the remoter source, particularly of the associated remark that the ancient fathers were shepherds of flocks not kings, is Augustine, in the *City of God*, Book XIX, 14–15. In the Church, commands are only given, Augustine teaches, with a view to ordered harmony, not from a lust for domination or from a pride in precedence. We must never forget, he adds, that in due course all human lordship and power will be annihilated, and God will be all in all (citing 1 Cor. 15:24,28).

Gregory draws the consequence that those who hold any office of leadership in the Church should always bear in mind their equality of nature with those in relation to whom they do not share equality of power. The point of the exercise of power of church is to rebuke the vices of evil doers. This is why Paul denied that he exercised dominion over the faith of his churches and presented himself as their servant (2 Cor. 1:23; 4:5); but at the same time was fierce with them when they erred ('Shall I come to you with a rod?' 1 Cor. 4:21). The danger of even that legitimate power, however, is, Gregory recognizes, its capacity for seepage into other less desirable traits, brilliantly described in the following passage:

> Usually, then, when the mind of a man is inflated with a multitude of subjects under him, he becomes corrupted and moved to pride by the eminence of his power which panders to his mind . . . For the human mind is prone to pride even when not supported by power; how much more, then, does it exalt itself when

> it has that support! But he disposes power aright, who knows how, with great care, both to derive from it what is profitable, and to subdue the temptations which it creates, and how, though in possession of it, to realize his equality with others, and at the same time to set himself above sinners in his zeal for retribution.[10]

It is in this connection that Gregory cites the famous passage from the Gospels where Jesus rebukes his disciples for quarrelling about places of eminence; 'he that will be the first among you must be your servant' (Mark 10:43–45). The interpretation he gives this passage is not that the Church has no business with inequality of power. There are, he simply presumes, those 'who would be first'; rulership, the office of people he calls 'superiors' (*praelati*), is simply a fact. Jesus' admonition is, rather, addressed to the mind and thought of one who would be first. The external manifestation of power 'must not so carry the mind away as to captivate it for itself'.[11] Indeed the whole subject-matter for the treatise is the spiritual dilemma created for one who simultaneously occupies high rank and yet truly desires to be humble. The difficulty is removed at a stroke if the premise of inequality of power is challenged. Has the Church made the dilemma in practice insoluble by developing the offices of bishop, archbishop and pope?

III

It is certainly true that since the Reformation the Protestant churches of Europe have developed different structures of leadership for their institutions. These structures have themselves changed with time, especially in response to advances in popular education and in democratic government. Nor have Episcopal churches remained static; there are striking national differences even within the bounds of a single world church family. Of course, it is not the intention of this book to examine the different structures of leadership, not even from the standpoint of how power is distributed and exercised within them.

However, if the argument of the earlier chapters has carried conviction, it is mistaken to suppose either that the life of the Church could be a power-free zone, or that it should be. The biblical resources which encourage us to be cautious about power should not lead us to its wholesale rejection. The rereading of Gregory's *Pastoral Care* in the context of the dilemma we have formulated is exceptionally instructive; but it does not absolve us from discriminating judgement about aspects of approach which modern conditions have rendered unavailable to us.

At the stage of theological history with which we are dealing, the late sixth century (and indeed for the next thousand years in the West), it was simply assumed that the Church's business was with power, *potestas.* This is made completely clear by Gregory in ways which make the modern reader uncomfortable; and to these we now turn. In the first place, Gregory simply asserts it to be the case that:

> There are those who are gifted with virtues (*virtutes*; the word could easily be translated 'powers') in a high degree and who are exalted by great endowments for the training of others.

His description of such persons is instructive; they are those:

> Who are unspotted in their zeal for chastity, strong in the vigour of their abstinence, replete with feasts of knowledge, humble in their long-suffering patience; erect in the fortitude of authority, gentle in the face of loving-kindness, strict and unbending in justice.[12]

It is simply God's will that such persons should rule in the Church, and we note that Gregory considers that proper humility demands of them submission to that will (I, 6). Naturally, therefore, 'the conduct of a prelate should so far surpass the conduct of the people, as the life of a pastor sets him apart from his flock' (II, 1). This unabashed affirmation of a double, if not a triple, standard, relates to conduct, of course, not to self-estimation. Once again Gregory sets up a spiritual dilemma for the office-holder. Those who become by office a model for others should also be deeply conscious of infirmity in themselves. They must also realize that their very qualities can be daunting and discouraging to others. Hence the need for compassion and, indeed, condescension in those who rule (II, 5). At the same time there should be no undue self-depreciation in case rulers should fail to be stern with the vices of evil-doers (not, one notes, with the evil-doers themselves).

It is not easy to feel entirely comfortable either with Gregory's exaltation of a leader's zeal for righteousness, which accords ill with the modern climate of tolerance and acceptance. But human inequality is, for him, the direct consequence of the Fall, and the need and point of power in the church, as in society, is the 'punishment of wickedness and vice', with authority, exactly as is prescribed in the Book of Common Prayer.[13] At this point, however, Gregory is at his most subtle. While recognizing that rulers like to be liked, and that this may undermine their willingness to confront misbehaviour, he counsels 'the great act of moderation', it being difficult for rulers to get a sympathetic hearing if they are detested. The resolution is that those who rule ought to aim at being sufficiently liked so that they may be listened to; but not on their own account, lest they displace the One whom they ostensibly serve.[14] Hounding people with bitter words and harsh rebukes is no part of a proper zeal for righteousness.

A further mitigating feature of Gregory's view at this point is his explicit acceptance of the possibility that those who govern should themselves be open to rebuke. Peter, he observes, willingly accepted the rebuke of Paul, and David of Nathan; 'good rulers who pay no regard to self-love, take as homage to their humility the free and sincere words of subjects'.[15] The fact that the word here is bluntly hierarchical *subditi*/subjects makes the point all the more remarkable. The social gulf separating 'rulers' from their 'subjects' is bridged by the radical theological egalitarianism of a common sinful human nature; and not just in theory, but in practice, it being a complement to the humility of those who rule if a subject feel able to address to them words of admonition.

IV

Nevertheless, no contemporary archbishop or bishop in his right mind will entertain for a moment the term 'subjects'/*subditi*, when it comes to thinking about fellow members of the church. Anglicans, as a matter of fact, know that this word survived into the twentieth century in the Book of Common Prayer, where it was used in reference to the 'subjects' of the sovereign – 'that we and all her subjects (duly considering whose authority she hath) may faithfully serve, honour and humbly obey her, in thee and for thee, according to thy blessed word and ordinance'.[16] The implicit reference to Scripture. we ought to remind ourselves, is the First Letter of Peter, where Christians are instructed to 'submit themselves to every human institution for the sake of the Lord, whether to the sovereign as supreme, or to the governor as his deputy for the punishment of criminals and the commendation of those who do right' (1 Peter 2:13). This passage, together with Romans 13:1 ('Every person must submit to the supreme authorities'), provided subsequent centuries with powerful warrants in the case for social conformism. Even so, they refer to the relations of rulers and their subjects in civil life, not to the Church. Why should the term 'subjects'/*subditi* have migrated from one context to the other?

To understand the reason for this shift we have to appreciate two matters, one relating specifically to Gregory's time and context, and one more general fact about church government.

(i) So far as Gregory is concerned it is quite evident for the reader of *Pastoral Care* that his mind naturally slips from general considerations relating to rule of any kind, and what is particularly the case for bishops.[17] His normal practice was to use the term 'rector' to apply to bishops. This, and the image of governing, had already been deployed with reference to bishops by a prominent Greek theologian of the fourth century, another Gregory (of Nazianzus). But civil governors and agents in charge of church lands were also *rectores*. And the fact was that from the fifth century onwards bishops and other clergy undertook very substantial roles of leadership in public life. The assumptions about good order in both contexts were at the time frankly hierarchical. The migration of terminology has to be seen in this setting; and it has to be recognized that one beneficial consequence of the shift was to create essentially Christian standards of service and humility in public life. The traffic between ideas was two-way.

(ii) The second, more general, point concerns the idea of a polity for the Church, a mode and structure for its governance. The Church has an absolutely unique task; it speaks of itself as 'apostolic' for this reason, that it was raised up and sent by God for the sake of the gospel, the good news of salvation. As a consequence it requires a form of governance fit for its mission at a given time and in a given place. The church became an institution and developed a form of governance as it expanded. It did so essentially from the resources it had been given; but the precise form and structure of the polity were always concrete and particular and embodied features which were adaptable, according to traditions and habits acceptable in given cultures. At the same time the forms of governance were not limitlessly accommodating. The very point of Jesus' rebuke to his disciples as they squabbled about power and precedence was that the mode of domineering authority on display in the surrounding culture was in contradiction to, and could not be adopted in the life of the Church. 'Not so with you', established firm limits.

Both these points help to illuminate our difficulty with the word subjects/*subditi* as applied to those over whom bishops ruled as rectors/*rectores.* It is pointless to blame Gregory as though he were guilty of some heinous mistake in his thinking about pastoral care. But by the same token, his times are not our times; and the mission of our Church in a very different cultural context requires and has rightly received a very different form. Broadly speaking, it is democracy and education which made the difference, a political and social order which has simply changed the traditions and habits of our society, and thus what is acceptable to it in its forms of governance.

Two examples from the history of the Church of England can be given of ways in which these churches have adapted their forms of governance, the impact of the late medieval theory termed 'conciliarism' upon sixteenth-century English thought, and the nineteenth- and twentieth-century adoption of synodical government, with their characteristic 'houses' of bishops, clergy and laity. Exclusive clerical, episcopal or papal control of decision making in the church has ceased to be generally acceptable to an educated and informed lay Christian public. Even a Church without a formal means of elected representation finds itself accountable in the media of a modern democracy, and failure to adapt to such conditions may seriously interfere with the Church's mission.

But we cannot be simple-minded about how this process has come about. It is tempting to depict the history of the Church as a two-act play. In the first act, foolish people hungry for power invented a hierarchical institution and justified it by arguing that God distributed power from above through serried ranks of intermediaries. In the second act, the people of God came to their senses and realized that power comes from below, from the people, and it is only with their permission and subject to their veto, that anyone can be temporarily entrusted with wider responsibilities.

It is, of course, true that hierarchy became a key intellectual resource for the Church of the medieval period. A late-fifth-century Syrian writer, under the pseudonym, Dionysius or Denis the Areopagite, wrote two immensely influential treatises on hierarchy, portraying the spread of the knowledge of God in a strongly neo-Platonic frame of reference through graded levels of angelic and human agencies. It was translated into Latin in the ninth century and had a major impact on the way in which both temporal and spiritual authority was portrayed. Some thought in terms of two parallel hierarchies in which pope and emperor were equivalent, partriarchs and *patricii*, archbishops and kings, metropolitans and dukes, bishops and counts and so forth. Others thought in terms of three orders, of laity to defend the Church, of monks to pray, and of bishops to rule both. The exaltation of the clerical order over the lay was the explicit purpose of eleventh-century reformers, especially of Pope Gregory VII and his supporters.

But even within this hierarchical framework it is not difficult to hear a different tone. In the middle of the twelfth century, in a remarkable treatise to a pope who had once been a novice under his direction, Bernard of Clairvaux bluntly denies that papal power involves any kind of secular rule. He contrasts the simplicity of Peter the apostle with the ceremony surrounding the papacy:

> In all this painted pomp you are not Peter's successor, but Constantine's. What I insist on is that while you may tolerate such pomp and glory to suit the time [one notes here the theme of adaptability], you must not claim it as a debt due to you . . . If on state occasions you are robed in purple and decked with gold, I am sure that this does not mean that you, the shepherd's heir, shrink from the shepherd's toil, or the shepherd's care; it does not imply that you are ashamed of the Gospel. Albeit, if you willingly preach the Gospel, you, too, have a glorious place among the apostles. To preach the gospel is to feed the sheep. Do the work of an evangelist, and you have done the work of a shepherd.[18]

We pinch ourselves when we realize that this is the Bernard for whom the pope possesses 'plenitude of power'. Perhaps the concept of an evangelical pope has securer roots in the medieval tradition than we might at first think.

V

If it is the case that both Gregory the Great and Bernard of Clairvaux are attempting to resolve the practical paradoxes of simultaneously governing the Church and yet remaining humble at heart, then the position of a modern archbishop in a democratic society is hardly less complex in practice and in theory. It is especially complex because of the divided mind we exhibit specifically about power and its exercise in our society. This ambivalence is evident in the way in which the media build up a particular person in a position of leadership, endowing them with sometimes imaginary star qualities, only to engage in their disparagement or even destruction at the first signs of human weakness. It is as if, simultaneously, we cannot be doing without personalities with superlative powers, and we cannot be doing with them. But the roots of this habit lie very deep in Western culture, and have to do with the systematic way in which what we have seen to be the very concept of power has been deformed in political philosophy, to the point where it has inherently negative connotations or is actually equated with 'domination'.

In this final part of my treatment of this question I want to highlight the contrast between this negativity and the more balanced view which we have inherited from our tradition, and which we have found in both Gregory the Great and Bernard. Let us start with the modern assault on what is called 'deference'. What lies behind the media's habit of unkind personal assault on public figures is a negative view of power. It is simply assumed that individuals engaged in a quest for political power are wholly motivated by self-interest. Hence (so the argument goes) it is reasonable to presume that they are no better than the rest of us, and probably worse. They deserve all the criticism which can be heaped on them, and if some of it happens to be unjust, let it serve as a warning. Any protestations they make about only wanting to serve the wider public or common good, any professions of personal humility or acknowledgements of past mistakes, are in all likelihood calculated, and thus hypocritical. Because all politicians are intent on their own advancement, all their patterns of behaviour are to be interpreted as aggressive or defensive strategies, best understood by a study of Machiavelli. Loyalty or trust are, on this view of human nature, forms of folly likely to be rewarded by assassination. One notes particularly that the implicit evaluation of human nature is bleaker by far than anything found in Gregory or other classical Christian authors.

It is an unmitigated disaster for the Christian Church when assumptions of this kind leak into the thinking and behaviour of Christian people towards their leaders, as they undoubtedly do. It is not that Christians are committed to defending the culture of deference. Indeed the notion of 'deference' is wholly at variance with what is recommended and taught in the New Testament, which is 'esteem'.

> We beg you, my brothers and sisters to acknowledge those who are working so hard among you, and in the Lord's fellowship are your leaders and counsellors. Hold them in the highest possible esteem and affection for the work they do. (1 Thess. 5:13, REB)

It is notable that 'esteem' is accompanied by the word 'affection'. Nothing is more characteristic of the tone of media comment on public figures than lack of anything resembling affection. Occasionally, indeed, it demonstrates an attitude of mind which borders upon the pitiless. But the atmosphere this creates has long-term, cumulative consequences. In survey after survey of public opinion it turns out that the two least-trusted professionals in the public domain are politicians and journalists. It seems that those who trade in the coinage of cynical ridicule and disparagement damage their own, and not merely their opponents' reputations. It would be a huge gain to public participation in democracy, which is at an alarmingly low ebb in our society, if politicians and the media exercised greater restraint in their rhetoric, if they stopped accusing each other of hypocrisy and bad faith.

The culture of esteem and affection for our leaders is not seen in the Church as an alternative for providing defences against the abuse of power. This is where the testimony of Gregory is so impressive. He has profound insight into the spiritual laziness which can so easily deflect a leader from the pathway of humility. He knows that discipline is needed to protect a leader from self-exaltation. His thought closely follows the teaching of the New Testament itself, where it is striking that a specific word for an overbearing kind of authority (*kata-kurieuo*), used in Mark and Matthew's versions of Jesus' rebuke to his disciples (and in 1 Peter 5), is matched by the use of the plain term *kurieuo*) in Luke's narrative. It is as if the moment someone starts to call you a *kurios* or master (or bishop, archbishop or pope – my lord, your grace, your holiness!) you are already resting upon a slope which will carry you downards (*kata* is the Greek preposition for that), unless you are very vigilant.

Why then be bothered with orders, offices and titles? Why not sweep the whole lot into the bin of history, throw the mitres (which are symbolic crowns made of cloth) into the Thames, and generally take the Magnificat literally for a change? I have already suggested that the New Testament does not give us a ready-made polity for the Church, as though the task simply consisted in fitting ourselves back into the kind of structures which the early communities were. What we have to do, it seems, is to develop and constantly adapt the structures to match and to facilitate the unique mission on which we are engaged. That is precisely the content of Bernard's advice to the pope of his day: 'Don't let the pomp get in the way of doing the work of an evangelist.' (He had other relevant advice, too, such as not allowing himself and his office to be dominated by the lawyers.)

There is a sociological argument about organizations which may give us pause before rushing to embrace egalitarianism; that is, that all large organizations are characterized by inequality of access to decision-making power. There are always, it seems, those with greater, and those with lesser opportunities for exercising influence. Within the Church, one could well argue, it is preferable to know who has the power to do what, by dressing them in purple and sticking funny hats on their heads, rather than having them slinking round the corridors anonymously in pale blouses and dark suits, casting votes in obscure communities. A justly celebrated piece of sociological research on a church that had officially embraced egalitarianism identified 'an influential hierarchy that is not legally legitimized'. The author concluded:

> It is of critical importance to recognize that the presence of power is not eliminated by noble purpose. Power in a social

> system is shared by those who are able and willing to mobilize the political, economic, psychological, and ideological resources of the community.[19]

Where these are formally acknowledged in the offices of a hierarchy, they are also formally constrained by rules. When they are informal, the danger is that they will be concealed, even from the consciousness of a person who possesses the requisite abilities.

But the issue is not one to be decided by sociological argument, which can describe (and so warn), but not prescribe what is appropriate for the mission of the Church. What the Church is constantly trying to do is to fashion, and, as I say, constantly to adapt its structures to make room for, and to give full rein to, the diversity of God's provision for that mission by his gracious gifts at a particular time. What creates the tension and complexity to which Gregory attends so carefully is not the assumptions of a grossly unequal social order, though that as we have seen plays a certain role. It is, rather, the fact of giftedness. In more than one strand of the New Testament this is quite overtly spoken of as 'power from on high' (Luke 24:49; Acts 1:8; 10:38; Rom. 15:13; 1 Cor. 2:4). The point of ordination is to recognize this giftedness in lay people, to give them the opportunity of nurturing the gift, and then to entrust them with the responsibility of exercising it. The gifts, we should note, are given to lay people. In the theology of giftedness they are specific gifts for a specific purpose, set in the context of all the gifts given to the people of God, to be used harmoniously and in co-operation with the full diversity of gifts of the whole people. In the context of the totality of giftedness, it only makes sense to say that those called 'clergy' and those called 'laity' are alike part of the people or *laos* of God.

Undoubtedly with the gifts come temptations. According to Paul 'articulate utterance' or 'wise speech' is one of the gifts of the Holy Spirit (1 Cor. 12:18). But in an earlier passage in the same letter he is at particular pains to distinguish such articulacy from the highly prized rhetorical style cultivated in a Graeco-Roman context; 'I did not come proclaiming the mystery of God to you in lofty words or wisdom' (1 Cor. 2:1). What was persuasive to his hearers, he insists, were not 'plausible words of wisdom', but the 'demonstration of the Spirit and of power' (1 Cor. 2:4).[20] It is not that Paul dispenses with rationality altogether. But there is, he warns, a misuse of it, which he is at pains to avoid. Because of the Church's commitment to teaching and preaching, eloquence is highly prized in the church. But it is capable of being abused; and even the right use of it in public can lead to vanity and private vices, as Gregory was well aware. To resist these temptations, one needs the protection of self-awareness and training in good habits. That is one of the purposes of the time and money spent in training for ordination. At least part of the invocation of the Holy Spirit needs to be a prayer of protection from those vices which accompany the giftedness for which those to be ordained were originally identified.

If it were the case that there was a clerical monopoly upon giftedness, then the simple division between those who have such gifts and those who do not would resolve the elements of complexity or tension we have noted. But this is certainly not the case, not even for Gregory the Great, whose society (and whose Church), was marked by huge discrepancies of influence between, for example, the literate and the illiterate. As we saw, Gregory preserves the possibility of 'subjects'/*subdicti* admonishing their rulers/*rectores*' for their errors. It is striking that this is reserved for relations within the Church. In the social order, Gregory warns 'subjects' against the vice of 'murmuring' against their rulers or what he calls the 'plague of disparagement'.[21] As we have seen, the reason why Gregory wants rulers in the Church to be open to admonition is his insistence that they share a common fallen nature. No matter what gift they have, they are not beyond falling into temptation; indeed, Gregory's point is that the very fact of giftedness can itself be that temptation.

VI

In what way does the discussion of this text contribute to the conclusions we have drawn from our study of the treatment of power in theological history?

In the first place, it is clear that although Gregory has no difficulty with the mere fact that some exercise power while others are their subjects, the temptations and dangers attending positions of leadership are virtually inseparable from them. This supports our contention that the sources of the Christian faith actually sponsor diverging views of power.

Second, Gregory's contention is that the requisite humility can only be practised when the individuals concerned are fully alert to their own failings and to the situation in which they have been placed. It is a disaster to be self-deceived. For Gregory the sources of insight seem largely to be psychological; since the rise of sociology, it would be reasonable to argue that they would be both psychological and sociological.

Third, it has been the argument of this study that Christian theology sets the whole of human existence in a deeply ambiguous context, a world of overlapping and intersecting powers in which we are enmeshed. The death of Christ illuminates and addresses the individual oppression, corporate manipulation and cosmic disorder which constitute the human situation.

Fourth, nothing in our study of Gregory's text or in the rest of the classical Christian tradition would suggest the idea that power is inherently corrupt. On the contrary, the Christian Church requires men and women of God-given gifts to lead it. The fact that they possess particular gifts, or powers (in the plural), is not inconsistent with their equality of nature with all others.

Fifth, the whole point of the exercise of powers in the Church is furtherance of its mission. Universal education and democracy change the context in which that mission is organized, enabling the participation of vastly more people in the processes of governance. This fact, however, does not mean that Gregory's insights into the nature of power exercised within the Church become redundant; but rather that it is imperative that a wider circle of people is alerted to its dangers and temptations. We need to resist the modern myth that power is something necessarily large scale and extraordinary. On the contrary, the formal abolition of hierarchy is compatible with the camouflaging of the structures and exercise of power.

Finally, the public exercise of leadership in the modern world contains some astonishing contradictions. Although it is a necessity, which we deeply desire to the point of wanting to idolize our leaders, we have also, culturally, succumbed to the habit of suspicion and mistrust. Both instincts are unjust to the men and women whose real talents are exercised in God's service. Their powers are best employed when they are recognized by them and by us as genuine and proper, not as a substitute for service or love, but as an expression of them; and when both we and they are conscious of the dangers which accompany them.

Notes

Foreword

1 Lord Acton first articulated this dictum in a letter to Bishop Mandell Creighton, dated 3 April, 1887. It is reproduced in *Life and Letters of Mandell Creighton*, Longmans, Green & Co., London, 1906, 372.
2 See J. Berry and G. Renner, *Vows of Silence: The Abuse of Power in the Papacy of John Paul II*, Free Press, New York, 2004. This work by two Catholic authors principally concerns the alleged abuse of power by the Vatican in seeking to cover up clerical misconduct.
3 See J. N. Poling, *The Abuse of Power: A Theological Problem*, Abingdon Press, Nashville, TN, 1991 and Parsons, S., *Ungodly Fear: Fundamentalist Christianity and the Abuse of Power*, Lion, Oxford, 2000.
4 See 2 Cor. 12:8.
5 See A. Kee, *Constantine Versus Christ: The Triumph of Ideology*, SCM Press, London, 1982 and N. G. Wright, *Disavowing Constantine: Mission, Church and the Social Order in the Theologies of John Howard Yoder and Jürgen Moltman*, Paternoster, Carlisle, 2000.
6 It is made absolutely explicit by Timothy Gorringe in his challenging work, *Furthering Humanity*, Ashgate, Aldershot, 2004, 173: '. . . the very idea of . . . the incorporation of bishops in the British "House of Lords" (an unchristian idea in itself), was a profound corruption'.
7 Robert Kagan, *Paradise and Power: America and Europe in the New World Order*, Atlantic Books, London, 2004, 11.
8 *Ibid.*, 38.
9 *Ibid.*, 56.
10 *Ibid.*, 27.
11 Joseph S. Nye Jr., *Soft Power: The Means to Success in World Politics*, Public Affairs, New York, 2004, 5.
12 *Ibid.*, 8.

Chapter 1

1 See the entry on 'power' in the *Oxford English Dictionary*, 2nd edn, Clarendon Press, Oxford, 1989.
2 R. Aron in S. Lukes (ed.), *Power*, Blackwell, Oxford, 1964, 253.
3 *Tyndale's New Testament* (Modern Spelling edn, ed. D. Daniell), Yale University Press, Newhaven, 1989, 238.
4 See C. K. Barrett, *The Holy Spirit and the Gospel Tradition*, SPCK, London, 1966, ch. 5.
5 *Tyndale's New Testament*, 253. Interestingly, this usage is most consistent with so-called 'critical language study', which concentrates on how power is exercised

by means of the ideological implications of language; see N. Fairclough, *Language and Power*, Longman, London, 1989, ch. 2.

6 E. D. Watt, *Authority*, Croom Helm, London, 1982, 11–17.

7 See below, pp. 35f. In a letter of Pope Gelasius to the Emperor Anastasius, cited in I. S. Robinson, 'Church and Papacy', in J. H. Burn (ed.), *The Cambridge History of Medieval Political Thought c.350–c.1450*, Cambridge University Press, Cambridge, 1988, 288f.

8 These were not abstract exercises in conceptual clarification, but related to highly specific issues, such as the taxation of clergy; see A. Black, *Political Thought in Europe, 1250–1450*, Cambridge University Press, Cambridge, 1992, 48–58.

9 Thomas Hobbes, *Leviathan*, ed. R. Tuck, Cambridge University Press, Cambridge, 1991, 34. See also 'Introduction', xvii.

10 B. Russell, *Power: A New Social Analysis*, G. Allen & Unwin, London, 1938, 10.

11 *Ibid.*

12 From W. G. Runciman (ed.) and E. Matthews (trans.), *Max Weber: Selections in Translation*, Cambridge University Press, Cambridge, 1978, 38; see also Max Weber, *Economy and Society*, Roth, G. and Wittich, C. (trans.), University of California Press, Berkeley, 1978, 53. *Herrschaft* has been variously translated as 'domination', 'rule', 'leadership', and 'authority'; and it has been suggested that there is no equivalent in English. There is no doubt that it is misleading to import into the meaning of the word American ideas of authority based on consent. The emphasis lies rather upon compliance with rule, grounded (in politics) upon the use of force or the threat of force. See J. P. Diggins, *Max Weber: Politics and the Spirit of Tragedy*, Basic Books, New York, 1996, 76f., and P. Lassman, 'The Rule of Man over Man: Politics, Power and Legitimation', in S. Turner, *The Cambridge Companion to Weber*, Cambridge University Press, Cambridge, 2000, 86ff.

13 T. Parsons, *Structures and Processes in Modern Societies*, Free Press, Glencoe, Ill., 1960, 242.

14 S. Lukes, 'Power and Authority', in T. Bottomore and R. Nisbet (eds), *A History of Sociological Analysis*, Heinemann, London, 1979, 638–639.

15 S. Lukes, *Power: A Radical View*, Macmillan, London, 1974.

16 W. B. Gallie, *Philosophy and the Historical Understanding*, Chatto & Windus, London, 1964, 158.

17 S. W. Sykes, *The Identity of Christianity: Theologians and the Identity of Christianity from Schleiermacher to Barth*, SPCK, London, 1984, 251–256.

18 S. Lukes (ed.), *Power*, Blackwell, Oxford, 1986, 4f.

19 As does Anthony Giddens in *Central Problems in Social Theory: Action, Structure and Contradiction in Social Analysis*, Macmillan, Basingstoke, 1979, 89.

20 I have already written on this topic in *The Identity of Christianity*, ch. 3, 'Power in the Church'. Here I argued that, because conflict in Christianity is not accidental or occasional, but intrinsic and chronic, there are, inevitably power-struggles in the Church, and theologians are necessarily involved in them. I adopted from a sociologist the definition of power as 'the capacity of some persons to produce intended or foreseen effects on others' [D. H. Wrong, *Power: Its Forms, Bases and Uses*, Blackwell, Oxford, 1979, 2]. It now is clear to me that this is too narrow a view; power is plainly being exercised when the interests of particular groups have become the normal presumptions of all parties to a discussion. But it is, I think, a mistake to say that I am proposing an 'identification of authority with power' [R. H. Roberts, *Religion, Theology and the Human Sciences*, Cambridge University Press, Cambridge, 2002, 142]. In *The Identity of Christianity*, I suggest (with Wrong) that authority may be an instance of the exercise of power, but so also is force, manipulation or persuasion. Authority cannot, therefore, be *identical* with

power. But I now think that the problem lies in attempting to elucidate the complexities by means of over-prescriptive definitions.

21 See Michael Walzer, *Thick and Thin Moral Argument at Home and Abroad*, University of Notre Dame Press, Notre Dame, Ind.; London, 1994.

22 An exemplary application of this method is to be found in Quentin Skinner's two-volumed *The Foundations of Modern Political Thought*, Cambridge University Press, Cambridge, 1978.

23 For example in A. P. D'Entrèves, *The Notion of the State*, The Clarendon Press, Oxford, 1967, followed by J. P. Mackey, *Power and Christian Ethics*, Cambridge University Press, Cambridge, 1994.

24 See D. H. Wrong, *Power, Its Forms, Bases, and Uses*, Blackwell, Oxford, 1979.

25 W. Brueggemann contrasts Psalm 146 with Psalm 150, arguing that, in the latter, the social reason for the praise of God has been lost and, as a consequence, doxology is in danger of becoming idolatry. *Israel's Praise*, Fortress Press, PA, 1988, pp. 92–4.

Chapter 2

1 Different forms of these words appear in versions of the text from the early second century onwards. They are modelled on the prayer of David, 1 Chron. 29:11, 'Thine, O Lord, is the greatness, the power and the glory, and the victory, and the majesty.' Matthew's text of the Lord's Prayer, which is longer than Luke's (Luke 11:2–4), was the version preferred for public prayer in the early church.

2 This familiar credal phrase conceals a host of complex questions. The combination of 'Father' with 'Almighty' (Gk. *pantocrator*) is rare before the fourth century. *Pantocrator* is the usual Greek translation for the Hebrew *Sebaoth* (rendered in English as '[Lord] of hosts'), but the term also had Hellenistic philosophical connotations. *Omnipotens*, the usual Latin word for *pantocrator*, is thought by some to have strengthened the abstract philosophical sense of the word. G. van den Brink, *Almighty God: A Study in the Doctrine of Divine Omnipotence*, Kok Pharos, Kampen, 1993, 43–67, has a useful discussion of the issues, with appropriate bibliography.

3 J. P. M. Walsh, *The Mighty from their Thrones: Power in the Biblical Tradition*, Fortress, Philadepia, 1987.

4 C. H. Powell, *The Biblical Concept of Power*, Epworth, London, 1963.

5 Kyle A. Pasewark, *A Theology of Power, Being Beyond Domination*, Fortress, Minneapolis, 1993. The point of this book is to escape from the association of the concept of power with that of domination. The liberator is, in effect, Michel Foucault, whose importance is first emphasized. Then is presented Luther's understanding of power in his eucharistic theology and in his political writings. Finally a switch is made to Paul Tillich's ontological understanding of power, which is broadly endorsed. There are objections to the undertaking, but it is undeniably heroic in scale and instructive in particulars.

6 Van den Brink, *op. cit.*, contains a careful analytic and philosophical discussion of the issues.

7 J. P. Stern, *Hitler: The Fuhrer and the People*, Fontana Books, London, 1984, rev. edn 1990.

8 The mingling of warlike sentiment, patriotism and Christianity, making reference to the 'sacrifice' of military or political 'martyrs', is common to English schools and Irish nationalism in the early twentieth century, as Sheridan Gilley makes clear, 'Pearce's sacrifice: Christ and Cuchulain crucified and risen in the Easter rising, 1916', in S. W. Sykes (ed.), *Sacrifice and Redemption: Durham Essays in Theology*, Cambridge University Press, Cambridge, 1991, 218–234.

9 L. G. Walsh, *The Sacraments of Initiation*, Geoffrey Chapman, London, 1988, 88. On martyrdom in the early Church, see R. L. Fox, *Pagans and Christians*, Penguin Books, Harmondsworth, 1986, ch. 9, 419–492.

10 In 'Sacrifice and the Ideology of War', ed. R. A. Hinde, *The Institution of War*, Macmillan, Basingstoke, 1991, 17, I discuss the use of 'sacrifice' in the context of the First World War, and Wilfred Owen's protest against it.

11 The destructive potential of sacrifice conceived in a certain way is brilliantly illustrated by Ann Loades in a comparison of St. Therese of Lisieux and Simone Weil, in 'Eucharistic Sacrifice: the problem of how to use a liturgical metaphor, with special reference to Simone Weil', in S. W. Sykes, *op. cit.*, 247–261.

12 J. Beattie in M. F. C. Bourdillon and M. Fortes (eds), *Sacrifice*, Academic Press for the Royal Anthropological Institute of Great Britain and Ireland, London, 1980, 37–8.

13 Josephus, *Antiquities of the Jews*, Bk XVII, 10, 10.

14 There is a connection between this scheme and the slightly more elaborate one devised by Dillistone in exposition of the Christian doctrine of the atonement, F. W. Dillistone, *The Christian Understanding of Atonement*, Westminster Press, Philadelphia, 1968.

15 In a classic essay Wilder wrote: 'What I would like to emphasize here is that the employment of the narrative mode – a combination of myth, saga, and history – provided not only orientation in the mysteries of time and existence, but therewith the structures of a human order against chaos, and of meaningfulness against unreason. The biblical epos secured life against death, being against non-being. In this sense again, language constituted a "house of being". Mythos and ethos were inseparable.' Amos N. Wilder, *Jesus' Parables and the War of Myths: Essays on Imagination in the Scripture*, Fortress, Philadelphia, 1982, 55.

Chapter 3

1 Note the shift from the KJV translation, 'there is no power but of God; the powers that be are ordained of God'. The Greek word translated as power/authority is *exousia*, which expresses the sense of power as a capacity or freedom to act; so the potter has *exousia* over the clay, Rom. 9:21.

2 R. Niebuhr, *Christ and Culture*, Faber & Faber, London, 1952. T. J. Gorringe (*Furthering Humanity: A Theology of Culture*, Ashgate, Aldershot, 2004, 12–16) offers good reasons for doubting the cogency of 'this immensely influential typology'. Implicitly he follows Raymond Whitehead in complaining that Niebuhr has failed to distinguish between cultural thought forms and the structures of economic and political power, 'Christ and Cultural Imperialism', in C. Lind and T. Brown (eds), *Justice as Mission: An Agenda for the Church*, Trinity Press, Burlington, 1985, 26. See also D. M. Yeager, 'The Social Self in a Pilgrim Church', in G. H. Stasser *et al.*, *Authentic Transformation: A New Vision of Christ and Culture*, Abingdon Press, Nashville, 1996, 100f.

3 See the account of this in Christopher Rowland, *Christian Origins: An Account of the Setting and Character of the More Important Messianic Sect of Judaism*, SPCK, London, 1985.

4 R. W. Dyson (ed. and trans.), *The City of God Against the Pagans*, Cambridge University Press, Cambridge, 1998, 900–904; H. Bettenson (trans.), *Concerning the City of God Against the Pagans*, Penguin, Harmondsworth, 1972, 835–838.

5 The words, 'Blessed be the one who comes in the name of the Lord' (Matt. 21:9) was used as a salutation of Christ's eucharistic presence from the fourth-century *Apostolic Constitutions*. See Jaroslav Jan Pelikan, *Emergence of the Catholic Tradition*, Corpus, New York, 1971, 122.

6 See Antonio Piñero and Jesús Peláez, *The Study of the New Testament*, Deo Pub-

lishing, Leiden, 2003, on the importance of the intertestamental literature, esp. 258ff.

7 On the origins and rise of the worship of Christ, see William Horbury, *Christianity in Ancient Jewish Tradition,* Cambridge University Press, Cambridge, 1999.

8 See especially Bruce Chilton, *Pure Kingdom: Jesus' Vision of God,* Eerdmans, Grand Rapids, Michigan,1996, 23–44, who emphasizes five dimensions of the Kingdom of God, its reference to eschatology, transcendence, judgement, purity and radiance.

9 These and other, contradictory assessments are listed by H. A. Drake in his study and translation of *In Praise of Constantine,* University of California Press, Berkeley, 1976, 131f., see footnote 3.

10 *Ibid.*, 87.

11 See Erwin Ramsden Goodenough, *An Introduction to Philo Judaeus,* Blackwell, Oxford, 1962, 65.

12 *1 Clement* 60–61; Tertullian, *Apologeticus* 30. This was consistent with the tradition of according 'honour' to those to whom it was due (Rom. 13:7, 1 Peter 2:17).

13 Per Beskow, *Rex Gloriae: The Kingship of Christ in the Early Church* (trans. Eric J. Sharpe), Almquist and Wiksall, Stockholm, 1962, 187–230, 261–275.

14 D. M. Nichol, 'Byzantine Political Thought' in J. H. Burns (ed.), *The Cambridge History of Medieval Political Thought c.350–1450,* Cambridge University Press, Cambridge, 1988, 52 and Francis Dvornik *Early Christian and Byzantine Political Philosophy: Origins and Background,* Vol. 1, Dumbarton Oaks Center for Byzantine Studies, Washington, 1966, 584 and 604.

15 F. Dvornik, *Byzantium and the Roman Primacy,* Vol. II, Fordham University Press, New York, 1966, 614ff, T. Barnes, *Constantine and Eusebius,* Harvard University Press, Cambridge, Mass., 1981, 254.

16 H. Chadwick, 'Christian Doctrine' in Burns (ed.), *op. cit.,* 19.

17 R. A. Markus, *Saeculum: History and Society in the Theology of St. Augustine,* Cambridge University Press, Cambridge, 1988, 95. H. Drake, *Constantine and the Bishops: The Politics of Intolerance,* John Hopkins University Press, Baltimore, 2000, 441–483.

18 *City of God,* 5, 24 (Dyson, *op. cit.*, 231–232).

19 *Ibid.*, 26 (Dyson, *op. cit.*, 235).

20 Henry Xavier Arquillière, *L'Augustinisme politique: Essai sur la formation des Théories du moyen-Age* (2nd edn), J. Vrin, Paris, 1955, 68–104; and see the still valuable treatment of John Neville Figgis, *The Political Aspects of Augustine's 'City of God',* Longmans, London, 1921.

21 Henry Xavier Arquillière, 'Origines de la théorie des deux glaives', *Studi Gregoriani* I (1947), 501–521; H. Hoffmann, 'Die beider Schwerter im hohen Mittelalter', *Deutsches Archiv* 20 (1964), 78–114; I. S. Robinson, 'Church and Papacy' in Burns (ed.), *op. cit,* 252–305; J. A. Watt,'Spiritual and Temporal Powers' in Burns (ed.), *op. cit.*, 370–372.

22 I. S. Robinson, *op. cit.*, 288f.

23 R. A. Markus, *Saeculum: History & Society in the Theology of St. Augustine,* Cambridge University Press, Cambridge, 1988, 102.

24 *Tractatus* IV, II; cited by Robinson, *op. cit.*, 289.

25 *Admonitio ad episcopus regni* 2; cited in Robinson, *op. cit.*, 297f.

26 Henry Bettenson (ed.), *Documents of the Christian Church,* Oxford University Press, London, 1943, 141–142, and in Brian Tierney, *Origins of Papal Infallibility, 1150–1350,* E. J. Brill, Leiden, 1988, 21–22. See the account in Walter Ullmann, *Law and Politics in the Middle Ages: An Introduction to the Sources of Medieval Political Thought,* Sources of History Limited, London, 1975, 58–66.

27 Sydney F. Ehler and John B. Morrall (eds and trans.), *Church and State Through the Centuries,* Newman, Westminster, Md., 1954, 33.

28 R. W. Dyson in his introduction to Giles of Rome, *On Ecclesiastical Power* (trans. R. W. Dyson), Boydell Press, Woodbridge, Suffolk, 1986, xiii.
29 Giles of Rome, *op. cit.*, 8.
30 Giles of Rome, *op. cit.*, 9. This has been well described as a 'Christological political logic', J. A. Watt in Burns, *op. cit.*, 402. But it did not elude Giles' contemporaries that, on any reasonable account, the powers of the 'Vicar of Christ' must differ from, and be less than, Christ himself. See, for example, R. W. Dyson, *Quaestio de Potestate Papae (Rex Pacificus): An Enquiry into the Power of the Pope*, E. Mellen, Lewiston, NJ, 1999, 72f.
31 A lucid account of these developments is to be found in G. van den Brink, *Almighty God: A Study in the Doctrine of Divine Omnipotence*, Pharos, Kampen, 1993, 68–91.
32 See Anna Case-Winters, *God's Power: Traditional Understanding and Contemporary Challenges*, Westminster/John Knox, Louisville, 1990, 39–62.
33 In *God's Power: Traditional Understanding & Contemporary Challenges*, 63–93, Case-Winters regards Calvin's understanding of the power of God as an instance of 'domination and control', a negative feature of the entire 'classical view' of omnipotence. In *Almighty God: A Study in the Doctrine of Divine Omnipotence*, 123f., G. van den Brink argues, successfully in my view, that this is to neglect the relationship between power-to and power-over, which is a characteristic of the tradition from Augustine onwards.
34 *Institutes of the Christian Religion* 4.8.9 (ed. and trans. Ford Lewis Battles, Baker, Grand Rapids 1986, 1156).
35 *Ibid.*, 4.9.13 (Battles, *op. cit.*, 1176).
36 *Ibid.*, 4.10.27 (Battles, *op. cit.*, 1205).
37 *Ibid.*, 4.11.1 (Battles, *op. cit.*, 1211).
38 *Ibid.*, 4.8.9 (Battles, *op. cit.*, 1156–1158). See also S. Wolin, *Politics and Vision: Continuity and Innovation in Western Political Thought*, Allen & Unwin, London, 1961, 191.
39 *Institutes* 4.20.3 (Battles, *op. cit.*, 1488).
40 *Ibid.*, 4.20.10 (Battles, *op. cit.*, 1497).
41 *Ibid.*, 4.20.23–4 (Battles, *op. cit.*, 1512).
42 *Ibid.*, 4.20.25 (Battles, *op. cit.*, 1512).
43 *Ibid.*, 4.20.32 (Battles, *op. cit.*, 1513). The section concerns the necessity of withholding obedience, if a superior commands a subject to do something contrary to God's law. God alone possesses the 'true, unique and supreme power' (*summa potestas*). The radicality of the idea that a Darius would have self-abrogated his power was seized on by Calvin's successors; see H. Höpfl (ed. and trans.), *Luther and Calvin on Secular Authority*, Cambridge University Press, Cambridge, 1991, 84.
44 For what follows see Christopher Elwood, *The Body Broken: The Calvinist Doctrine of the Eucharist and the Symbolization of Power in 16th Century France*, Oxford University Press, New York, 1999.
45 The development of the theory of just resistance to tyranny is described in Q. Skinner, *The Foundations of Modern Political Thought*, Vol. 2, Cambridge University Press, Cambridge, 1978, 189–238.
46 Höpfl (ed.), *op. cit.*, xxxviiiff.
47 Bernard Cottret, *Calvin: A Biography* (trans. M. Wallace McDonald), Eerdmans, Grand Rapids, Michigan, 2000, 159–168.
48 *Institutes*, 4.20.2 (Battles, *op. cit.*, 1487).
49 *Ibid.*, 4.20.4 (Battles, *op. cit.*, 1489)
50 D. Rensenberger, *Johannine Faith and Liberating Community*, Westminster, PA, 1988, esp. ch. 7, 135–52.

51 Oliver O'Donovan, *The Desire of the Nations: Rediscovering the Roots of Political Thought*, Cambridge University Press, Cambridge, 1996, 2.
52 Erik Peterson, *Der Monotheismus als politisches problem*, (1935) in *Theologische Traktate*, München, 1951, 45–147; H. G. Williams, 'Christology and Church–State Relations in the Fourth Century', *Church History* 20 (1951), nr. 3, 1–33, and nr. 4, 1–26.
53 See Alfred Schindler (ed.), *Monotheismus als politisches Problem?*, Gütersloher Verlaghaus Mohn, Gütersloh, 1978. Moltmann cites this work but offers no comment on the fact that it undermines the point he is making; see *The Trinity and the Kingdom of God*, SCM Press, London, 1981, 248, see footnote 2.
54 P. Beskow, *Rex Gloriae: The Kingship of Christ in the Early Church* (trans. E. J. Sharpe), Almquist & Wiksell, Stockholm, 1962, 314. The reviewer was F. J. Dolger, *Byzantinishe Zeitschrift* 36 (1936), 225–226.
55 Williams, *op. cit.*, nr. 4, 18; see Beskow, *op. cit.*, 319.
56 P. Beskow, *op. cit.*, 324f.
57 F. Dvornik, *Early Christian and Byzantine Political Philosophy: Origins and Background*, Vol. II, Dumbarton Oaks Center for Byzantine Studies, Washington, 1966, 772.
58 *Ibid.*, 782–783.
59 For what follows see Steven Runciman, *The Byzantine Theocracy*, Cambridge University Press, Cambridge, 1977, 135–164.
60 Walter Ullmann, *Law & Politics in the Middle Ages: An Introduction to the Sources of Medieval Political Thought*, Sources of History Limited, London, 1975, 13.
61 *Ibid.*, 32.
62 *Institutes*, 4.20.4 (Battles, *op. cit.*, 1489)
63 See Isaiah 10:5–19, where Assyria is said to be God's punishment.
64 J. Colet, *An Exposition of St. Paul's Epistle to the Romans* (trans. and ed. J. H. Lupton), Bell & Daldy, London, 1873, 94; cited in Q. Skinner, *The Foundations of Modern Political Thought*, Vol. I, Cambridge University Press, Cambridge, 1978, 209f.
65 Henry Chadwick, *Christian Doctrine*, in Burns (ed.), *op. cit.*, 18.
66 See O'Donovan, *op. cit.*, 197f.; 'it is as though the eschatological horizon of all political theology has, in a moment of astonishment, come to be spoken of as present'.
67 Runciman, *op. cit.*, 23.
68 J. N. Figgis, *The Political Aspects of Augustine's 'City of God'*, Longmans, London, 1921, 56, 77.
69 Reinhold Niebuhr, *Christian Realism and Political Problems*, Faber & Faber, London, 1954, 114–39.
70 *City of God*, 2, 29 (Bettenson, H. [trans.], *Concerning the City of God Against the Pagans*, Penguin, Harmondsworth, 1972, 86–88; Dyson, *op. cit.*, 91–93).
71 *City of God*, 4.31 (Bettenson, *op. cit.*, 174–176; Dyson, *op. cit.*, 182–184).
72 *City of God*, 11.1 (Bettenson, *op. cit.*, 429–430; Dyson *op. cit.*, 449–450).
73 *City of God*, 11.9 (Bettenson, *op. cit.*, 438–440; Dyson *op. cit.*, 459–461).
74 *City of God*, 11.18 (Dyson, *op. cit.*, 472; Bettenson 1972, 449).
75 *City of God*, 11.23 (Bettenson, *op. cit.*, 455–456; Dyson, *op. cit.*, 479).
76 *City of God*, 5.11; 7.30; 11.24; 22.24.
77 *City of God*, 5.12–19 (Bettenson, *op. cit.*, 196–214; Dyson, *op. cit.*, 207–226).
78 *City of God*, 5.19 (Dyson, *op. cit.*, 225–226).
79 *City of God*, 11.24 (Dyson, *op. cit.*, 482).
80 *City of God*, 12.8 (Dyson, *op. cit.*, 509).
81 *City of God*, 5.24 (Bettenson, *op. cit.*, 219–220; Dyson, *op. cit.*, 231–232).
82 *City of God*, 15.4 (Bettenson, *op. cit.*, 599–600; Dyson, *op. cit.*, 638–639).

83 *City of God*, 4.4 (Dyson, *op. cit.*, 147).
84 *City of God*, 19.24 (Dyson, *op. cit.*, 960).
85 *City of God*, 2.21 (Bettenson, *op. cit.*, 72–75; Dyson, *op. cit.*, 76–80).

Chapter 4

1 J. N. Collins, *Diakonia: Reinterpreting the Ancient Sources*, Oxford University Press, New York, 1990.
2 See the work of the Dutch theologian, Robert Adolfs, *The Grave of God*, Burns & Oates, London, 1967, esp. chs 4 and 5.
3 St. Gregory the Great, *Pastoral Care* (trans. and ed. H. Davis), Newman Press, Maryland, 1950. On the influence of Gregory see Jeffery Richards, *Consul of God: The Life and Times of Gregory the Great*, Routledge & Kegan Paul, London, 1980, and R. A. Markus,'The Latin Fathers' in J. H. Burns (ed.), *The Cambridge History of Medieval Political Thought c.350–1450*, Cambridge University Press, Cambridge, 1988, 92–122 and R. A. Markus, *Gregory the Great and His World*, Cambridge University Press, Cambridge, 1997.
4 On *rectores* see Markus, 1997, *op. cit.*, 26–33.
5 Translation in Henry Sweet, *King Alfred's West-Saxon Version of Gregory's Pastoral Care*, 2 vols, Oxford University Press, Oxford,1958; but see the introduction in Charles P. Carlson Jr., *Justification in Earlier Medieval Theology*, Nijhoff, The Hague, 1975. The work is judged by H. R. Loyn in *Alfred the Great*, Oxford University Press, London, 1967, 55, to be 'one of the most important books of the Early Middle Ages'.
6 Marsilius of Padua, *Defensor Pacis* (trans. and introd. Alan Gerwirth), Toronto University Press, Toronto, 1980, 114–115.
7 Marsilius of Padua, *ibid.*, 125.
8 Cited in Q. Skinner., *The Foundations of Modern Political Thought*, Vol. II, Cambridge University Press, Cambridge, 1978, 101.
9 Marsilius of Padua, *op. cit.*, 114.
10 *Ibid.*
11 A. Gewirth, Preface, Marsilius of Padua, *op. cit.*, xxxi f.
12 Marsilius of Padua, *op. cit.*, 125.
13 A. Black, *Political Thought in Europe, 1250–1450*, Cambridge University Press, Cambridge, 1992, 188.
14 See the account of the pontificate of Alexander VI, and his use of money and force, in *The Prince* (Q. Skinner and R. Price eds), Cambridge University Press, Cambridge, 1988, 41.
15 B. Lohse, *Martin Luther's Theology: Its Historical and Systematice Development*, T & T Clark, Edinburgh, 1999, 317.
16 N. J. Figgis, *Studies of Political Thought from Gerson to Grotios 1414–1625* (1907), 2nd edn, Cambridge University Press, Cambridge, 1925, 27.
17 Was written in the midst of the agrarian revolution of 1525; *Luther's Works*, Vol. 46, The Christian in Society III, ed. R. C. Schultz, Fortress Press, Philadelphia, 1967, 47–55.
18 The difficulty for Dietrich Bonhoeffer, a Lutheran theologian, in achieving the transition from silent opposition to Hitler's regime, to open protest, and from there to active participation in underground resistance, is sensitively portrayed in E. Bethge, *Dietrich Bonhoeffer*, Collins, London, 1970, 526 and *passim.*
19 Lohse, *op. cit.*, 314–320, warns against imposing a systematic consistency upon Luther's flexible use of the distinction.
20 H. Höpfl (ed.) introduction, *Luther and Calvin on Secular Authority*, Cambridge University Press, Cambridge, 1991, xii, xxxiii and xxviii.
21 'Admonition to Peace' (1525), *Luther's Works*, Vol. 46, 39.

22 H. Höpfl, introduction, *Luther and Calvin on Secular Authority*, xvf. 'The crucial point is that Gewalt erodes the distinction between "power" and "authority",' xxxvii.

23 *Ibid.*, 6. See the earlier translation in Brandt, W. I. (ed.), *Luther's Works*, Vol. 45, Fortress Press, Philadelphia, 1962, 86. Luther is referring to Rom. 13:4.

24 *Ibid.*, xvi.

25 *Ibid.*, 15; *Luther's Works*, Vol. 45, 95.

26 *Ibid.*, 11; *Luther's Works*, Vol. 45, 91.

27 *Ibid.*, 12; *Luther's Works*, Vol. 45, 92.

28 *Ibid.*, 21; *Luther's Works*, Vol. 45, 103.

29 *Ibid.*, 30–33; *Luther's Works*, Vol. 45, 113–116.

30 *Ibid.*, 33; *Luther's Works*, Vol. 45, 117.

31 *Luther's Works*, Vol. 44, J. Atkinson (ed.), Fortress Press, Philadelphia, 1966 and *Luther's Works*, Vol. 36, A. R. Wehtz (ed.), Fortres Press, Philadelphia, 1959.

32 *Luther's Works*, Vol. 46, R. C. Schultz (ed.), Fortress Press, Philadelphia, 1967, 75.

33 *Luther's Works*, Vol. 46, 49.

34 Höpfl, *op. cit.*, 36; *Luther's Works*, Vol. 45, 120.

35 Lohse, *op. cit.*, 319.

36 Anabaptist historiography has changed markedly since the 1980s, and is helpfully reviewed by J. M. Stayer, in 'The Anabaptists', ed. S. Osment, *Reformation Europe: A Guide to Research*, Center for Reformation Research, St. Louis, 1982. See also J. M. Stayer, *The German Peasants' War and Anabaptist Community of Goods*, McGill-Queens University Press, Montreal, 1991; C. A. Snyder, *Anabaptist History and Theology: An Introduction*, Pandora Press, Kitchener, Ontario, 1995; and H. J. Goetz, *The Anabaptists*, Routledge, London, 1996.

37 'A highly provoked defence and answer to the spiritless, soft-living flesh at Wittenberg [i.e. Luther], who has most lamentably befouled pitiable Christianity in a perverted way by his theft of Holy Scripture' (1524). Text in Michael G. Baylor (ed. and trans.), *The Radical Reformation*, Cambridge University Press, Cambridge, 1991, 74–79.

38 *Ibid.*, xivf.

39 *Luther's Works*, Vol. 46, 22.

40 G. R. Potter, *Zwingli*, Cambridge University Press, Cambridge, 1976, 160–197.

41 H. Zwingli, in *Ulrich Zwingli Selected Works*, ed. S. M. Jackson, University of Pennsylvania Press, Philadelphia, 1972, 123–258; and J. Calvin, *A Short Instruction for to Arme all Good Christian People*, Jhon Daye and W. Beres, London, 1549.

42 Sattler had been a Benedictine monk and perhaps Prior of a monastery in the Black Forest. He married and lived in Zurich, from which he was expelled in 1525. See J. Yoder, *The Legacy of Michael Sattler*, Herald Press, Scotdale, Pa, 1973; and C. Snyder, *The Life and Thought of Michael Sattler*, Herald Press, Scottdale, Pa, 1984.

43 Text in M. G. Baylor (ed.), *The Radical Reformation*, Cambridge University Press, Cambridge, 1991, 172–180; also in O. O'Donovan and J. L. O'Donovan (eds), *A Sourcebook in Christian Political Thought*, Eerdmans, Grand Rapids, Michigan, 1999, 631–637.

44 Baylor, *op. cit.*, 176; O'Donovan and O'Donovan, *op. cit.*, 4.

45 Baylor, *ibid.*, 177f.; O'Donovan and O'Donovan, *op. cit.*, 635f.

46 'Let Every Soul be Subject: Romans 13 and the Authority of the State', in J. H. Yoder, *The Politics of Jesus*, 1972; reprinted Eerdmans, Grand Rapids, Michigan, 1994, 193–211; see 202.

47 *Ibid*, 210.

48 'Christ and Power', in Yoder, *op. cit.*, 134–161.

49 *Ibid.*, 158. It remains ambiguous in Yoder's thought to what extent the Church

is bound to be involved in 'wordly power', and whether a Christian can be called to a career in the power struggles for the well-being of society. See the discussion in N. G. Wright, *Disavowing Constantine: Mission, Church and the Social Order in the Theologies of John Howard Yoder and Jürgen Moltmann*, Paternoster, Carlisle, 2000, esp. chs 4 and 5.

50 Y. Congar, *Vrai et fausse réforme dans l'Eglise*, Du Cerf, Paris, 1950; rev. edn 1969. For a brief introduction to Congar's theology, see A. Nichols, *Yves Congar*, Morehouse-Barlow, Wilton, Conn, 1989.

51 Y. Congar, *Martin Luther. Sa vie, sa foie, sa réforme*, Paris.

52 Y. Congar, *Power and Poverty in the Church*, Editions du Cerf, Paris, 1963. English translation, Chapman, London, 1964.

53 *Ibid.*, 17.

54 art. diakoneo, diakonia, diakonos in G. Kittel and G. Friedrich, *Theological Dictionary of the New Testament* (ET, Bromley, GN) II, Eerdmans, Grand Rapids, 1964, 81–93.

55 Congar, 1963, *op. cit.*, 98.

56 *Ibid.*, 81.

57 *Ibid.*, 121f.

58 *Ibid.*, 82–100.

59 *Ibid.*, 81.

60 *Ibid.*, 55.

61 *Ibid.*, 61.

62 *Ibid.*, 70–72.

63 *Ibid.*, 79.

64 *Ibid.*, 123.

65 Y. Congar, 'Moving Towards a Pilgrim Church', in A. Stackpole (ed.), *Vatican II by Those Who were There*, Chapman, London, 1986, 129–152.

66 Compare this absence with the work of a Catholic theologian who is also a professional political scientist, which makes rather clear the kind of structural changes needed if anything like the theology of Congar were to provide the rationale for the institutional reality of the Catholic Church. T. J. Reese, *Inside the Vatican: The Politics and Organization of the Catholic Church*, Harvard University Press, Cambridge, Mass., 1996.

67 Congar, *op. cit.*, 75.

68 *Ibid.*, 96.

69 N. M. Healy, *Church, World, and the Christian Life: Practical-Prophetic Ecclesiology*, Cambridge University Press, Cambridge, 2000, 37.

70 The phrase 'the crucified God' is Luther's, see J. Moltmann, *The Crucified God: The Cross of Christ as the Foundation and Criticism of Christian Theology*, SCM Press, London, 1974, 47. The *theologia crucies* 'is not a single chapter in theology, but the key signature for all Christian theology', *ibid.*, 72.

71 There is a careful and interesting discussion of the implications for political ethics of Luther's Doctrine of the Two Kingdoms in J. Moltmann, *Politische Theologie, Politische Ethik*, Kaiser, München, 1984, 61–77. To the separation of the Kingdoms Moltmann traces the tendency of Lutheran theology to conservatism or apoliticism. But to the other aspect of the same inheritance, namely that the Church should and could be a powerfree zone, Moltmann is implicitly much more sympathetic.

72 On the importance of Hegel for Moltmann's theology, see, for example, *The Crucified God*, 235f.

73 J. Moltmann, *The Theology of Hope: On the Ground and Implications of a Christian Theology*, Harper & Row, New York, 1967; J. Moltmann, *The Church in the Power of*

the Spirit: A Contribution of Messianic Ecclesiology, SCM Press, London, 1977; J. Moltmann, *The Trinity and the Kingdom: The Doctrine of God*, Harper & Row, San Francisco, 1981. A recent outline of Moltmann's theology was entitled, in English, *The Kingdom and the Power*, but contained no analysis of the understanding of power; its German title was *Phantasie für das Reich Gottes*: Geiko Müller-Fahrenholz, *The Kingdom and the Power: The Theology of Jürgen Moltmann*, SCM Press, London, 2000.

74 *The Trinity and the Kingdom of God*, 192.
75 *Ibid.*, 192.
76 *Ibid.*, 195.
77 See Chapter 3, note 53, above.
78 *The Trinity and the Kingdom of God*, 197.
79 *Ibid.*, 200–202.
80 *The Church in the Power of the Spirit*, 396f.
81 *The Trinity and the Kingdom of God*, 197f.
82 *Ibid.*, 198.
83 *Ibid.*, 199.
84 *Ibid.*, 202.
85 *Ibid.*, 202.
86 *Ibid.*, 217.
87 *Ibid.*, 220.
88 *Ibid.*, 221.
89 *The Crucified God*, 215f.
90 *The Church in the Power of the Spirit*, 298.
91 *Ibid.*, 305.
92 H. von Campenhausen, *Ecclesiastical Authority and Spiritual Power in the Church of the First Three Centuries*, A. & C. Black, London, 1969.
93 The 1970s saw a burgeoning of interest in the application of sociological categories to the study of the New Testament. See John Howard Schültz, *Paul and the Anatomy of Apostolic Authority*, Cambridge University Press, Cambridge, 1975; Bengt Holmberg, *Paul and Power: The Structure of Authority in the Primitive Church as Reflected in the Pauline Epistles*, Lieber Läromedel, Gleerup, 1978; and below, Chapter 5.
94 A. Thistleton argues, against most interpreters, who consider that Paul expects the guilty man to die, that the 'destruction of the body' envisaged is of his 'fleshly self-satisfaction', *The First Epistle to the Corinthians*, Eerdmans, Grand Rapids, Michigan; Paternoster, Carlisle, 2000, 392–400.
95 *The Crucified God*, 168; for a discussion of this treatment, see S. W. Sykes, 'Life after Death: the Christian Doctrine of Heaven', in *Creation, Christ and Culture*, ed. R. W. A. McKinney, T & T Clark, Edinburgh, 1976, 255–266. There is a subsequent revaluation of personal eschatology in J. Moltmann, *The Coming of Christ: Christian Eschatology*, Fortress, Minneapolis, 1966, 47–128.
96 *Ibid.*, 171.
97 *The Church in the Power of the Spirit*, 33f.
98 *The Crucified God*, 253f; and see 307 on 'knowledge and acceptance of the new salvation'.
99 *Ibid.*, 249.
100 In J. Moltmann, *The Experiment of Hope*, SCM Press, London, 1975, 137.
101 J. Moltmann, *Creating a Just Future: The Politics of Peace and the Ethics of Creation in a Threatened World*, SCM Press, London, 1989, 45. It is clear that Moltmann departs from Yoder's view of this matter; see N. G. Wright, *Disavowing Constantine*, 115f.

102 Arne Rasmusson, *The Church as Polis: From Political Theology to Theological Politics as Exemplified by Jürgen Moltmann and Stanley Hauerwas*, Lund University Press, Lund, 1994.

103 I am myself the object of suspicion in R. Roberts, *Religion, Theology, And the Human Sciences*, Cambridge University Press, Cambridge, 2002, 113–160.

104 An interesting attempt to relate Moltmann's political ethics to the Anabaptist tradition is to be found in A. D. Wright, *The Early Modern Papacy: From the Council of Trent to the French Revolution, 1564–1789*, Longman, Harlow, 2000. Wright makes clear that, although Moltmann inclines strongly towards the radical strand of the reformation, he appears to have no detailed knowledge of Anabaptist history.

Chapter 5

1 See D. Martin, 'Comparing Different Maps of the Same Ground', *Reflections on Sociology and Theology*, Clarendon Press, Oxford, 1997, 74–88.

2 John Milbank, *Theology and Social Theory: Beyond Secular Reason*, Blackwell, Oxford, 1990, 4. Both David B. Burrell, 'An Introduction to Theology and Social Theory: Beyond Secular Reason', *Modern Theology*, 8.4, 1992, 319–329; and R. H. Roberts, *Religion, Theology and the Human Sciences*, Cambridge University Press, Cambridge, 2002, provide useful brief accounts of the major theses of the book.

3 Milbank, *op. cit.*, 3.

4 Roberts, for example, accuses a Church of England Report, *Working as One Body: the Report of the Archbishops' Commission on the organision of the Church of England*, Church House Publishing, London, 1995, of capitulating to 'managerialism', a situation he regards as similar to that in contemporary British universities. Whether the strictures are justified or not, it is social theory which warns us of the inherent conservatism of all 'one body' metaphors.

5 The point is made effectively by Nicholas Lash, 'Not Exactly Politics or Power', *Modern Theology*, 8.4, 1992, 353–364, in response to Milbank.

6 Notably demonstrated in Wayne A. Meeks, *The Origins of Christian Morality*, Yale University Press, New Haven, 1993.

7 *Cyril of Jerusalem and Nemesius of Emesa*, ed. W. Telfer (1950), SCM Press, London, 1955.

8 Tertullian (c.170–c.215) received a classical education in Carthage, and plainly used it to defend Christianity. But he rejected the attempt to reconcile faith with Stoicism or Platonism. See T. D. Barnes, *Tertullian: A Historical and Literary Study*, Clarendon Press, Oxford, 1971, 187–210.

9 A. Giddens, *Sociology* 2nd edn, Polity Press, Cambridge, 1993, 7.

10 R. L. Fox, *Pagans and Christians*, ch. 10, 'Bishops and Authority', argues that the Church adopted the pattern of authority unknown to pagan cults, and a break from synagogue practice, 495.

11 Michael Mann, *The Sources of Social Power*, Vol. 1, Cambridge University Press, Cambridge, 1986, 328.

12 A. Giddens, *op. cit.*, 706f.

13 T. Bottomore and R. Nisbet (eds), *A History of Sociological Analysis*, Heinemann, London, 1979.

14 R. Bierstedt, 'Sociological Thought in the Eighteenth Century' in Bottomore and Nisbet (eds), *op. cit.*, 5.

15 *Ibid.*, 12.

16 Note the dismissive sentence, 'Although making many obeisances to Providence, and never failing to emphasize the significance of religion in human societies, Vico nevertheless gave a scientific cast to history', Bierstedt, *op. cit.*, 24. Contrast this with 'heretical perhaps; but unswervingly religious', I. Berlin, *Vico*

& Herder, Hogarth, Press, London, 1976, 80. A recent attempt to give a thorough interpretation of Vico's theological views can be found in M. Lilla, *G. B. Vico: The Making of an Anti-modern*, Harvard University Press, Cambridge, Mass., 1993, 14–56, 144–151.

17 H. Arendt, *On Violence*, Penguin Press, London, 1970. The quotation is from d'Entrèves, *The Notion of the State: An Introduction to Political Theory*, The Clarendon Press, Oxford, 1967, 64. She concludes, wrongly as it turns out, that d'Entrèves' definition of power is 'a kind of mitigated violence'.

18 On the spread of Lutheran political thought see esp. Q. Skinner, *The Foundations of Modern Political Thought*, Vol. 2, Cambridge University Press, Cambridge, 1978, 65–108.

19 Luther and Machiavelli were identified by Italian and Spanish Jesuits of the late sixteenth and early seventeenth centuries as the founding fathers of the impious modern State, *ibid.*, 143. The same coupling is already found in J. N. Figgis, *Political Thought from Gerson to Grotius, 1414–1625*, 2nd edn, 1907, reprint, Cambridge University Press, Cambridge.

20 See especially G. Bonner., *Saint Augustine of Hippo*, SCM Press, London, 1963, 294–311; P. Brown, 'St. Augustine's Attitude to Religious Coercion', in *Religion and Society in the Age of St. Augustine*, Faber & Faber, London, 1972, 260–278; P. Brown, *Augustine of Hippo: A Biography*, Faber & Faber, London, 1967, 233–243; R. A. Markus, *Saeculum: History and Society in the Theology of St. Augustine*, Cambridge University Press, Cambridge, 1970, 133–153.

21 *Contra Gaudentium* I, 22, 25; cited in Bonner, *op. cit.*, 308. See also Brown, 1967, *op. cit.*, 335f.

22 Brown, *op. cit.*, 272.

23 *Confessions* 3, 7, 13, trans. Maria Boulding, Vintage Books, New York, 1998, 84.

24 Brown, *op. cit.*, 268.

25 *Ibid.*, 263.

26 Bonner, *op. cit.*, 306f.

27 Brown, *op. cit.*, 266 and 275.

28 The vivid phrase is Peter Brown's; 'the man of Augustine is always about to be engulfed in vast, mysterious solidarites', *ibid.*, 365.

29 Milbank argues that by justifying coercion in some circumstances Augustine contradicts his own ontology, Milbank, *op. cit.*, 417–422. But the issue is really about the fall and human sinfulness; this is why Augustine believed that severity could be justified.

30 Bernard of Clairvaux, *de Consideratione* IV, iii, 7; cited by J. A. Watt in J. H. Burns, *Medieval Political Thought*, 373.

31 Bonner, *op. cit.*, 303.

32 Letter 93, V, 18; cited in *ibid.*, 305f.

33 I. S. Robinsin in Burns, *op. cit.*, 293; on the theory of the 'righteous persecution' of heretics, see further, *The Papacy 1073–1198: Continuity and Innovation*, Cambridge University Press, Cambridge, 1990, 317.

34 Watt, *op. cit.*, 400.

35 *Ibid.*, 402.

36 *de Regno* 1.14, cited in *ibid.*, 402.

37 *On Ecclesiastical Power*, Pt 2, X, 19, *Giles of Rome on Ecclesiastical Power: The De ecclesiastica potestate of Aegidius Romanus* (trans. R. W. Dyson), Boydell Press, London, 1986, 88.

38 *Monarchia* 3.15. In *Dante's Monarchia* (trans. R. Kay), Pontifical Institute of Medieval Studies, Toronto, 1998, 309–325.

39 H. Bettenson, *Documents of the Christian Church*, 2nd edn, Oxford University Press, Oxford, 1963, 115f.

40 Q. Skinner, *The Foundations of Modern Political Thought*, II, Cambridge University Press, Cambridge, 1978, 101.
41 N. Machiavelli, *The Prince* 18 (trans. Quentin Skinner and Russell Price), Cambridge University Press, Cambridge, 1982, 62; *The Portable Machiavelli* (trans. Peter Bondanella and Mark Musa), Penguin, Harmondsworth, 1979, 134.
42 Stephen Lukes, 'Power and Authority' in T. Bottomore and R. Nisbet (eds), *A History of Sociological Analysis*, Heinemann, London, 1979, 633.
43 Machiavelli, trans. Price and Skinner, *op. cit.*, 59.
44 *Ibid.*, 55.
45 See the meticulous account of the historical setting of Hobbes' ideas in R. Tuck, *Philosophy and Government, 1572–1651*, Cambridge University Press, Cambridge, 1993, 279–348.
46 *Leviathan*, Part I, ch. 13, 'Of the Natural Condition of Mankind', R. Tuck (ed.), Cambridge University Press, Cambridge, 1991, 89.
47 A contemporary Anglican theologian, Henry Hammond (1605–1660) described Leviathan as 'a farrago of Christian atheism'. The term 'Christian' is justified in as much as Hobbes continued to assert belief in Christ as Messiah and redeemer, the one fundamental article of faith; see Tuck, 1993, *op. cit.*, 329f.
48 Hobbes' brief and unsatisfactory treatment of trinitarian theology reduces this doctrine to a mode of representing the one God; *Leviathan*, Part 3, ch. 42 (ed. Tuck, 339f.). Riches, reputation, friends and 'good luck' are all described as forms of 'instrumental power' by which 'natural powers' of body and mind are increased; *Leviathan*, Part I, ch. 10 (ed. Tuck, 62).
49 *Leviathan*, Part II, ch. 31 (ed. Tuck, 247).
50 'The value, or worth of a man, is as of all other things, his price; that is to say, so much as would be given for the use of his power: and therefore is not absolute; but a thing dependent on the need and judgement of another'; *Leviathan*, Part I, ch. 10 (ed. Tuck, 63).
51 'Hobbes' ethical starting-point was thus one of avowed and extreme relativism'; so Tuck, *ibid.*, 304.
52 *Leviathan*, Part IV, ch. 47 (ed. Tuck, 479–480). It was not, of course, the independency envisaged by the Anabaptists.
53 *Leviathan*, Part IV, ch. 42 (*ibid.*, 338–402). On the relation to seventeenth-century politics, especially religion, see J. S. McClelland, *A History of Western Political Thought*, Routledge, London, 1996, 208–214.
54 Stewart Clegg, *Frameworks of Power*, Sage Publications, London, 1989, 31.
55 Q. Skinner, *The Foundations of Modern Political Thought*, Vol. I, 250–251; Vol. II, 171–173, 307–309. Pole, indeed, claimed that *The Prince* was the inspiration behind Henry VIII's break with Rome, and a sign of the coming Antichrist; Peter S. Donaldson, *Machiavelli and the Mystery of State*, Cambridge University Press, New York, 1988, 1–35.
56 'It is the duty of rulers of a republic or of a kingdom ro maintain the foundations of the religion that sustains them', *The Discourse*, ch. 12, in *The Portable Machiavelli*; ed. and trans. P. Bondanella and M. Musa, Penguin, Harmondsworth, 1979, 211.
57 The 'shocking the Christian Sensibilities' view of Machiavelli is discussed with some pungency by McClelland, *op. cit.*, 151–153.
58 Jacob J. Golomb, *Nietzsche's Enticing Psychology of Power*, Iowa State University Press, Ames, Iowa, 1989, is an extended study of Nietzsche's psychology, seeing it as an essential precondition for understanding Freud on repression.
59 A selection of these texts have now been retranslated under the title, *Writings from the Late Notebooks*, R. Bittner ed., K. Sturge trans., Cambridge University Press, Cambridge, 2003). Based on the new critical edition of the works of Niet-

zsche, it replaces the 1967 translation of the earlier German work, *The Will to Power*, ed. W. Kaufman and R. I. Hollingdale (Weidenfeld & Nicolson, London, 1968).

60 Neitzsche, ed. Bittner and trans. Sturge, *op. cit.*, 68.

61 Darwin, Nietzsche holds, 'absurdly *overestimates* the influence of "external circumstances"; the essential thing about the life process is precisely the tremendous force which shapes, creation from within, which *utilizes* and *exploits* "external circumstances" . . .', ed. Bittner and trans. Sturge, *op. cit.*, 135.

62 As, for example, by P. Lassman, 'The Rule of Man over Man: Politics, Power and Legitimation' in S. Turner (ed.), *The Cambridge Companion to Weber*, Cambridge University Press, Cambridge, 2000, 83–98, who also stresses the affinity of Weber with Machiavelli.

63 T. Bottomore, 'Marxism and Sociology' in Bottomore and Nisbet (eds), *op. cit.*, 118–148.

64 See the exposition of 'hegemony' in R. Bellamy and D. Schecter, *Gramsci and the Italian State*, Manchester University Press, Manchester, 1993, 112–136. For a critical discussion, see N. Abercrombie and S. B. Turner, *The Dominant Ideology Thesis*, G. Allen & Unwin, London, 1980.

65 On the theologian as 'organic intellectual', see R. H. Roberts, *Reform, Theology and the Human Sciences*, Cambridge University Press, Cambridge, 2002, 213f.

66 *The Power of the Poor in History*, Orbis Books, Maryknoll, NY, 1983, 76.

67 S. Lukes in Bottomore and Nisbet (eds), *op. cit.*, 662.

68 See Dirk Käsler, *Max Weber: An Introduction to his Life and Work*, Polity Press, Cambridge, 1988. Two recently published studies of Weber from the standpoint of Christian theology arrive at completely opposite standpoints, Milbank, *op. cit.* and Thomas Ekstrand, *Max Weber in a Theological Perspective*, Leuven, Peeters, 2000.

69 See the discussion in Fritz K. Ringer., *Max Weber's Methodology: The Unification of the Culture and Social Sciences*, Harvard University Press, Cambridge , Mass., 1997.

70 See A. Giddens, *Politics and Sociology in the Thought of Max Weber*, Macmillan Press, London, 1972.

71 Alternatives have included 'rule', 'authority', 'leadership' and 'imperative coordination'; the term is also said to have no English equivalent or to be untranslatable, Lassman, *op. cit.*, 85.

72 Lassman, *op. cit.*, 96–98.

73 C. Charles Mills, *The Power Elite*, Oxford University Press, New York, 1956.

74 T. Parsons, *Social Structure and Personality*, Free Press of Glencoe, New York, 1964, 103.

75 See S. Lukes in Bottomore and Nisbet (eds), *op. cit.*, 665f.

76 M. Foucault, *Power/Knowledge: Selected Interviews and Other Writings, 1972–1977* (E. Gordon *et al.* eds), Harvester Press, Brighton, Sussex, 1980, 151.

77 *Ibid.*, 89f. See the discussion in P. Miller, *Domination and Power*, Routledge & Kegan Paul, London, 1987, ch. 7.

78 José Guilherme Merquior, *Foucault*, Fontana Press, London, 1985, 141–160.

79 Merquior describes Foucault as a 'neo-anarchist' because of his anti-utopianism and irrationalism, *ibid.*, 155ff.

80 See J. R. Carette (ed.), *Religion and Culture. Michel Foucault*, Routledge, New York, 1999.

81 L. de Bonald, *Théorie du pouvoir politique et religieux*, Le Clerc, Paris, 1843.

82 This is the view of Robert A. Nisbet, *The Sociological Tradition*, Basic Books, New York, 1966.

83 Second General Conference of Latin-American Bishops, Medellía, August/September 1968 in A. T. Hennelly, *Liberation Theology: A Documentary History*, Orbis, Maryknoll, New York, 1990, 89–119.

84 James H. Cone, *Black Theology and Black Power*, Seabury, New York, 1969. See also the work of the South African theologian, Boesak, A. A.
85 See the extracts from Thomasius and other German theologians in C. Welch (ed.), *God and Incarnation in Mid-Nineteenth Century German Theology*, Oxford University Press, New York, 1965.
86 See S. W. Sykes, 'The Strange Persistence of Kenotic Christology', in A. Kee and E. T. Long (eds), *Being and Truth: Essays in Honour of John Macquarrie*, SCM Press, London, 1986; and S. Coakley, *Powers and Submissions*, Blackwell, Oxford, 2002, 3–39.
87 See especially the chapter on 'The Power of the Institutional Church', in Leonardo Boff, *Church, Charism and Power: Liberation Theology and the Institutional Church*, SCM Press, London, 1985, 47–64. Boff's target is frequently the centralization of power, rather than power itself. His hope is for 'institutions whose power will be pure service' (63).
88 The blindness of reformers to the power of publicity and rhetoric is a feature of this tradition from the days of Luther.
89 J. Wimber, *Power Evangelism*, Hodder and Stoughton, London, 1985, 47.
90 But now see Martyn Percy, *Words, Wonders and Power*, SPCK, London, 1996 and *Power in the Church*, Cassell, London, 1998.
91 *Max Weber: Selections in Translation*, ed. W. G. Runciman, trans. E. Matthews, Cambridge University Press, Cambridge, 1978, 246. See also the discussion in T. Ekstrand, *Max Weber in a Theological Perspective*, Peeters, Leuven, 2000, 167–196. Milbank views Weber's contrast between 'charisma' and 'routine' as a rehearsal of 'the historic prejudices of liberal protestantism', J. Milbank., *Theology and Social Theory*, 87–92. Weber's interpretation of early Christianity is given thorough discussion in the collection of essays, Wolfgang Schluchter, *Max Webers Sicht des antiken Christentumis*, Suhrkamp, Frankfurt-am-Main, 1985.
92 Ernst Troeltsch, *Die Bedeutung des Protestantismus für die Entstehung der modernen Welt*, Oldenburg, München, 1911.
93 *Weber* 1978 [1968], *op. cit.*, 215–216.
94 *Ecclesiastical Authority and Spiritual Power in the Church of the First Three Centuries*, trans. J. A. Baker, A & C Black, London, 1969.
95 P. Worsley, *The Trumpet Shall Sound: A Study of 'Cargo' Cults in Melanesia*, Paladin, London, 1970.
96 G. Theissen, *Sociology of Early Palestinian Christianity*, trans. J. Bowden, Fortress Press, Minn, 1978.
97 See, esp., R. A. Horsley, *Sociology and the Jesus Movement*, Crossroad, New York, 1989.
98 Esp. Gerhard E. Lenski, *Power and Privilege*, McGraw-Hill, New York, 1966 and J. H. Kautsky , *The Politics of Aristocratic Empires*, University of North Carolina Press, Chapel Hill, 1982.
99 P. L. Berger and T. Luckman, *The Social Construction of Reality: A Treatise in the Sociology of Knowledge*, Doubleday, Garden City, NY, 1967.
100 Yale University Press, New Haven, 1983.
101 Norman R. Petersen, *Rediscovering Paul: Philemon and the Sociology of Paul's Narrative World*, Fortress Press, Philadelphia, 1985.
102 Milbank objects that sociology purports to explain the phenomena in terms of regularities, whereas in fact it is more than historiography, Milbank, *op. cit.*, 110–143.
103 J. Schütz, *Paul and the Anatomy of Apostolic Authority*, Cambridge University Press, Cambridge, 1975 and Bengt Holmberg, *Paul and Power*, Fortress Press, Philadelphia, 1978.

104 Wayne A. Meeks (ed.), *The Writings of St. Paul*, Norton, New York, 1972, 295; the reference is to the Antichrist.
105 G. Shaw, *The Cost of Authority: Manipulation and Freedom in the New Testament*, SCM Press, London, 1982.
106 Elizabeth A. Castelli, *Imitating Paul: A Discourse of Power*, Westminster/John Knox, Louisville, 1991.
107 Herbert L. Dreyfus and Paul Rabinow, *Michel Foucault: Beyond Structuralism and Hermaneutics*, University of Chicago Press, Chicago, 1982, 214f.
108 Castelli, *op. cit.*, 134.
109 In an interview, *Nouvelle littéraires*, 2477 (17–23 March 1975), cited by J. G. Merquior, *Foucault*, 118.
110 S. H. Polaski, *Paul and the Discourse of Power*, Sheffield Academic Press, Sheffield, 1999, 124–136, contains a moving autobiographical account of the implications for the hermeneutics of suspicion of a woman growing up in the Southern Baptist Church, and coming to appreciate its 'hidden practices of power', 131.
111 Ralph Dahrendorf, *Soziale Klassen und Klassenkonflikt in der industriellen Gesellschaft*, F. Enke, Stuttgart, 1957.
112 S. Lukes, 'Power and Authority' in Bottomore and Nisbet (eds), *op. cit.*, 654–665.
113 *Ibid.*, 650; citing T. Parsons, 'Authority, Legitimation and Political Action' in C. J. Friedrich (ed.), *Authority, Nomos 1*, Harvard University Press, Cambridge, Mass., 1958, 206.
114 R. Dahrendorf, *Class and Class Conflict in Industrial Society*, Routledge & Kegan Paul, London, 1959, esp. ch. 5.
115 Maurice Duverger, *The Idea of Politics: The Use of Power in Society*, Methuen, London, 1966.
116 The most obvious example is the use of the title 'Servant of the servants of God' by the Pope. It is neither a paradox nor a contradiction that the title should have been employed by St. Bernard, the same writer who attributes to the Pope 'plenitude of power'.

Chapter 6

1 F. Nietzsche,, *The Will to Power* (trans. Kaufman, W. and Hollingdale, R. J.), Viking Books, New York, 1968, 142.
2 A. N. Wilder, *Jesus' Parables and the War of Myths*, SPCK, London, 1982, 55.
3 Justin Martyr, *Apology* I, 41. 1–4 *Dialogue* 73. 1–4.
4 *Apology* I, 23.
5 Tertullian, *Against Marcian*, III, 19, 2; 'The one new king of the new ages, Jesus Christ, carried on his shoulder both the power and the excellence of his new glory, even his cross' (English translation by A. Roberts and J. Donaldson), T & T Clark, Edinburgh, 1868, 157. See R. Kearsley, *Tertullian's Theology of Divine Power*, Paternoster Press, Carlisle, 1998, ch. 5, 'Divine Power and Incarnation'.
6 Justin Martyr, *Dialogue* 36.5f. This motif recurs in many later expositions of the Psalm; see P. Beskow, *Rex Gloriae*, Almqvist & Wiksell, Stockholm, 1962, 279.
7 Gregory of Nyssa, *In Christi Resurrectionem*, Orat. 1 (D.G. 46, 624); discussed by J. Daníelon, *The Theology of Jewish Christianity* I, Darton, Longman & Todd, London, 1964, 290. For the Son to be identified with the Power of God was an argument in favour of the theology of Nicaea in the controversies of the fourth century. See M. R. Barnes, *The Power of God, Dynamis in Gregory of Nyssa's Trinitarian Theology*, The Catholic University of America Press, Washington, 2001, ch. 7, 260–307.
8 K. Rahner, 'The Theology of Power', in *Theological Investigations*, Vol. IV, Darton, Longman & Todd, London, 1966, 391–409, see esp. 408.

9 'On Understanding Sacrifice' in M. F. C. Bourdillon and M. Fortes (eds), *Sacrifice,* Academic Press, London, 1980, 37.
10 *Ibid.*, 38.
11 'Preface' in Bourdillon and Fortes, *op. cit.*, xiv.
12 *Ibid.*, xiv.
13 *Ibid.*, xv.
14 J. W. Rogerson, 'Sacrifice in the Old Testament: Problems of Method and Approach' in *ibid.*, 45–59.
15 R. Girard, *Violence and the Sacred,* Johns Hopkins University Press, Baltimore, 1977, 31.
16 *Ibid.*, 20–21.
17 *Ibid.*, 23.
18 R. Girard, *The Scapegoat,* trans. Y. Freccero, Athlone Press, London, 1986, 100–116.
19 *Ibid.*, 114.
20 *Ibid.*, 116.
21 *Ibid.*, 125.
22 *Ibid.*, 126.
23 *Ibid.*, 201.
24 *Ibid.*, 205.
25 *Ibid.*, 207.
26 *Ibid.*, 212.
27 J. Beattie, rev., 'Violence and the Sacred' in *Rain,* No. 29 (Dec. 1978), 7–8.
28 A. Macintyre, *After Virtue,* Duckworth, London, 1981, 201.
29 See S. W. Sykes, 'Outline of a Theology of Sacrifice', in S. W. Sykes (ed.), *Sacrifice and Redemption, Durham Essays in Theology,* Cambridge University Press, Cambridge, 1991, 282–298.
30 R. Williams, *Resurrection,* Darton, Longman & Todd, London, 1982, 13.
31 *Ibid.*, 15.
32 *Ibid.*, 24.
33 *Ibid.*, 25.
34 See S. W. Sykes, 'Sacrifice and the Theology of War', in R. A. Hinde (ed.), *The Institution of War,* Macmillan, London, 1991, 87–98.
35 A. L. Loades, 'Eucharistic Sacrifice: The problem of how to use a liturgical metaphor with special reference to Simone Weil', in Sykes (ed.), *op. cit.*, 247–261.
36 So Mary Daly, 'the qualities that Christianity *idealizes,* especially for women, are also those of a victim: sacrificial love, passive acceptance of suffering, humility, meekness', *Beyond God the Father,* Beacon Press, Boston, 1973, 75–77. See also L. S. Cahill, 'Feminism and Christian Ethics' in C. M. La Cugna (ed.), *Freeing Theology: The Essentials of Theology in Feminist Perspective,* Harper, San Francisco, 1993, 211–234 (see esp. 216f.).
37 See the discussion of the election of Judas in K. Bourth, *Church Dogmatics* II, 2, ed. and trans. by G. W. Bromiley *et al.*, T and T Clark, Edinburgh, 1957, 458–506.
38 'Man is the world's high Priest: he doth present
The sacrifice for all; while they below
Unto the service mutter an assent,
Such as springs use that fall, and winds that blow.
(Providence)

George Herbert, *The Complete English Works,* ed. A. P. Slater, David Campbell Publishers, London, 1995, 113.

Chapter 7

1 The substance of this chapter was given as the 6th Archbishop Blanch Memorial Lecture, in Liverpool Hope University College (now Liverpool Hope University) in October 2002.
2 Stuart Blanch, *Future Patterns of Episcopacy*, Latimer Studies 37, Latimer House, Oxford, 1991, 41.
3 *Ibid.*
4 *St. Gregory the Great, Pastoral Care*, Ancient Christian Writers II, trans. and ed. H. Davis, Newman Press, New York, 1950. Latin text with French translation in Grégoire le Grand, *Règle Pastorale*, 2 vols, du Cerf, Paris, 1992.
5 See the introduction of B. Judie to the *Règle Pastorale*, Vol. I, 91–100.
6 Cited from Alcuin, *Epistolae* 116 by Davis, *op. cit.*, 10–11.
7 *Ibid.*, I, 8, 35f.
8 *Ibid.*, I, 9, 35.
9 *Ibid.*, II, 6, 61.
10 *Ibid.*, II, 6, 62.
11 *Ibid.*, II, 6, 65.
12 *Ibid.*, I, 5, 29.
13 'And grant unto her [the Queen's] whole Council, and to all that are put in authority under her, that they may truly and indifferently minister justice, to the punishment of wickedness and vice, and to the maintenance of thy true religion, and virtue'. Prayer for the Church, Order of the Administration of Holy Communion, Book of Common Prayer.
14 Davis, *op. cit.*, II, 8, 70f.
15 *Ibid.*, II, 8, 76f.
16 Collect for the Sovereign, Order of the Administration of Holy Communion, Book of Common Prayer.
17 For what follows see R. A. Marcus, *Gregory the Great and this World*, Cambridge University Press, Cambridge, 1997.
18 Bernard of Clairvaux, *On Consideration*, Book IV, iii, trans. E. T. G. Lewis, The Clarendon Press, Oxford, 1908, 103f.
19 P. M. Harrison, *Authority and Power in the Free Church Tradition: A Social Case Study of the American Baptist Convention*, Princeton University Press, Princeton, 1959.
20 See the thorough discussion of this passage in A. C. Thistleton, *The First Epistle to the Corinthians*, Paternoster Press, Carlisle, 2000, 204–223.
21 *Ibid.*, III, 4 (citing Exod. 16:8); 100.

Index of Biblical References

Note: Where notes for two chapters appear on the same page, notes are distinguished by the addition of the letters a or b.

Index of Names and Subjects

Note: Where notes for two chapters appear on the same page, notes are distinguished by the addition of the letters a or b. Page references in italics indicate a diagram.